Jeremy Black is one of the UK's most respected and prolific historians. He is Emeritus Professor of History at the University of Exeter and a renowned expert on the history of war. He is a Senior Fellow at both Policy Exchange and the Foreign Policy Research Institute. His recent books include *Military Strategy: A Global History*, *A History of the Second World War in 100 Maps*, *Tank Warfare* and *The World of James Bond*. He appears regularly on TV and radio, including BBC Radio 4's *In Our Time*.

A BRIEF HISTORY OF

The Caribbean

····················

JEREMY BLACK

ROBINSON

ROBINSON

First published in Great Britain in 2021 by Robinson

1 3 5 7 9 10 8 6 4 2

Copyright © Jeremy Black, 2021
Map © iStock

A CIP catalogue record for this book
is available from the British Library.

ISBN: 978-1-40871-348-8

Typeset in Scala by Hewer Text UK Ltd, Edinburgh
Printed and bound in Great Britain by Clays Ltd, Elcograf S.p.A.

Papers used by Robinson are from well-managed
forests and other responsible sources.

MIX
Paper from
responsible sources
FSC® C104740

Robinson
An imprint of
Little, Brown Book Group
Carmelite House
50 Victoria Embankment
London EC4Y 0DZ

An Hachette UK Company
www.hachette.co.uk

www.littlebrown.co.uk

For Azzie and Derek Partridge

Contents

....

	Preface: Light on Water	ix
	Introduction: The Caribbean as a Frontier Region	1
CHAPTER ONE	The Sea and Its Shores	15
CHAPTER TWO	'Pre-European/Contact' Civilisations	27
CHAPTER THREE	The Europeans Arrive, 1492–1600	39
CHAPTER FOUR	The Seventeenth Century	63
CHAPTER FIVE	Competing to Run an Economy of Misery, 1700–50	95
CHAPTER SIX	Britain to the Fore, 1750–90	121
CHAPTER SEVEN	The End of Slavery, 1790–1850	145
CHAPTER EIGHT	A New Age of Capital, 1848–98	189
CHAPTER NINE	The Age of American Power, 1898–1945	221
CHAPTER TEN	The Cold War, 1945–90	241
CHAPTER ELEVEN	The Caribbean Today, 1990–	267
CHAPTER TWELVE	Contingencies and Conclusions	283
	Selected Further Reading	291
	Index	295

Preface:
Light on Water

....

I bade an eternal farewell to Barbados. In it I ate, drank,
laughed, danced and perspired as much as ever I expect to
do again.

Henry Nelson Coleridge,
Six Months in the West Indies in 1825 (1826)

From childhood, the sight of light on water has always been
special for me. It has brought me the purest pleasure, only
equalled by that of a smile on a child's face. Light on water has its
own flow, born of the water but moving on its own, alike but
different to light on the eye. So, travel to places with water – its
mass and flow, colour and depth – has always fascinated me. The
sights of great seas, a sunset slipping like a yolk into the sudden
dark of the water, or pelicans flying low to fish by the islands off
the coast of Belize, are both intoxicating and magical.

The Caribbean, the sea and its shores, are a setting for the
imagination, a magnet for travellers, and the focus of much of the
modern cruise world. Here we give a history. We will engage not
only with the sea and the islands, but also with the continental
shores, what some people call the circum-Caribbean. This will be
as much about Cartagena, Pensacola, New Orleans, Galveston
and Veracruz as about the islands. Indeed, the history of the latter
does not make much sense without the coasts and, in particular,
their mercantile cities and the ambitions of their states, notably
the United States. There may have been little in common between
the eastern Caribbean and Mexico in the age of the British empire,

but now they are both affected by American economic and political power. Moreover, there are many close connections between the history of individual islands and the mainland, most notably Haiti and Louisiana, and Cuban history cannot readily be detached from that of Spanish America and later the United States.

British readers may find this inclusion a surprising one, but their view of the Caribbean is overly insular in a double respect. The islands, irrespective of the identity of the former imperial power, share a history of sugar and slavery, which gives them a strong cultural similarity, but it does not make them distinct as it is one that the Guianas (Guyana, Cayenne, Surinam) and northeast Brazil also share; while the plantation economies and labour coercion of the islands were scarcely absent from the circum-Caribbean. If an imperial-strategic framework highlights the islands of the archipelago, it does the same for the coasts, and both note the extension of island traditions to the mainland littoral, as at Cartagena, Veracruz and New Orleans, and emphasise the mainland territories as a potential and fluctuating base of regional economic and political power.

Although partly covered in the upcoming sequel volume, *A Brief History of the Atlantic*, embracing the mainland Americas as critical to the Caribbean story enables us to consider comparisons between empires which is appropriate because the specifics of Caribbean history benefit from being set in a global perspective. Indeed, interpretations of social and cultural history, as well as histories emphasising environment and the specifics of the region, benefit from attention to imperial and strategic issues. To that here is added comparison with the empires of the East Indies, an approach that helps underline the distinctive character of the Caribbean's development. At the same time, from the 1490s, the Caribbean has been a part of a wider history born of the globalisation enforced by European voyagers, and the ambitions for adventure, power, control and wealth they brought in their wake. The concept of frontier serves to tie the very varied geographies and the peoples of the Caribbean together, especially to highlight the essential impermanence of life in the region.

While providing a history, this book is intended to be of particular value to travellers, whether on cruises, using other means to travel, or staying at home and travelling through time and space in their imagination and mind. The history will be end-loaded, focusing on recent centuries, for it is the last half-millennium that has made the Caribbean societies that we see today.

I have had the good fortune to travel widely in the region over the last thirty years, both at sea and on land, and would like to thank all those who have provided company and hospitality. The high point for me has been visiting islands in the western Caribbean, notably Providence and Roatán, but, throughout, I have been attracted by people and place, life and setting.

I have benefited greatly from the comments of Roger Billis, Olwyn Blouet, Steve Bodger, Trevor Burnard, Guy Chet, Eileen Cox, Perry Gauci, William Gibson, John Gilmore, Mark Hanna, Richard Harding, Herb Kaplan, Patrick Manning, Angela Murray and Tobias Rupprecht on an earlier draft and from advice on particular points by Kathy Burk and Thomas Otte. Duncan Proudfoot has been a most supportive editor. It is a great pleasure to dedicate this book to Azzie and Derek Partridge who have offered Sarah and myself a quarter-century of most welcome friendship.

Stately Spanish Galleon

Stately Spanish galleon coming from the Isthmus,
Dipping through the Tropics by the palm-green shores,
With a cargo of diamonds,
Emeralds, amethysts,
Topazes, and cinnamon, and gold moidores.

I would be hard-pressed to say whether it was Ursula Andress coming from the sea as a bikini-clad Botticelli heroine in *Dr No* (1962) or John Masefield's poem 'Cargoes' (1903) that was my very first contact with the Caribbean. We had to learn 'Cargoes' as children at school, and I was mesmerised, although, in truth, more with the first magical verse . . .

Quinquireme of Nineveh from distant Ophir
Rowing home to haven in sunny Palestine,
With a cargo of ivory,
And apes and peacocks,
Sandalwood, cedarwood, and sweet white wine

. . . than by the bathetic third . . .

Dirty British coaster with a salt-caked smoke stack,
Butting through the Channel in the mad March days,
With a cargo of Tyne coal,
Road-rails, pig-lead,
Firewood, iron-ware, and cheap tin trays.

The Spanish galleon second verse, however, stuck in the imagination, and now that I have seen the shores in a sailing ship, I feel more the resonance of these lines.

THE

CUBA

Cayman Islands
(U.K.)

JAMA

GUATEMALA

EL SALVADOR

PANAMA

COSTA RICA

Bermuda
(U.K.)

MAS

Turks and
Caicos Islands
(U.K.)

Puerto Rico
(U.S.)

Anguilla
(U.K.)

Virgin
Islands

ANTIGUA &
BARBUDA

TI

DOMINICAN
REPUBLIC

ST. KITTS
AND NEVIS

Guadeloupe
(FRANCE)

DOMINICA

Martinique
(FRANCE)

ST. LUCIA

Aruba
(NETH.)

Curaçao
(NETH.)

ST. VINCENT AND
THE GRENADINES

BARBADOS

GRENADA

TRINIDAD AND
TOBAGO

VENEZUELA

GUYANA

Introduction: The Caribbean as a Frontier Region

The Caribbean as a frontier may not seem obvious to those slipping through its generally calm waters, but that has been its geological destiny, one dramatically present today with volcanic peaks and earthquakes. Hurricanes, of which there have been over 4000, and on some counts over 5000, since 1492, and which help bring the Caribbean today to the attention of outsiders, notably in the United States, are a demonstration of the precariousness of life. This precariousness was greatly accentuated by the tendency of Europeans, who came by sea and in their continuing need for maritime links, to locate settlements and plantations on and near the coast. This frontier character extends to species, populations, crops, economic institutions and governance; all of which were very much in flux, and, indeed, remain so. It was a hard place for imperial powers to assert and maintain their will, and particularly order, in the face of all that flux.

A High Wind in Jamaica

Richard Hughes's first novel, published in 1929 and, for me, an early, albeit indirect, contact with the Caribbean, was a highly successful book that provided a flavour of Caribbean life, and a mixed account of the interaction of piracy and civilisation that in part reflected the shift to a period when pirates were no longer really feared. Set in

Jamaica after slave emancipation, the plot's source is a transformative hurricane that destroys the home in which the Bas-Thornton children grow up, leading to them being sent back to the apparent safety of England. Seized by Cuba-based pirates, the children have a variety of difficult experiences, including exposure to risk, death both accidental and violent, sexuality and uncertainty. The pirates are eventually captured, tried and executed by the British. This is not childhood as a romance, but as a setting for tension and the breakdown of conventional frontiers of behaviour, as such prefiguring William Golding's *Lord of the Flies* (1954), which was set on an uninhabited Pacific island. *A High Wind in Jamaica* appeared in stage, radio and, in 1965, film versions.

Humanity brought its full share of frontiers, notably the inhumane division between white and enslaved black. Alongside that from the outset, but increasingly with time, came the multiple gradations that sought to register the complexities of ethnic intermingling, marital convention, sexual practice, legal differentiation, status assertion and religious affiliation. The frontier world was also seen in the escapees from Europe (and later also the United States), those seeking new opportunities in a world that was, in promise, appearance and often reality, unregulated or less regulated. This character helped lead to a sense of the Caribbean being on the edge, a region where morals and mores were looser, and more critically, and notably to outside observers, morality, souls and salvation under challenge.

Indeed, interracial sex repeatedly contributed greatly to the moral panic posed to many outsiders by the Caribbean, not least because it challenged concepts of purity, concepts that had been strengthened in the case of Spain from the late fifteenth century by brutal campaigns, legislation and prohibition against those

with Arab or Jewish blood. Racist notions were greatly strengthened by the exposure to natives and black people in the Caribbean,
an exposure to non-Europeans that was particularly novel to the
British, the Dutch and the French, but not to Spaniards. Moreover,
the scale of the contrast in numbers, with the white people very
much in a minority, in large part due to their dependence on
slaves, strengthened alarm and thus ideas of a frontier. Very
frequently, female black slaves were held responsible for the
actions of white masters. Sin was personified accordingly, and
lust blamed on the victim, as Shakespeare had noted in a different
context in *King Lear*.

At the Edge: Bertha Mason in Charlotte Brontë's *Jane Eyre* (1847)

The daughter of a merchant-planter 'creole' wife, meaning
in this case of racially mixed origins, Bertha is married to
Edward Rochester in Spanish-Town Jamaica in pursuit of
his father's interest in the £30,000 dowry. Rochester subsequently decries her as a woman of:

> giant propensities . . . the true daughter of an infam-
> ous mother . . . a wife at once intemperate and
> unchaste . . . her excesses . . . prematurely devel-
> oped the germs of insanity . . . One night I had been
> awakened by her yells . . . it was a fiery West-Indian
> night . . . The air was like sulphur-steams – I could
> find no refreshment anywhere. Mosquitoes came
> buzzing in and hummed sullenly round the room;
> the sea, which I could hear from thence, rumbled
> dull like an earthquake – black clouds were casting
> up over it; the moon was setting in the waves, broad
> and red, like a hot cannon-ball – she threw her last

3

bloody glance over a world quivering with the ferment of tempest . . . A wind fresh from Europe blew over the ocean and rushed through the open casement: the storm broke, streamed, thundered, blazed, and the air grew pure . . . I walked under the dripping orange-trees of my wet garden, and amongst its drenched pomegranates and pine-apples, and while the refulgent dawn of the tropics kindled round me . . . the sweet wind from Europe was still whispering . . . my soul thirsted for a pure draught . . . the old world was beyond; clear pros-pects opened thus: 'Go,' said Hope, 'and live again in Europe: there is not known what a sullied name you bear, nor what a filthy burden is bound to you.'

One of the most-read novels in English, *Jane Eyre* presents a negative account of the Caribbean as a sickly beautiful world. The lunacy in the novel is rooted there, and the impli-cation is that slavery in the shape of miscegenation is the root cause; while the fortune derived from slavery is the basis for the mistake imposed on Rochester by his relatives. A marginal world of dark secrets is transposed to England.

Wide Sargasso Sea (1966)

Written by Jean Rhys (1890–1979), a British author born in Dominica, this 1966 novel of which there were film versions in 1993 and 2006, was a view of the world created in Charlotte Brontë's novel *Jane Eyre* from the perspective of

Antoinette Cosway, the mad creole heiress. Beginning on Coulibri Estate, a rundown Jamaican plantation, after the 1833 Emancipation Act – 'I did not remember the place when it was prosperous' – this is a critique directed against male control and patriarchy. The depiction of the West Indies captures the hierarchy of racial difference, although the blacks now refer to 'white niggers' or 'white cockroaches', as well as the multiple forms of control present in society, notably sexual control, and the resulting harsh experience, material and psychological, that defines the position of women, although the latter are not free from criticism: 'The Jamaican ladies had never approved of my mother . . . far too young . . . and, worse still, a Martinique girl', the last capturing the suspicion of those from a French and Catholic background, and, notably, the lack of fellow-feelings between the islands. Rhys's mother's family, creoles of Scots ancestry, owned a former plantation, while her brother Oscar had illegitimate children by an island mixed-race woman.

Sexual freedom, and the violence, predation, threat and frisson involved, were also part of the perception of piracy, and, more generally, of both an unlicensed masculinity and of a femininity at the edge. Sexual freedom was given an even darker edge with syphilis and other venereal diseases, which were debilitating, if not deadly, for most of history. These were important elements of the relationship between the frontier and illegality that defined, or at least affected, the attitude of many to the Caribbean. This relationship was seen in responses to particular places that were held to be dens of iniquity, such as Port Royal in the 1670s, Havana in the 1820s and 1950s, and Mustique in the 1970s. When Port Royal was devastated by an earthquake in 1692, providential judgement was seen at work, although, by the 1680s, Jamaica's governors had begun to crack down on the island's support of piracy and most pirates began to head north at that point, taking their goods to Charleston, Newport and New York. By the 1690s, it was dangerous to try to bring illicit plunder into Jamaica, so the divine vengeance seen at work in 1692 was somewhat late.

In part, the contemporary presentation of divine intervention captured the dual nature of the Caribbean as a religious frontier, a factor that it is all-too-easy to overlook in a more secular age, but one that has left a powerful legacy in terms of the religious commitment that is readily apparent in the Caribbean and notably so at Sunday church services. In the Caribbean, there was the clash between Catholicism and Protestantism, and also that between Christianity and non-Christian practices, each clash important in itself and also overlapping with other causes of division. The clash between Catholicism and Protestantism was very much born of the hostility, indeed hatred, between Catholic powers, in the shape of Spain and France, that offered no tolerance to Protestantism and Protestant challengers, particularly the English, the Dutch, and Huguenots (French Protestants). Providence was seen as playing a role, as in the *Monitor*, an influential London newspaper, urging Caribbean conquests in its issue of 3 April 1762 and declaring: 'The late conquest of Martinique is such a peculiar mark of Providence, that we might, without presumption, look upon all the other islands in those seas, belonging to our arms ... permitted to pursue the course of Providence.' The Americans inherited this challenge from the British.

This hatred between Catholics and Protestants played a role in the murder of prisoners, as of Huguenots by the Spaniards in Florida in 1565, and in the repeated desecration of churches and religious items. Thus, the two missions established by the Franciscans among the Muzul Maya of central Belize in 1641 were sacked by Dutch pirates within a year. The English (from 1707 British) and Dutch developed a toleration of Catholicism long before the reverse; but in the Caribbean, a frontier region, there was both the continuation of the practices of hatred, yet also the degree of accommodation otherwise seen in smuggling and similar illegal, but nevertheless semi-accepted, activities.

As a variant on relations between Protestantism and Catholicism, there were also tensions between Protestant sects, notably between Dutch Calvinists and English Anglicans. In British colonies in the early nineteenth century, Anglican settlers were hostile to Nonconformists, whom they saw as a key source of support for Abolitionism; and, notably so, with Nonconformist missionaries.

Religious Frontiers

The interaction and melding of different religions underlined the role of the Caribbean as a frontier, and necessarily so as natives and slaves had to adapt to Christianity. There was also adaptation as well as hostility within the Christian world. Thus, William Stapleton, Governor of the Leeward Islands (1671–83), was an Irish Catholic, and observant of his faith. Yet he called on Bishop Compton of London to send out Anglican chaplains from England and he supported their work on the islands. As governor, Stapleton acted as the 'ordinary' in issuing marriage licences, proving wills and licensing clergy; and on occasion he was called on to exert discipline over the clergy. This was clearly a world in which the domestic fault lines of the Test Act and the persecution of Dissenters were pretty much unknown.

As far as the clash between Christianity and non-Christian practices were concerned, there were important overlaps with issues of cultural and social control over slaves, both newly arrived and their descendants, and over native peoples. Non-Christian religious practices were also linked to different social customs, for example polygamy. The focus has long been on vodou or voodoo, a practice almost as elusive as its spelling is unfixed, but that is only one aspect of the situation. Moreover, this clash was present from the arrival of the Europeans in the 1490s because Christianity, as a monotheistic religion with intolerant practices toward what was seen as idolatry, was both destructive of other religions or cultural-religious activities, and paranoid about them. The presence of an Inquisition, the belief that cultural activities among slaves and natives were covers for other religions, and that the latter were inherently anti-Christian; and the legacy of treating other religions in Europe, notably Islam and Judaism, in this fashion; all proved a potent mixture. Christian proselytism, based on sites such as the sixteenth-century Franciscan convent in Havana, contributed powerfully to this attitude, as failure in proselytism, or the only partial success that was an aspect of accommodation, could be attributed to purposeful resistance on behalf of a covert and sinister set of beliefs. Moreover, the presence of churches across the region provided sites for an energisation of what was at once, depending on circumstances and personalities, accommodation and hostility. Thus, the frontier character of the Caribbean was taken further by missionary activity.

The polytheistic nature of African religions ensured a range of deities, some of whom could be assimilated with Christian saints, a practice also seen with some native peoples. This process helped give a particular character both to Caribbean Catholicism (a character the Church sought to contain and in part extirpate) and to African diaspora faiths. Thus, on Cuba, Santería, an Afro-Cuban religion, had particular *orishas*, gods or goddesses, as well as priests, and religious ceremonies in which divination and propitiation played a major role. In 2020, the attempt in Nicaragua to ignore the COVID-19 epidemic was widely attributed to Rosario

Murillo, the Vice-President (and wife of Daniel Ortega, the President), a mystic who wore turquoise rings on every finger to ward off evil spirits.

More subtly have come the frontiers within, and between, states as government authority has been obstructed, opposed or, more commonly, ignored when local communities have thought appropriate. This attitude and practice, seen with both blacks and whites, very much feeds into the culture. As part of this opposition to government authority has come the maintenance of links, and sometimes loyalties, across the formal frontiers, a situation which itself helps create the informal frontiers within states. This situation, which was central to illicit trans-imperial commerce that often had official connivance, was dramatised with smuggling and piracy, but was, in practice, more widespread in Caribbean life, indeed helping to provide a habit of mind that was different to that on the surrounding continental landmasses, even while each influenced the other.

In part, this difference was because the sea itself offered far greater possibilities for such intermingling; and this situation has remained a pattern until the present. Indeed, this helps to differentiate the frontier nature of the Caribbean from that of many other regions. So also did the legacy of large-scale population movements into the Caribbean, and the experience of long being a fracture zone of imperial presence, contact and reaction; a situation that with the United States has reached to the present. Due to the population movements and to the attraction of the Caribbean as a frontier region, many individuals came from mixed backgrounds. Thus, Moses Cohen Henriques, a Dutch pirate of Portuguese Sephardic Jewish origin, fought with the Dutch against the Spaniards in 1628, and subsequently against the Portuguese in Brazil, and later became an advisor to Sir Henry Morgan, the leading English privateer in the Caribbean. Creole societies are inherently disrespectful of boundaries, but they do have their own boundaries.

Smuggling and piracy dramatised the extent to which ineffective law enforcement was a factor, at sea, on land and now also in the air. This issue with law enforcement was a matter not only of opportunities for smuggling and piracy, by their bridging the barriers to entrepreneurs between prosperity and poverty, but also of the impact of low living standards on the recruitment of active support for smuggling and piracy, as well as the complicity of communities and officials. The latter corresponded to a longstanding tension toward central authority, one in which local practice rested on traditions related to the limited, even parlous, material conditions of life and livelihood. Moreover, modern states have distinct economic and fiscal systems, and smuggling helps ensure that the differences between them are overcome in the cause of supplying need as well as profit. Similarly for the past age of empires, inter-imperial exchanges helped compensate for the deficiencies of protectionist mercantilist systems, both in peace and in war. The British breach in Spanish imperial protectionism was an aspect of this but so, far less attractively, was slave trading once it became illegal. In the 1920s, protectionism in the United States greatly encouraged the production of alcohol in the Caribbean and smuggling into America, for example from the Bahamas and Cuba. This was a continuing aspect of the movement of Caribbean rum into North America, one that began in the seventeenth century and persisted whatever the politics. In this, as in so much else, environmental contrasts in terms of products and production capability, and thus opportunities for producers and consumers, overcame the frontiers provided by regulation and prohibition.

There is an instructive contrast with the East Indies, a theme that will be pursued across the book for it throws a comparative light on the West Indies, notably by focusing the spotlight on difference. The East Indies is now largely the state of Indonesia; although East Timor, Brunei and part of Malaysia are also involved.

In many respects, characteristics seen in the West Indies were also present in the East Indies, notably piracy, which has continued to the present day. Moreover, Charles Kingsley co-dedicated his novel set in the Caribbean, *Westward Ho!* (1855), to Sir James Brooke, Rajah of Sarawak (r. 1841–68), whom he regarded as a modern representative of the heroic character traits of the sixteenth-century English buccaneers in the Caribbean; the other being George Selwyn, the first Bishop of New Zealand, which included Melanesia. Brooke, an adventurer of enterprise and success, who also provided Britain with a naval base at Labuan, battled local pirates while he established his own territory.

Yet, although there were English traders in the East Indies from the early seventeenth century, and, indeed, Britain conquered the region in 1810–14, there was no gripping of the imagination comparable to that of the Caribbean, and no British 'deep history' of the East Indies comparable in any respects to that of the Caribbean. The nearest comparison, instead, was with India, where the British presence was far more significant, both for India and for the British. However, even India lacked a comparable 'deep history' for Europeans, in part because there was not the same background of settlement by Europeans and, at their behest, the latter principally being by African slaves. Moreover, although there were offshore islands, most prominently Ceylon (Sri Lanka), the centre of British activity, military, political and economic, was the Indian interior, and there was no physical counterpart to the island character and maritime setting of the Caribbean. Such contrasts help to explain the particular character of the Caribbean and its role in the Western imagination.

The theme of the frontier can be variously presented for Caribbean history and identity. It is both opportunity and threat, and it certainly provides contrasts, as, very differently, in the work of the poet Derek Walcott and in the Agatha Christie murder story set there.

Derek Walcott (1930–2017)

St Lucian poet and expert wordsmith, from an African, Dutch and English background, and Methodist-educated, he won the 1992 Nobel Prize in Literature; his work included *Omeros* (1990), an epic poem that captured an ability to link an account of the Caribbean with major themes in Classical literature. He pursued most of his career in North America and Britain. In his Nobel acceptance speech, Walcott emphasised the discordant nature of the diasporic identity that he felt was that of the Caribbean with its 'broken fragments' and the struggle between groundedness and amnesia. Mostly set in St Lucia, *Omeros* presented its beauty but also the disturbing weight of colonialism. To describe the Caribbean, he used the metaphors of shipwreck in some of his work. Another Nobel Laureate of the islands, the Trinidad-born V. S. Naipaul (1932–2018), set a number of works, including *A House for Mr Biswas* (1961) and *The Middle Passage* (1962), in the Caribbean.

Agatha Christie in the Caribbean:
A Caribbean Mystery *(1964)*

'The dining room was a large room open on three sides to the soft warm scented air of the West Indies . . . The steel bands were one of the main attractions of the islands . . . The pleasure that everyone else took in them was undeniable . . . The weather was always the same

– fine . . . hurricanes were not weather in Miss Marple's sense of the word. They were more in the nature of an Act of God.'

Set in the Golden Palm resort on the fictional island of St Honoré, this Miss Marple adventure drew on a visit Agatha Christie made to the Caribbean. The 1989 BBC adaptation was shot in Barbados, whereas Cape Town was used for the 2013 ITV version. The Caribbean as a frontier attractive to marginal characters in search of fortune was very much seen in the murderer.

1

The Sea and Its Shores

....

The Chicxulub Crater

Buried in Yucatán beneath a kilometre-thick sequence of subsequently deposited limestone, the Chicxulub crater is 25,450 kilometres square (9826 square miles), 193 kilometres (120 miles) in diameter and 20 kilometres (12 miles) deep. It is an impact crater formed when a large asteroid or comet hit the Earth about 66 million years ago, probably leading to the extinction of the dinosaurs, notably due to a soot cloud blocking out the sun. Chicxulub is the only known well-preserved crater on Earth with a peak ring, and the results, published in 2016, of drilling into the crater, beneath the Caribbean off north-western Yucatán, reveal shocked, granite rocks that are out of the expected geological sequence.

Bisected as well as defined by the boundaries of geological plates, the Caribbean is the name of a plate but also has the northern half of its sea as part of a separate one, the North American plate. This situation helps explain the volcanic arcs that have produced the consequent distribution of the islands of the Greater and Lesser Antilles. To the south, the relationship of the Caribbean and South American plates has been linked to the formation of islands to the north of South America. Central America is part of the Caribbean plate, and Mexico of the North American. The frontier character of the region is indicated by the differences found, past and present, over naming it, more particularly the extent to which the Gulf of Mexico should be seen as part of the Caribbean. Following the example of my *Brief History of the Mediterranean* (2020), which included the Adriatic and the Aegean, the decision here has been to include the Gulf. The alternative, in leaving it out, would be to divide Cuba and Yucatán between two bodies of water.

Theories of the origin of the Caribbean plate provide alternatively a Pacific or an Atlantic origin of the 'Caribbean large igneous province' that became the plate. The usual view suggests an eastward migration of the plate from 80 million years ago, which is relatively recent in geological terms, with the result being a volcanic arc from South America to Yucatán via the Antilles, leading to a land bridge along the eastern and northern sides of the plate that survives today in the shape of islands and underwater features. In turn, the western margin of the plate was lifted up, becoming Central America about 3 million years ago.

Geological instability has left an often deadly legacy of volcanoes and earthquakes, both above and below the sea; although not so for the Gulf of Mexico, where, instead, long-term sedimentary loading lowered the underlying crust. Similarly, the Bahamas are built on the basement rock of the Florida–Bahamas platform, which has subsided under its own weight. The Bahama Banks were dry land during past Ice Ages, and some of the banks are wholly submerged, notably the Mouchoir, Silver and Navidad banks, all of which are north of the Dominican Republic.

Volcanoes and earthquakes have had a devastating impact on particular places in recorded time and would also have done earlier. Thus, Port Royal, Jamaica, a major English settlement on a natural harbour, was crippled by an earthquake in 1692, which led to the founding in 1693 of Kingston across the bay. Many of its first settlers were refugees from Port Royal which, now a fishing village, became one of the many dead cities found across the Caribbean.

The geological history of the Caribbean left it with more islands than similar areas of ocean-linked sea, notably the Arabian Sea and the Bay of Bengal to the west and east of India, and more than all other parts of the Atlantic or the eastern Pacific; points that are particularly apparent if readily inhabitable islands are considered. Indeed, the Caribbean approach to the Americas contrasts notably with that in inhabitable climes to the Americas from the west, for, in the latter, there are no similar island groups.

There is no uniformity on the islands or shores of the Caribbean, or in its waters. Indeed, of the 87,000 square miles (225,000 square kilometres) of the West Indies, Cuba occupies 40,852 square miles, Hispaniola 29,529, Jamaica 4320, Puerto Rico 3435, Trinidad 1864 and North Andros Island in the Bahamas 1328; but the remainder are less than 900, and, among them, Grand Turk and Saba only 6.7 and 5 respectively. The complex geology and geological history of the region ensure an enormous diversity in islands, notably, depending on their age, between volcanic ones and others, some of which are older. Thus, on Trinidad, there are two mountain ranges as well as lower land. Islands are variously limestone, for example Barbados or the flat south-west of Tobago, young volcanic, such as Grenada, or older volcanic rocks, as with the Blue Mountains of Jamaica and the Sierra Maestra of Cuba. Erosion has affected some of the older volcanic terrain, for example on St Martin; but volcanic plugs remain prominent, as with the two dramatic and photogenic Pitons on St Lucia. On Dominica, the steam-covered Boiling Lake is volcanically heated. Marine sediments are also important to the surface and submarine geology of the region, a geology that greatly affects the soil and therefore agricultural landscapes; with alluvial plains leading to fertile, brown soil, while windward slopes tend to have red clay. Islands can range from lush to barren.

In turn, the climate produces major variations on land, not least with rainfall; and many islands have, within a surprisingly small area, very contrasting wet and dry sides. The windward sides are cooler. Rainfall supporting rainforest is seen on the continental coast from Colombia to Belize and in some of the islands, but drier conditions are the case in Venezuela, its offshore islands, Cuba and Yucatán, and from the last northwards into Texas. In dry areas, savanna grasslands are conducive for animal husbandry, and cotton responds well to constant heat, but it requires water, well-drained soils and fairly dry conditions. Wetter areas are used for sugar, bananas, coffee and the growing of food crops, but their humidity makes work very tiring and, depending on the season, can make life oppressive.

Alongside variations due to the latitude of the islands and related wind conditions, come those linked to altitude, which leads to higher rainfall, as on Guadeloupe, and to exposure, notably to the wet trade wind. In contrast, there is less rainfall on the leeward side of islands and on low land. These microclimates can ensure major differences, and related consequences for vegetations, in some islands such as Martinique, let alone larger Hispaniola, which, as a legacy of the colonial division between the French and Spanish empires formalised in 1697, is now divided between Haiti and the Dominican Republic. Linked to the varied rainfall come major contrasts in vegetation, fauna and exposure to disease; all of which were of great consequence for human life.

Geological diversity is not only seen on land, for there are underwater ridges and troughs, with the sea shallow on the whole, but also, in the Cayman Trough, with a depth of about 7600 metres (25,000 feet). The complex pattern of islands and underwater ridges creates a series of basins, the whole leading to particular passages and distinctive currents and winds. These were of great significance in the age of sail, as well as for those relying on vessels powered by rowing; and names, such as Windward Passage (between Cuba and Hispaniola) and Leeward

Islands, capture this significance. On the lee side, ships could take shelter from storms, but could also be becalmed. So also with the importance of these features for fishing.

Whales in the Caribbean

The Caribbean is a prime area for whale watching, and notably so for humpback whales off the Dominican Republic and in the eastern Caribbean, for example off Grenada, Martinique, Grand Turk and St Lucia from mid-January to mid-March and more generally for whales between December and April, as a result of seasonal migrations, although some whales have a year-long presence. Other whales seen include sperm whales, beaked whales, pilot whales and, less frequently, orcas (killer whales). These, however, are not the only areas with whales. Thus, humpbacks, orcas, pilot whales, sperm whales, Bryde's whales and fin whales are seen off Curaçao. Dolphins are also seen, for example off St Lucia and Curaçao.

Shallowness, complexity and storms have combined to ensure numerous shipwrecks; and notably so before the waters were reliably charted. Wooden warships were holed when driven onto rocks, and could be badly damaged by coral reefs. The poorly charted nature of inshore waters made entering and leaving harbours, as well as enforcing blockades, particularly hazardous, and shoals were also a problem when attacking enemy warships sheltering in coastal waters. Once aground, ships were vulnerable to attack and to the weather.

At sea, wind-powered ships were heavily dependent on the weather, with too much or insufficient wind both serious problems, and ships only able to sail up to a certain angle to the wind.

The powerful easterly trade wind created a particular difficulty, and it could be very difficult to beat back from the leeward. As a result of these problems, which could cause real difficulties and even danger, the significance of certain passages, the shelter they offered and the winds they required, greatly increased. This was particularly because the major channels could be hazardous, for example the Florida or Bahamas Channel between Florida and the Bahamas, which offered the westerly support of the Gulf Stream, and the Anegada Passage between the Virgin Islands and the rest of the Lower Antilles. The pattern of the winds led to a particular circuit for ships sailing from Europe and then returning to it, for, even after steam power came into play, prevailing winds and currents remained of great significance, affecting ease of navigation, speed and fuel usage.

The hazardous nature of channels and coasts increased the importance of skilful navigation and the accumulation of accurate information about winds and currents for charts. Thus, in 1762, Captain John Elphinstone of HMS *Richmond*, who led the British fleet through difficult waters to Havana, presented the Admiralty with a chart of the north side of Cuba that showed the route of the fleet and the degree of detailed information the Royal Navy could command. However, and unsurprisingly so given the scale of the task arising from the number of islands, much of the Caribbean remained poorly charted until the late nineteenth century. Thus, the Spanish Hydrographic Office mapped the north coast of Cuba in the 1860s and Puerto Rico in the 1890s: Spain had ruled both for centuries. Poor charting increased the need for navigational skill and the ability to read the waters; yet both, in turn, were heavily dependent on good weather and related visibility.

Navigational issues were not the sole problems affecting ships, for general conditions of service were bleak. Aside from cramped living conditions and poor sanitation, both of which encouraged the spread of infections, food supplies could be inadequate and inappropriate. The cumulative impact was to make naval service unattractive and to ensure heavy losses among those already in service, notably due to infectious diseases, such as yellow fever. This hit operational effectiveness. Thus, in the War of Jenkins's Ear (1739–48), the British Admiralty's failure to keep the fleet in the Caribbean adequately manned was exacerbated by the effects of disease, however the Royal Navy could generally get the seamen it needed, particularly the relatively unskilled waisters (men stationed in the 'waist' (middle) of a warship), although doing so involved stripping the transport ships of men and also using soldiers in the process. As seamen did not go ashore as much as soldiers, they were not so exposed to the mosquito that was the vector for yellow fever, and death rates for soldiers were consequently generally higher than on warships. Moreover, for the Royal Navy, the Sick and Hurt Board supplied all the medicines it was asked to, the Admiralty consented to the building of a new hospital, and the sick were given the best treatment that the medical knowledge of the day allowed, but, crucially, the nature of the diseases was not understood.

Measures to improve the situation made the Caribbean less of a hazard. During the American War of Independence (1775–83), British Admiral George Rodney took great care of the health of his fleet, supporting the efforts of Gilbert Blane, a ship's doctor who emphasised the use of fresh fruit, notably lemon juice, to deal with scurvy, and the importance of sanitation. As deaths due to disease fell, so it became easier to support military operations; although the major breakthroughs occurred only in the late nineteenth century, a period for Europeans of limited conflict with the exception of the Spanish–American War of 1898.

The naming by the English of the Mosquito Coast, which takes its name from the Miskito or Mosquito Indians, for that of Nicaragua and Honduras, reflects in large part the impact of the environment. So also with the far higher death rates among European settlers in the Caribbean than in North America; but for which difference, the demographic history, both of the Caribbean and of the New World as a whole, would have been very different.

This was not only a matter for settlers and those on land, for sickness was cited as a factor in seamen's grievances and in the decay of social order aboard ships generally. Ships with a lot of sick men were undermanned, and the sailors expected officers to do something about it. The sources do not always give the specific illnesses, but the big killer seems to have been yellow fever. A Spanish fleet from the Caribbean brought to Cádiz in 1730 the first European cases of yellow fever.

Disease was also a major factor affecting military operations, not least because the troops were close-packed, in ships and encampments, while many of the men, whether from Europe or from North America, were new to the region and had no immunity. In 1703, Lieutenant-Colonel James Rivers wrote of his wish to leave Jamaica: 'to get out of this unhealthy climate as soon as possible which diminishes the forces both sea and land very considerably every day ... for fear of this service several of the officers quitted their commission'. Proposing an attack on Havana in the event of war with Spain in 1727, Lieutenant-Colonel Alexander Spotswood warned of the need to have troops inured to the climate and to tropical illness; while disease and the effects of rum caused heavy losses among the British troops who arrived to garrison Jamaica in 1731. 'They will fight well at first, but soon they will fall sick and die like flies', correctly predicted Toussaint L'Ouverture, the leader of the rebels on Saint-Domingue, of the French forces unsuccessfully sent in 1801–2 to suppress the slave rebellion. 'My fears on that subject are the climate, the climate, the climate' (which was seen as responsible for heavy losses from disease) reflected Colonel Gordon in 1808 about the possibility of a campaign on the Caribbean coast of South America that did not in the end occur. In 1837–8, the French naval blockade of Tampico, a significant Mexican Caribbean port not least because of its customs dues, was hit hard by yellow fever, while the French unit dispatched there in August 1863 during the Mexican Civil War was sent back to France the following March, due to the impact on it of tropical disease. In 1898, the American forces in Cuba lost over three times as many men through disease as in battle with the Spaniards.

Far from being a constant across time, disease was an important part of the history of the Caribbean. Yellow fever, which first definitely struck there in 1647, was to be a particular scourge and was especially virulent in whites previously unexposed to the disease; which helped give particular value, for family (inheritance and marital) and business purposes, to those who had been exposed and had survived. The ships that brought the slaves from West Africa carried mosquitoes that had the yellow fever virus. Because the *Aedes aegypti* mosquito that passed on yellow fever only lives thirty days and does not fly far from where it hatches, the mosquitoes initially did not survive the transatlantic crossing, or, if they did, the virus could not find opportunities in the Caribbean. This changed in 1647 as Barbados began to receive many black slaves, and the mosquitoes discovered that the watering holes built to catch the rains in lieu of running water provided excellent breeding grounds for their eggs, so that large numbers hatched after rainfall. The insects found ready victims for the virus, which began with flu-like symptoms, moving on to vomiting a black discharge, and then, with eyes and skin turning yellow as livers were infected, to, in many cases, unconsciousness and death. The virus hit European workers hardest as many slaves had already survived the virus in Africa. From Barbados, the other islands were infected in the 1650s.

As part of a general process of ecological change seen for example with the introduction of rats, the cutting down of forests to clear land for sugar cultivation, and to provide fuel for sugar refining, hit the birds that were predators of mosquitoes. This cutting down of the forests continued, being seen in the nineteenth century on Cuba as sugar cultivation spread eastward on the island. More generally, the cutting down of trees produced major environmental changes, not least a marked lessening in biodiversity, as well as local alterations in drainage. Both the cutting down of forests and the challenge from mosquitoes were aspects of the Caribbean as a frontier world. Moreover, clay pots used for sugar refining, once discarded and filled with rainwater, became breeding grounds for mosquitoes, and the latter also fed off sugar. Water for drinking and cooking had to be boiled to get the mosquito eggs out, and familiarity with tropical diseases was an important impact of the African-American and Native American contribution to the life of Caribbean societies; one that European-Americans were inclined to underplay, if not overlook. Disease continued to be a major killer in the late nineteenth century, hitting hard the abortive French attempt to build the Panama Canal; but American success in tackling disease, a success reflecting applied knowledge and an engineering approach, helped ensure that they completed the canal.

Earlier, alongside insects, parasites and disease attacking humans and their plants, for example the boll weevil with cotton, came the impact of *Teredo navalis*, the shipworm, a species of salt-water clam that was spread on ship hulls and attacked both them and harbour piers. Adding to the problems created by barnacles and weeds, there was a consequent loss of speed for ships. As a result, after other attempts to prevent the ravages of the shipworm, the British resorted to copper sheathing their warships, and this helped with both speed and refitting, Charles, 2nd Marquess of Rockingham claiming in 1781: 'the copper bottoms occasioning our ships to sail so much better enables us either to go and attack if we should see an inferior fleet or to decline the attempt if we should see a superior fleet'.

The advantages for power projection brought by shipping, however, were lost when approaching shorelines made difficult by shoals, cliffs, dense forest or marshes, which, between them, covered much of the Caribbean shoreline. Thus, Thomas

Wentworth, a young British naval officer, wrote in January 1815 about the British advance on New Orleans: 'the place seems naturally unfavourable to our operations, almost the whole country consisting of one impassable morass'.

Success against disease in the twentieth century has thrown attention even more on natural disasters such as volcanic eruptions, for example of the explosive Mount Pelée on Martinique in 1902 and 1929, and hurricanes, as in the Dominican Republic in 1930 and 1979, and Cuba in 1926. Early settlers struggled to understand the formation and patterns of hurricanes. Now that they are better understood, they can still be devastating, even if warnings are possible.

Their impact persists. For St Martin, Hurricane Donna (1960) was succeeded by Luis (1995) and Irma (2017), while Hurricane Flora badly hit Tobago's banana, coconut and cacao plantations in 1963, encouraging a turn to tourism, and Hurricane Katrina in 2006 dramatically cut the population of New Orleans from 484,674 in April 2000 to 230,172. The poor, mostly black, population of East New Orleans found their homes flooded and lacked insurance. Many moved away, in that they chose to settle where they were taken to emergency accommodation, largely in Dallas and Houston; an option that is not open for the inhabitants of Caribbean islands. The population of New Orleans by July 2015 was back up to 386,612, but the impact of Katrina is still apparent. In 2020, an earthquake on Puerto Rico caused severe damage, including the collapse of a prominent coastal feature, the stone arch of the Punta Ventana, as well as widespread power cuts. There was an unprecedented number of hurricanes that year, breaking the 2005 record, with Eta for example hitting coastal communities in Nicaragua, Honduras and Guatemala.

Meanwhile, the coastline of Louisiana was greatly affected by the combination, with the more general process of global warming, of specific human activity, in the shape of the channelling of the flow of the River Mississippi, to deal with floods, such as the major one on the German Coast (named after German settlers) of the Mississippi in 1927. This channelling resulted in more of the river-borne silt being deposited deeper into the Gulf of Mexico. The net effect was that the shoreline receded, while former offshore islands became sandbanks, which was significant both economically and for natural life, as the mudflats were where many animals seeded, for example providing a major source of oysters.

A more widespread environmental crisis has arisen from recent global climate warming. That has caused rising seas, which are a threat to low-lying islands, such as the San Blas archipelago off Panama, as well as greater evaporation. Combined with lower rainfall, and even, as in 2016 and 2019, drought, this has helped cause a fall in the level of Lake Gatun, which makes up two-fifths of the Panama Canal, and thus has threatened the depth of the ships that can transit, as well as plans for upgrades. Panama's income and water supply are both threatened as a result. Global warming is also a significant issue in the East Indies, but the Caribbean is more exposed, not least because its low-lying islands and shores are very vulnerable to hurricanes.

2

'Pre-European/Contact' Civilisations

....

Like dangling emerald pendants the two humming-birds were making their last rounds of the hibiscus and a mocking bird had started on its evening song, sweeter than a nightingale's, from the summit of a bush of night-scented jasmine.

Ian Fleming, *Live and Let Die* (1954)

The land bridges, the remains of which currently in part frame the Caribbean, offered ways for mammals and other species to travel; and humans eventually became part of the process. Theories of human origin and spread in the New World vary, and will continue to do so, but the usual view is that humans crossed from north-east Siberia via a land bridge where the Bering Strait is today; although there is also the suggestion that the first colonisers from Asia were seaborne. At any rate, these humans moved south, eventually to populate Central and South America, neither of which was populated at this stage nor settled from across the Atlantic. The overall situation was made more complex by the period of cooling that resulted in the Pleistocene glaciation, or Ice Ages, as, during the cold spells, ice caps advanced from the poles while, with so much water held in the ice caps, sea levels fell. The southward movement of humans into Central America was affected by the ice, while a large part of what is now the Caribbean was then land, notably the northern section of the Gulf of Mexico. Variations in the Caribbean coastline are a significant part of its more recent geological history.

The melting of the ice and the rising of the sea levels were linked to warmer climes that opened up more land for human habitation. Hunting was dominant at this stage and remained very important, and, as a result, hunting can be found in Mayan art. Animals were also important to religion, as with the Mayan jaguar deities, including the God of the Underworld. A Maya site in Chiapas, Mexico, yielded a terracotta lidded bowl of *c.* 200 to *c.* 600 CE depicting the water bird fishing on the waters of the world.

So also with other cultures. Thus, finds from the Veracruz Culture of about 100 to 1000 CE include a frog yoke stone (*c.* 600 to *c.* 900 CE), a head with a serpent helmet (*c.* 300 to 900 CE) and a palma depicting a ball player and flying bats (*c.* 200 to *c.* 900 CE). El Tajín, near but not on the sea, was the major site of this culture, and ball games were important, including to ritual, as they also were for the Olmecs and the Maya.

Agriculture, meanwhile, spread, with maize, beans and squash being cultivated, maize being the staple for the Olmec, Maya and the Veracruz; and sweet potato and amaranth grown on the Caribbean islands. Agriculture is believed to have diffused to the islands from South America where cultigens were domesticated, and then spread northward along the islands.

This followed the spread into and through the islands, by means of rowing boats, of humans. Trinidad was settled in the mid-sixth millennium BCE, and humans reached Hispaniola and Cuba by the mid-fifth, with major consequences for other animals as humans proved the most successful predator. Subsequently, other peoples took the same route, the Saladoid from 400 BCE, the Barrancoid from 250 CE, the Arauquinoid (later called Taíno and Arawaks) from 650 CE, and the Mayoid (later called Caribs) from 1200 CE. However, this account underplays the complexity of the range of migrant groups; and the conventional categorisation can be actively misleading, a point supported by research on other areas of human settlement. This earlier sequence was not necessarily peaceful. In particular, the

Caribs killed or enslaved the Arawaks where they encountered them. Separately, settlement on particular islands may have been affected by volcanism.

Other peoples appear to have come to the islands from the American mainland further north, either from Florida or Yucatán, both of which are close and with easy sea crossings. This was notably so to Cuba across the Yucatán channel, which could well have been a settlement 'lifeline' whether or not it subsequently became the basis for an exchange network. The net effect was to produce considerable ethnic diversity and, as in the Pacific, very varied settlement histories, with Jamaica and the Bahamas not apparently settled until about 600 CE. Language studies show early migrations around the Caribbean. In addition, to the Arawak/Taíno and Caribs, the Chibchan-language family based in the Costa Rica–Panama border area extended to Colombia, while Mayan languages indicated movement of both people and language. Language studies remain an active area of fresh hypothesis for Caribbean history.

From the perspective of diversity and change, the Spaniards in the 1490s represented another stage in the settlement history of the Caribbean, and, again, a disruptive one; although the scale of the disruption was greater to human society and to animals and plants. On the other hand, conquest by Caribs would have been experienced by humans in a similar fashion. Meanwhile, animals moved with humans, guinea pigs being found in Puerto Rico after around 600 CE.

There was far more human settlement on the continental shores than on the islands. Surviving sites of early settlement include Taima-Taima in Venezuela and El Bosque in Nicaragua. The former suggests human occupation back in 12,200 to 10,980 BCE, and archaeological evidence includes a mastodon bone pierced by spearpoint. Seasonal hunting and gathering were the nutritional base of these peoples, who also started growing squash, avocadoes and chillies in Central America by

5500 BCE, and sunflower, sumpweed and tepary bean in the Mississippi basin from about 4500 BCE. Pottery followed in north-western South America by about 3000 BCE, and in Mexico by about 2400 BCE; and there was a transition to permanent settlements, and the farming that went with them, with cotton cultivated in Central America by about 3500 BCE. Trade links followed, producing revenues and encouraging urbanisations, and, by 1200 BCE, the Olmec civilisation was flourishing.

The Olmecs, the earliest civilisation in Central America of which there is much knowledge, developed on the Caribbean coast of Mexico on the Isthmus of Tehuantepec in about 1150 BCE, and remained significant until about 400 BCE, trading widely in Central America and producing impressive sculptures and pottery, as well as developing a pantheon of gods, a calendar and a writing system. Other sites further north on the coast included Taxla, Remojadas, El Trapiche and Pavón.

To the east, a jungle-based Maya civilisation developed from about 1000 BCE and came to dominate Yucatán, which became the centre of their impressive and more far-reaching civilisation. The goods produced extended to books made of bark paper and covered in jaguar skins. Ritual and ceremonial played an important part in culture and society, as with ritual dances. Boxing and a game with rubber balls were leisure activities. The Maya staple was maize, and their ceremonials included the consumption of cacao in the shape of liquid chocolate. Force was part of the equation. Thus, from Yucatán comes a terracotta standing warrior who is depicted wearing armour and a removable mask bearing an image to create terror, and holding an axe and a circular shield. Discoveries about the Maya continue, as with the excavation from the late 2010s of the capital of the Sak Tz'i' (White Dog) kingdom.

The bulk of Maya cities were inland, with additional sites revealed recently beneath the forest cover through the use of pulses of light from lasers mounted on an aircraft to create a three-dimensional map of the surface hidden beneath vegetation, as with the astronomical site at Aguada Fénix in the Mexican province of Tabasco, the discovery of which was revealed in 2020; and there will be more finds. There were also coastal settlements such as Bellote, Jaina Island, Cozumel and Tancah, and ports such as Chaktumal, Tulum, Moho Cay and Wild Cane Cay; and, necessarily so because of the impassable nature of much of the interior, coastal trade routes both westwards and eastwards. These routes appear to have hugged the coastline where water and food could be taken on by the crew and goods traded. Ports were located where coastal and inland routes converged, notably the latter in the shape of navigable rivers, and the absence of wheeled vehicles and draught animals encouraged reliance on water transport. Breaks in the sea cliffs, when accompanied by coves and landing beaches, were important for access to canoes. A major product of the Caribbean coast was salt, with brine boiled in ceramic pots, as in Punta Ycacos Lagoon in Belize, and the salt then traded. So also with maize, honey, fish, textiles, ceramics, cacao, gold, feathers and obsidian, the last of which has been found in particular at Tulum.

The extent to which the Maya navigated the Caribbean is unclear. Dugout canoes were probably made from hollowed-out cedar trunks made watertight with pitch, although archaeological evidence on the islands of the results of trade is limited. Ferdinand Columbus described one canoe encountered near the Bay Islands during his father's fourth voyage in 1504. It was 'as long as a galley and eight feet wide' and 'in the middle' had a 'shelter of palm matting'. It contained up to twenty-five men as well as women and children and was full of trade merchandise from Yucatán. This was an impressive boat, but the Bay Islands were not far offshore. Moreover, watercraft designs and navigational techniques seen in many of the world's seas were not present, while seafaring traditions on the islands further from the shore may have waned after initial colonisation.

The Huastec civilisation on the Caribbean coast of northern Mexico, whose remains include shell-made discoidal ear flares of about 900 to 1200 CE, had artistic and cultural similarities with the Maya. The latter, however, may have suffered from climate change, notably desertification as well as war; both of which could have brought down the Classic period of their civilisation in the ninth to tenth centuries. The Maya were, in part, replaced by the Mexican-based Toltecs, who created an empire from about 900 to 1200 CE that had numerous coastal sites on the Gulf including Las Flores, Cempoala, the Isla de Sacrificios and Atasta, that settled Yucatán, and that traded widely.

In contrast, the eventual replacement of the Toltecs, the fifteenth-century Aztec empire, was based in the Valley of Mexico and had scant presence on the coast other than to obtain tribute. This was very different to the pattern of European colonisation that was to supervene, and, like the Inca empire of the Andean chain, the Aztecs had no global linkages, although it is possible that the Aztecs relied in part on Mayan traders. Their adaptation to local crops included the drinking of *pulque*, a fermented beverage made from the maguey (agave) plant.

At the same time, in the Post-Classical period (*c.* 950–1696), the Maya cities of northern Yucatán continued to be inhabited even though much of the central Maya area further south was abandoned. Mayapan is an example of a major city from this period, although it appears to have been partly destroyed in conflict in the mid-fifteenth century.

On the North American shores of the Caribbean, the Hopewell culture of the Mississippi Valley (*c.* 100 to *c.* 400 CE) was centred further north, but reached and traded to the Gulf (Caribbean) coast, from which turtles, fish and shells were obtained. In turn, from about 800 CE, the Mississippian culture was also centred further north, but its influence extended to the Gulf. Coastal settlements from the period included Fort Walton, Weeden Island, Safety Harbor, Madira Bickel Mound, Englewood and Key Marco in Florida. There have been controversies over the dating of sites and cultures, and concerning the classification of peoples, for example the relationship between Weeden Island and Mississippian cultures. A key element was adaptation to the subsistence possibilities of particular sites, in the shape of the relationship between fishing, hunter-gathering and agriculture. Ceremonials also varied. The Weeden Island culture is dated from 200 to 1200 CE and came to be characterised by chiefdoms. Used for ritual and/or adornment, and thus also as a form of currency, stingray spines and seashells were traded from the coast. They were also used by other cultures, such as the Olmec.

On the South American coast of the Caribbean, there are few sites prior to 10,000 BCE, notably Taima-Taima, and then, with the spread of agriculture, notably manioc and then maize, the development of sites round Lake Maracaibo and in the Lower Orinoco basin. Banwari Trace and Barrancas are early sites. Subsequently, the coastline saw some autonomous chiefdoms, notably the Tairona ones in modern Colombia, and the Orinqueponi and Llanos in Venezuela. Such chiefdoms shaded off into tropical forest farming villages, and the latter into hunter-gatherers, whether sedentary or nomadic.

Traditionally, attention has focused, instead, on the 'highly developed civilisations', such as the Aztec. This approach, however, underplays the role of other cultures, and the degree to which their fitness for purpose ensured what was their level of necessary development and adaptation which should not, therefore, be judged critically. The chiefdom areas, moreover, could include appreciable numbers of people. The religions tended to be animist, with the addition of ancestor cults in which the remains of chiefs played an important role. Animals played a major role in the culture, as with the *incensario* or stand for burning incense with double alligator heads of *c.* 60 to *c.* 110 CE from Caribbean Costa Rica, from which *metate*, or ceremonial grinding stones carved from volcanic heads, survive, as do gold and jade pendants and jewellery.

An attempt to link back to these cultures is important to modern states seeking to find an appropriate early history that does not simply present them as imperial subjects, notably of Spain, and this attempt can be seen in Costa Rica's National Museum in San José which has a good holding of pre-Columbian material. However, this attempt is complicated by the longstanding tension between the descendants of indigenous peoples and those, in whole or part, of Hispanic origin who tend to remain socially dominant. Tourists are usually shown Maya sites, which are truly impressive and well worth a visit, and where the pyramidal structures exist and can be climbed, this should be done, albeit with care. Having visited Maya sites in Belize and Mexico, I prefer the former as there are fewer tourists: Caracol is the largest, and Altun Ha, Xunantunich and Lamanai are all worth visiting.

There was a parallel in the Caribbean with the systems of settlement and trade within, and between, archipelagos in the western Pacific. As there, overpopulation could encourage migration and thus lead to conflict; although the evidence for this overpopulation is necessarily indirect. It was in part inherent to 'slash-and-burn' or patterns of shifting cultivation as soil nutrients were exhausted. These patterns, which increased the environmental impact and damage brought by humans, also brought human groups into hostile contact with each other.

'Slash-and-burn' agriculture was also to be seen later in Caribbean history, including by the Maroons (escaped slaves, from the Spanish *cimarrones* for mountaineers) who evaded European control, for example on Jamaica; as well, separately, as by former slaves in the late nineteenth century. The system relied on the need for clearing forest to create a field termed a swidden, being combined with the value of burning the trees in order to produce ash rich in nutrients. Moreover, burning was a way to destroy weeds and pests for a period of time. The combination of benefits was an aspect of human adaptation to the environment, one that, alongside legacy patterns of behaviour, was important to 'pre-contact' and European societies, as well as to Africans and other settlers. Characterised by shifting cultivation, 'slash-and-burn', and particularly the land demands of its shifting nature, it was also, however, a source of social and political tension, as it could clash with existing assumptions about land control and use. This issue captures a source of the interaction of change with continuity that helps make Caribbean history so fascinating. On the one hand comes the continuity of the practice of slash-and-burn, which is a response not only to environmental conditions but also to social factors, notably individual and collective resources and opportunities, both of which have been limited, as they remain. The context, however, also changes, notably with attitudes toward land ownership and access. We should not assume an idyllic situation of 'pre-contact' harmony as it would be naive to overlook violent practices of tribal control and contention. But with European settlement, land ownership and access became differently fixed and contentious and this was very much at the expense of the indigenous populations, who were largely wiped out or enslaved in the Caribbean. As a result, the issues of land ownership and access involved in control over 'slash-and-burn' became an aspect of the European settlers' response to areas of continued independent native presence. Moreover, the issues swiftly became involved with the question of the livelihood of escaped slaves. This was seen on Jamaica where, although the first Maroon War began in 1728, there had been earlier conflict. Control at many levels over land, people and activity was therefore involved.

The value of land for cultivation varied by group. To Europeans, land was important if it could be used for plantation agriculture, a usefulness which in part was a matter of transport links. Lacking those, areas which could be used simply for growing food were of far less value to Europeans, whereas the situation was different for local populations and for slaves who had struggled to win and retain freedom.

This contrast then changed after the emancipation of slaves, as, with the decline of the plantation economy, the pattern of cultivation altered, and so did the value of land. Thus, with the strengthening of practices of self-sufficiency, there was more of a zone of limited outside control over activity. That situation continued into the twentieth century but, in turn, was affected by the marked rise in the population, while the issue of land access and control was also placed under strain by the development of mass tourism from the late twentieth century.

The pre-European political pattern on the islands was of generally small units, as also in the forested parts of the mainland; and this pattern was linked to separate tribal deities. In Hispaniola, aside from the more recent Caribs to the east, there were five tribal areas among the Taíno, each under a chieftain, and there was communal working of the land. As iron was not known, sharpened sticks or stone-headed axes were used in agriculture, which was primarily based on the cultivation of yucca, from which cassava bread was produced. Pre-Columbian stone axes can be found for example in the *Museo Castillo de la Real Fuerza* in Havana, situated in an old fort. The technological development at the time was limited: there were no horses or oxen or llamas, and no wheeled transport.

The Taíno are commonly divided between the Classic Taíno, based in Hispaniola, Puerto Rico and the eastern tip of Cuba; the Eastern Taíno on the islands from Guadeloupe to the Virgin Islands; and the Western Taíno on Jamaica, the Bahamas, most of Cuba and westernmost Hispaniola. These cultural areas underline the significance of maritime links. The extent to which the Taíno had large chiefdoms varied, being less with the Western than the Classic Taíno. Taíno remains include, from Haiti, a wooden inhaler with the face of a bird that was supposedly used to inhale a drug in order to help messages with the dead, and, from Cuba, an idol that is thought to have been for the ritual preparation of tobacco leaves. The non-Taíno Guanahatabey, a hunter-gatherer people unlike the farming Taíno, were on western Cuba, and may have been descendants of an earlier culture, like those in other areas, for example southern Florida. The Guanahatabey had no pottery and constructed no dwellings, living instead in caves or outdoors.

The accounts of native societies offered by Europeans were of varied value, and also contradictory. Thus, Colonel John Scott (c. 1634–96) wrote of cannibalism: 'They rather eat out of malice, chewing only one mouthful and spitting it out again, and animating one another thereby to be fierce and cruel to their enemies, as a thing pleasing to their Gods, and it hath been a great mistake in those that have reported the Southern Indians eat one another as food.'

Aside from links with the Maya and the Toltecs, there was trade between what is now Costa Rica and the Caribbean in c. 500 to c. 1500, but nothing that offered any preparation for European impact. Thus, the notion, based on a degree of facial resemblance, that the Olmecs were Africans who had emigrated is widely rejected. More modestly, Cuba is only about 219 kilometres (130 miles) from Yucatán, the Bahamas 100 kilometres (60 miles) from Florida, and Trinidad 11 kilometres (7 miles) from Venezuela; but these distances did not see a power projection that was to compare with those of the Europeans.

The geopolitical situation was very different in the East Indies where, although there was no state in control of what is an enormous area, there were empires, notably Srivijaya, which, from the late seventh century to the thirteenth, was based on Sumatra, dominated Java and Malaya, and was much involved in trade, including with China, and was important to the expansion of Buddhism. There was no equivalent to the Taíno position. Srivijayan ships also reached to Madagascar, Borneo and the Philippines. In turn, the Srivijaya were hit hard by the Chola

kingdom of Sri Lanka in the eleventh century, and, more seriously, by the Singhasari empire of eastern Java in the thirteenth.
This trading power was followed by the Javan-based Majapahit
empire (1293–1527) that had or at least sought influence across
much of the East Indies, and control certainly of eastern Java,
Malaya, Sumatra, Sulawesi and coastal Borneo. The warfare of the
period required large-scale naval movements. Muslim prosely-
tisers and traders benefited from the Majapahit hegemony, and
there was no equivalent in the Caribbean. Another instructive
contrast is that between the Ming Chinese naval presence in the
early fifteenth century and that of Spain in the Caribbean. The
Ming imposed a degree of hegemony, and helped local protégés,
notably the Sultanate of Malacca; but, on the part of Ming China,
there was neither a search for more permanent control nor persis-
tence. The situation was to be totally different for the Caribbean
in the case of the Spanish empire.

3

The Europeans Arrive, 1492–1600

....

Our ship being so tossed, that she opened at the stern a [fathom: six feet] under water ... and for fear of sinking we threw into the sea all the goods we had or could come by: but that would not serve. Then we cut our main mast and threw all our ordinance [cannon] into the sea saving one piece ... And then we began to embrace one another, every man his friend, every wife her husband, and the children their fathers and mothers, committing our souls to Almighty God, thinking never to escape alive.

> Robert Thompson, 1555. He was rescued
> off the coast of Mexico by a passing ship.

By sailing west from Spain to discover a route to Asia, Christopher Columbus (*c.* 1451–1506) hoped to raise money to retake the Holy Land, a goal that was a crucial preliminary, in the widespread millenarian views of the period, to the Second Coming of Christ; and, thus, to the redemption of the Christian world. In his *Book of Prophecies*, compiled before his fourth voyage to the Caribbean, in 1502, Columbus argued that the end of the world would occur in 155 years, and that his own discoveries had been foretold in the Bible. Drawing on the up-to-date geographical information of the period, information greatly enhanced by the Renaissance and its emphasis on Classical understanding, notably that the world was a sphere, Columbus set sail westwards in 1492. With three lightly-armed and relatively small ships, he thought he was bound for Japan, which Marco Polo, although he had not got there, had reported about because the Chinese knew of Japan, which they had unsuccessfully tried to invade. Using Ptolemy's second-century ideas as a guide, Columbus, who was sponsored by Queen Isabella of Castile, had expected the voyage from Europe to be around 2400 nautical miles (4450 kilometres), not the 10,000 it really entailed. In the event, Columbus found (the natives already knew it was there) what was to be termed the West Indies.

Born around 1451 in Genoa, a key trading city, Columbus took part in Portuguese trading missions, being shipwrecked off Portugal in 1476, before entering the service of Spain. This was not easy; he faced mutinous sailors on his voyage in 1492, and in 1500 was removed from office and sent back to Spain in chains. Columbus was part of a pattern of Iberian expansion supported by Italian navigators and driven in part by economic interest. Drawing on their longstanding ideological crusading role in driving Islam from Iberia, a task achieved with the fall of Granada in 1492, the crowns of Portugal and Castile had already been looking further afield.

Territorial claims followed Columbus's first voyage, and in the Papal division of 1493, followed by the Treaty of Tordesillas of 1494, the Atlantic world was divided between Portuguese and Spanish zones, with Africa awarded to Portugal and what was then known as the Americas to Spain (the product of joining the inheritances of Castile and Aragon); although subsequent exploration revealed that Brazil was in the Portuguese zone. This Papal division was to be rejected by France as well as by Protestant powers.

Sailing west across the Atlantic benefiting from the speeding Trade Wind might sound relatively easy, but, in practice, voyagers faced major difficulties, especially in terms of supplies, routes, certainty, safety and maintenance. For supplies, the need to collect fresh water from rain was a particular issue, as was preventing food from spoiling totally, and delays at sea that might jeopardise the supply situation. Separately, navigation was tricky, and it was hard to assess dead reckoning. Storms were a major problem, indeed leading to the death of Pánfilo de Narváez and most of his men near Galveston in 1528. Equipment included log and line (for speed and distance measurement), the traverse board (for recording the ship's movement), the sandglass (for timing), and lead and line (to identify location by water depth and the nature of the seabed). The thirty-two-point compass was used to help navigation, tidal prediction and timekeeping.

Despite multiple difficulties, the lure of opportunities encouraged repeated voyages which, through a process of accumulation and checking, brought experience including knowledge of navigational conditions, notably winds, currents and channels. As a result, the Spanish presence in the Caribbean was inherently incremental, and knowledge came from repeated expedition, as when Hernando de Soto failed to find a route to the Pacific, both along the Yucatán coast in 1530 and in the southern United States in 1539–42.

From exploration on, conflict defined the history of the region, as Spanish authority was imposed both by individual enterprisers of power and by the monarchy. The enterprisers competed with each other; and the monarchy, which benefited from their efforts, had, nevertheless, to bring them under control, which it did by punishment or patronage, or both. At first, the focus for both enterprisers and monarchy was on the islands, with Hispaniola and, then, more distant Cuba rapidly conquered. The initial cooperation, indeed friendship, of the Taíno of Hispaniola had in part been obtained by Columbus's promise to help them against the fierce Caribs. However, this cooperation was rapidly exhausted by serious mistreatment. In 1495, the Taíno were heavily defeated at Santo Cerro by Columbus on his second voyage. Subsequently, invaded from Hispaniola in 1509 by Diego Velázquez de Cuéllar, Cuba was rapidly conquered from east to west by 1514, with the population, already warned by the fate of Hispaniola, enslaved or killed. The most significant opponent, the Taíno chief Hatuey, was captured and burned at the stake in 1512, only now to be acclaimed as Cuba's first national hero: there are monuments to him in the towns of Baracoa and Yara, he appears on the logo of the cigar and cigarette brand Cohiba, and he plays an indirect role in the Spanish film *Even the Rain* (2010), which ahistorically brought the story into the social tensions in modern-day Bolivia.

There could be effective resistance: the Caribs and Arawaks of the Guianas thwarted Spanish attacks, and mounted counter-raids with fast, manoeuvrable shallow-draft boats carved from tropical trees. Indeed, the Caribs of St Vincent kept the Spaniards out. Nor was there necessarily an easy arrival on the coasts. When the Spaniards first arrived in Florida in 1513, they had been obliged to withdraw by Timucua and Calusa archers, while Pánfilo de Narváez's expedition of 1528 was repelled there by Apalachees and Autes whose accurate archers used arrows capable of penetrating Spanish armour. Maya warriors equipped with quilted cotton armour, and carrying bows, slings, stone-tipped spears and flint or obsidian-edged swords, all deadly, drove back at Champotón a smaller Spanish force under Francisco Hernández de Córdoba. In 1517, Hernández left Cuba to seek new lands and, in particular, slaves, finding, after a storm, the Yucatán coast with the first major urban centre encountered in the New World. Initially, the Mayas met the expedition with ten large canoes that were equipped with oars and sails. The Spanish expedition suffered from a shortage of water, and that led to later landings. Beaten in battle, the Spaniards fled, naming the area 'the coast of the evil battle'. The survivors reached Havana where the wounded Hernández died. However, the report to Mexico that Yucatán contained a city termed *El Gran Cairo*, and of gold, led to strong interest, with expeditions in 1518 under Juan de Grijalva, and in 1519 under Hernán Cortés.

What became the key Spanish move was the conquest of the Aztec empire from 1519. Montezuma, the panicky Aztec ruler, was fascinated by the Spanish leader, Cortés, worried that he might be an envoy from a powerful potentate (despite Spanish claims, he was not seen as a god), and unwilling to act decisively against him. Supported only by about 450 soldiers, Cortés reached the impressive lake-sited Aztec capital, Tenochtitlán, without having to fight his way there. In 1520, however, tensions mounted. A massacre of Aztec nobles in the courtyard of the Great Temple led to an Aztec rising and Cortés had to flee Tenochtitlán. Montezuma was killed and his successor, his ener-getic brother, Cuitláhuac, died that year from smallpox, which killed at least half of the Aztecs and weakened the morale of the survivors. Divisions among native peoples also helped the Spaniards gain allies, there and elsewhere. Aztec expansion, and the lack of a theory and practice of assimilation, had left conquered peoples, such as the Totonacs and Tlaxcalans, ready to ally with, and fight alongside, Cortés, offsetting what would otherwise have been the massive numerical superiority of the Aztecs when they were in fact finally beaten in 1521. So also in Central America. The excessive violence of Cortés's men was linked to their brutalisation during long periods of fighting in the Caribbean before they landed in Mexico.

The conquest of the Aztec empire proved decisive for the Caribbean as it cemented the dominance of the Europeans, later European-Americans or *criollos* (creoles), that was to last until the present. This dominance cut short any alternative in which a native empire based in Central America, notably a successor to the Aztecs that was more committed to coastal regions, developed the technol-ogy, force and interest able to project power to the islands. Crucially drawing on already developed Chinese naval capabilities, Mongol China was to try to do with Japan and Java, and Manchu China was to do so successfully with the closer and more vulnerable target of Taiwan. That was not a prospect in 1492; but it is misleading to think that it might not have become so, either within a develop-ment of the technological parameters of the period, or as a consequence of borrowing, buying or copying Western technology, as happened with the unification of the Hawai'ian archipelago in the late eighteenth and early nineteenth centuries.

In the end, there was to be a fault line in the nineteenth-century Caribbean between still European colonial islands (bar Haiti) and (with the exception of the British presence in British Honduras and on the Mosquito Coast) the largely independent mainland; but this fault line had no relationship to the potential for such a division in the early sixteenth century. There were, initially, however, tensions between Spaniards focused on Cuba and those keen to conquer Mexico and control the consequences, and notably so in 1519, and Cortés's expedition very much took place in this context.

Technological superiority, notably firearms, steel swords and steel helmets, is widely held to have helped the Spaniards, as their opponents could not match them in range, killing power, protection and effectiveness; a situation accentuated by the Spaniards having horses, which provided mobility, presence and height for the cavalry. Yet, weaponry did not give the Spaniards with the necessary mass, as the 1517 expedition discovered, and could anyway be countered, not least by dispersed fighting techniques; and conquest was not always easy, typically due to a combination of local resistance, difficult environmental conditions, insufficient interest in expansion and limited manpower. As the Spaniards were most successful in the Caribbean in regions where there was much for them to gain, their failure to expand elsewhere was not necessarily due to military factors, as the Spaniards never devoted military resources to the New World that in any way compared with their efforts either in European struggles or against Islam.

Spanish control of the extensive jungle regions south-east of Mexico was limited, and the absence of major imperial states that provided a ready target that could be overthrown complicated the Spanish task. Replacing native religious images with those of the

Virgin Mary, Cortés led a costly campaign in Honduras in 1524, while, resuming pre-Spanish patterns of attempted expansion from central Mexico, Pedro de Alvarado invaded Guatemala with native allies, overrunning the area only to undermine his success (and that of his allies) by excessive violence and harsh demands for tribute and labour. As a result of continuing opposition, his brother Jorge recruited 5000 to 10,000 native warriors for his invasion of Guatemala in 1527, but only succeeded in 1529 after large-scale butchery of the population. Native support, which provided fighting power, intelligence and the logistics of porterage, as well as obtaining and preparing supplies, was extremely important. In Yucatán, the Xiu Maya of Maní allied with the Spaniards against their mutual enemy, the Cocom Maya of Sotuta. Helped by their support, and by the smallpox, measles and influenza the Spaniards unwittingly introduced, much of northern Yucatán was brought under Spanish rule in 1527-42, and a rebellion in 1546 was defeated, but the rest of Yucatán did not follow until the 1690s.

Meanwhile, setting off from Havana, and landing initially on the west coast of Florida, Hernando de Soto who, between 1539 and 1542, brutally pillaged local peoples in what is now the southern United States, defeated the Mobilian tribe in 1540, his cavalry dominating the open ground, but he did not consolidate a Spanish presence in the region and died on the banks of the Mississippi. Under Luis de Moscoso, in 1542-3, the survivors made it across eastern Texas to Mexico City having taken more casualties, but the expedition caused epidemics of measles, smallpox and chicken pox.

The checks encountered by the Spaniards highlight the contrast with some, but by no means all, of the Caribbean islands. Superficially, the issue may seem to be one of the greater vulnerability of natives on islands. They contained few places to hide, and were particularly exposed to the maritime power of the Europeans. In contrast, the Spaniards encountered limits to their expansion on land, notably in northern Mexico and central Chile. Yet, while this contrast was indeed important, it was not the complete story, because several of the islands were not conquered, in part due to fear about the Caribs combined with an absence of ostensible attractions for settlers.

Intended to be more than raiding, conquest was not solely a matter of initial military success; although that success was very important. Potential resistance to Spanish control in areas that had been conquered was greatly lessened by enslavement and disease, with enslavement disrupting social structures and household and communal economies, leading to famine and population decline. The herding together of enslaved peoples, for example Arawaks brought from the Bahamas to work the goldmines of Hispaniola in the 1510s, exacerbated the impact of disease, both new and old. Even without enslavement, disease imported by Europeans, particularly smallpox, led to a major fall in indigenous populations who lacked any immunity to it. Smallpox decimated the population of Hispaniola in 1519 and cut that of the island of Cozumel, a major Maya trading and religious site, from up to 10,000 to 358 by 1570. The advent of smallpox was a key aspect of the role of the Caribbean as the conduit for the abrupt transmission, mixing and homogenising of biological and human societies that had hitherto been distinctive because of the physical separation of continents.

Conquest was followed by the arrival of colonists and their livestock, by Christian proselytisation and the destruction of rival religious rituals, by the introduction of administrative and tenurial structures, and by a degree of Spanish acceptance of local élites and local material cultures, not least through intermarriage with prominent local families, as well as of adaptation to the Spaniards. This mutual adaptation was most pronounced in rural areas, and least so in the new towns such as Panama, which was founded in 1517 and served first as the base for expeditions to Peru and, later, as a key site on the transhipment from the Pacific to the Caribbean. To take advantage of the deep water of the largest natural port in the Caribbean, Spain established Havana in 1519. An earlier attempt in 1515, at nearby Batabanó, had been abandoned because of infested swampland and the lack of a sheltered harbour. In 1533, the governor moved his capital from Santiago to Havana. The new cities were also places from which Christianity could be preached. Thus, in 1544, the cathedral of Santa María la Menor was completed at the heart of Santo Domingo, the capital of Hispaniola and the oldest European city in the New World, which had been founded by Columbus's brother Bartholomew in 1496 on the bank of the Ozama River. The university there had been established in 1538. The grid layout of colonial cities was emblematic of imperial control and of the lack of any interest in pre-existing possession of the land. A *Plaza de Armas* for military drill was at the centre of the grid, as in Havana.

Cities were very much affected by the dynamic character of colonisation that responded to dramatically changing opportunities. Thus, Cuba, while attractive initially, not least because of gold, rapidly became much less so, both because the accessible gold deposits were exhausted and due to the greater opportunities on the American mainland. Thus, founded in 1514 as a gold-mining colony, Trinidad had similarly declined within three decades. The population of Havana also fell after its foundation; only to benefit when the harbour of Havana, the Florida Channel and the Gulf Stream became important to the shipment back of goods from the Americas to Spain. The key bullion sources became those of Mexico and Potosi, the 'silver mountain' in what is now Bolivia. Land for settlement was also more plentiful on the mainland, as was native labour, and a more pleasant and healthy living environment for Europeans. The Caribbean islands had less of an appeal on all three heads, and there was a shift of emphasis to the mainland under Spain that, to a degree, prefigured the situation under American dominance. This ensured that the islands were not fully controlled by Spain, which created opportunities for other Europeans to insert themselves into the Caribbean, a process facilitated by their stake in the slave trade. The later insertion of American power into a Caribbean dominated by European empires in the 1780s, of Soviet influence into the American-dominated Caribbean in the 1960s to 1980s, and of Chinese influence likewise in the 2010s and 2020s, were very different in geopolitical terms, but also reflected the limitations of the hegemonic state.

Alongside the often brutal treatment of Native American society, which was seen as heathen and evil, there was the syncretic character of Spanish imperialism, its ability to adopt and adapt as part of its conquest and, even more, rule. This was a policy and practice observed in the way in which, after a period of destructiveness, native religious cults, although not their priests, were given a place within Christianity. Indeed, however much changed by conquest, indigenous communities shaped the Spanish encounter with the Caribbean. Yet, attitudes towards these communities were also affected by traditional Christian ideas, such as the belief in the capacity for human fall from grace which was then applied to the natives, presenting them as, at best, irrational and, more commonly, as primitive. While Christian worship in the Spanish Caribbean might contain elements of compromise, there was no compromise about Christianity, although there were disagreements among the Spaniards about the treatment of the local population.

Their generally harsh treatment was a key element of the political economy of work that was to have a lasting impact in Caribbean population dynamics. Disease and resistance limited the labour force. Natives who were willing to supply goods to the Spaniards by barter were not prepared to provide continuous labour on plantations, which were introduced to Hispaniola from 1503; although the key need for labour there initially was for the goldmines, and the Taíno were oppressed accordingly.

The search for yet more labour encouraged the Spaniards to resort to raiding into unconquered areas, a practice that continued for centuries, and of which today there are still echoes. Thus, the Spaniards conducted large-scale slaving among native peoples in Honduras and Nicaragua, in large part to satisfy a demand for labour in the Caribbean that they had created. The consequences were devastating, with areas of Nicaragua under Spanish control losing more than half of their population. Raiding, however, faced many difficulties, with natives fleeing or resisting. In addition, there were costs to the process, not least those involved in walking the prisoners long distances.

Moreover, control over native labour was at least in theory greatly affected by royal legislation addressing clerical pressure to treat the native peoples as subjects ready for Christianisation, rather than as slaves. This pressure reflected the intention that was to be crucial for Caribbean societies, that Christianity should be a world religion open to all, rather than the religion of an ethnic group. Transoceanic expansion, indeed, was both opportunity and problem, and the linkage of Church and state ensured that each became a subject for royal action. In a key distinction, freedom was seen as an opportunity for proselytism, rather than simply as a reward for becoming Christian. The New Laws for the Good Treatment and Preservation of the Indians (natives) issued in 1542 banned their future enslavement and ordered the freeing of slaves whose owners could not prove legal ownership; although landowners, as well as officials concerned about their views, frequently ignored them. Moreover, de facto slavery was permitted in the form of the *encomienda*, a system of tied labour under which land and, crucially, native families were allocated to colonists, and the *repartimiento*, under which a part of the male population had to work away from home. Making service an element of debt repayment also ensured labour control.

Alongside extensive intermarriage, these methods contributed to a caste system based on ethnicity that became hardwired into society; a caste system that in some respects replicated features in 'pre-contact' native societies, but that was more complex. Intermarriage led to a rapid lessening of the value of these racial categories, not that this prevented their use as part of the incessant process of classification in what was intended to be a very hierarchical society. Indeed, the classification necessarily came to include different categories arising from intermarriage, including *mestizos* (mixed race), *moriscos* (three-quarters Spanish, one-quarter black), *cholos* (one-quarter Spanish, three-quarters Indian) and *castizos* (children of a Spaniard and a *mestiza*). The Taíno are usually referred to as becoming extinct, but many Taíno women raised families headed by European men, and passed on genes and cultural practices that remained parts of Caribbean society. Since the 1990s, the Taíno heritage has attracted more attention.

At the outset, African slavery was not primarily to do with the needs of agriculture, as it was initially more expensive to use this source of labour supply rather than the native peoples. Instead, the Africans were often employed as house slaves. In 1518, however, *asientos* (licences) were granted for the import of slaves direct from Africa, rather than via existing Spanish bases, which enabled a more rapid and profitable supply of slaves. In 1522, a small and rapidly suppressed revolt of African slaves occurred near Santo Domingo on Hispaniola, an island that, thanks largely to sugar plantations, had 25,000 African slaves by the 1550s. Profits from cash crops, such as sugar in Mexico near Veracruz and cacao in Costa Rica, provided liquidity and covered the cost of purchasing slaves. Cacao had been cultivated in pre-Columbian times, having value as currency.

Africans were considered more suited to the heat and humidity of the coastal valleys and lowlands than native peoples, who were generally used as labour in higher and drier terrain; and the slave trade was part of the process by which the Spaniards responded to Caribbean geography and demographics, and acquired, processed and constructed information accordingly. The coastlands were also more dangerous, as infectious disease was a major and far greater problem there; which, in turn, meant the need for more slaves.

Slaves were also crucial to the urban economy, landed at leading ports, notably Cartagena, Veracruz and Havana, employed there as craftsmen, servants and labourers, and used to grow the necessary food for the urban population. There were also Crown slaves, as in Havana, for the construction and maintenance of fortifications (and later with the British naval dockyards), and they could be rented out for use by private labour. However, the availability of native labour, as well as the lack of Spanish bases in Africa from which slaves could be obtained, helped ensure that Africans were a smaller group on much of the mainland than on the islands where disease had ravaged the native population, as in Puerto Rico and Hispaniola, where the black population by 1600 was greater than that of the surviving Taínos. While the Europeans had disproportionate agency in the (Spanish) Caribbean, the Africans were already numerous in the sixteenth century, and outnumbered European immigrants in the seventeenth and eighteenth.

ENGLAND VERSUS SPAIN

The wealth of the Indies encouraged interest and envy from others, most prominently the French who raided Spanish shipping and possessions in the Caribbean from 1528, and increasingly so in the mid-1530s. There were French raids on Santiago in 1537 and 1538, and Havana in 1537, 1538 and 1543. English interest, in contrast, was delayed by Henry VIII's focus on European power politics, and by the marriage in 1554 of Queen Mary (r. 1553–8) to Philip II of Spain; but, in the 1560s, under Elizabeth I (r. 1558–1603) the situation changed: an attempt to take a share in the profitable slave trade to the Spanish New

World was an important aspect of a search for overseas opportunities that in part reflected difficulties with trade to the Low Countries. John Hawkins sold slaves from 1562, finding the Spaniards in Hispaniola very ready to buy, until, at San Juan de Ulúa near Veracruz in September 1568, the presence of the Viceroy of New Spain, Don Martín Enríquez, led to an attack on what was, in the official view, an unwelcome interloper. This attack ensured that the venture made a large loss, and made it unlikely that there could be a peaceful means to enter the trade by establishing respective value. Moreover, the harsh treatment of the English prisoners helped encourage a hardening of English attitudes.

Commercial exclusivity once enforced created major issues for outsiders who wished to enter the trade. As tension between England and Spain rose in the 1570s, privateering attacks on Spanish trade and settlements in the New World became more common, and imposed risk and costs on Spanish trade, activity and governance. This was a transoceanic conflict of wooden sailing ships equipped with cannon, one of the first between Europeans. The introduction of large numbers of cannon on individual ships was a challenge for ship design, made maritime technology more complex, and greatly increased the operational and fighting demands on crews. The need for cannon also accentuated the extent to which the construction, equipment, manning and supply of a fleet required considerable financial and logistical efforts. Alongside new provision, maintenance was a problem, as wood and canvas rotted, while the iron used for weapons and armour corroded. Moreover these were particular risks in the unfamiliar heat and humidity of the Caribbean, and there were no available countermeasures other than replacement. The acute strains on materiel were different to those on people, but each was significant.

Large sailing ships required fewer bases than galleys, which relied on human power: thanks to a reliance on the wind, the crews of sailing ships were smaller, their larger hull capacity allowing them to carry more food and water, and they could also sail closer to the wind. Able, as a result of their relatively small crews, to transport a large cargo over a long distance at an acceptable cost, sailing ships, thanks to their cannon (called 'guns' while on deck), could also defend themselves against attack, and without requiring a large crew or the support of soldiers to do so.

Nevertheless, the capture of prizes, usually by boarding, remained a fundamental of maritime conflict, and certainly so in the Caribbean. There was scant incentive to sink an enemy, which was, anyway, difficult because of the problems of depressing cannon so as to hole a ship below the waterline. It was always better to capture the ship and take its cargo, which could be sold. Prizes could be taken by artillery, often striking their colours when the rig was severely damaged and the ship could not escape, nor turn its guns on the enemy. Boarding could also follow an exchange of fire.

The English constructed purpose-built warships along new lines focused on firepower from the 1570s, as did the Portuguese and, from the 1590s, the Spaniards. In addition, Francis Drake and other English private men of war (the term privateers was coined later) took small, oared, prefabricated raiding vessels with them to assist with operations against Spain in the inshore waters of the Caribbean. From the 1540s, cheap cast-iron cannon able to fire iron shot with a high muzzle velocity were produced in England, although bronze cannon remained dominant.

Benefiting from assistance from the natives who were locally numerous, Drake attacked the Spanish silver route bringing bullion from South America across the Panama isthmus for transhipment to Europe in 1573, although he encountered serious difficulties, including disease and a stronger resistance than had been anticipated. In 1576, his former companion John

Oxenham sailed for Panama with one ship and fifty-seven men. After capturing some prizes, he allied with the Cimarron natives and crossed the isthmus to the Pacific where he seized two bullion ships, only to be pursued, captured in 1578, and executed in 1580. At this stage, Elizabeth I was hesitant about overtly offending Spain too much. Privateering offered deniability as well as the attraction of a profitable asymmetrical conflict. In contrast, after war formally broke out in 1585, campaigning was not restricted. Yet, the capture of Santo Domingo and Cartagena by Drake in 1585–6 yielded only transient gains, notably substantial ransoms from the two cities that did not match the cost of the fleet; and such attacks were increasingly challenged by the strength of imperial defence, particularly at Veracruz and Havana.

The destruction by a French Huguenot (Protestant) pirate Jacques de Sores in 1555 of the original, rather modest, fort in Havana, and of the city as a whole, led in 1577 to the building of the *Castillo de la Real Fuerza* with its thick stone walls. Subsequently, to protect the entrance to the harbour, the castles of San Salvador de la Punta and El Morro were built on its opposite sides between 1589 and 1630.

Pirates: The Later View

Based on a 1915 novel by the prolific Rafael Sabatini, *The Sea Hawk* was the title of an American silent film made in 1924 that was set in the Mediterranean. For the 1940 version, an American blockbuster with Errol Flynn in the title role, there was a very different plot, set in the 1580s and with part of the action in the New World, where there is a planned attack on a Spanish gold caravan on the isthmus of Panama. Flynn had already appeared in *Captain Blood* (1935), again based on a Sabatini novel, which had earlier led to a 1924 silent version. In *Captain Blood*, Flynn is an imprisoned and enslaved doctor punished for his role in the treating of the wounded in the Monmouth Rebellion of 1685 against the autocratic Catholic king, Joseph II. With the others thus enslaved and sent to the Caribbean, Flynn seizes a Spanish warship and becomes a successful pirate. The overthrow of the Catholic James II in 1688–9 means that he can return to his loyalty and save the colony from French attack. The film, a great commercial success, launched Flynn's fame. At the end of his career, Flynn wrote and narrated *Cuban Rebel Girls* (1959), a B-picture reflecting his support for Castro, on whose behalf he also wrote newspaper and magazine pieces. Rafael Sabatini (1875–1940) was an Italian-English novelist who lived most of his life in Britain.

Improved Spanish fortifications in the Caribbean were a factor for Drake in 1586, and in 1595 when Drake and Hawkins led an expedition against San Juan, Puerto Rico, it failed in the face of the strong defence; both English commanders died of disease. In 1598, George, 3rd Earl of Cumberland, by attacking the landward approaches, captured the heavily fortified San Juan that had repelled Drake in 1595; but he could not sustain a garrison there, and, consequently, the overall result was minimal and degenerated into acrimonious arguments with Elizabeth over the division of the booty. This was a clear demonstration of the tension on the English part between operations and conquest and, therefore, of the distinctive aspect of the Spanish presence at this period.

This Spanish presence emerged clearly both in contrast to the more ephemeral efforts of England and France, and, more obviously, thanks to the ability to dominate major areas, notably Cuba, which existed in an important strategic relationship with New

Spain, particularly Mexico. The Spaniards had both an effective practice of grounding control and an integrated imperial system, which was not the case for any of their opponents. Profiting from an economy that generated a strong revenue stream in the New World, Spain benefited from Atlantic and Caribbean way-bases, notably the Canaries and, from 1583 to 1640, the Azores, where they could replenish supplies and take shelter from the weather, whereas the English had no equivalent until Bermuda was settled from 1609.

No Caribbean bases were established by the English in the sixteenth-century period; but, nevertheless, a model of success was created, and, as a strong recovered memory, was subsequently held up as the correct course for English action, and notably so in periods of crisis in the 1620s, 1650s, 1720s and 1730s. In his poem *London* (1738), Samuel Johnson used these campaigns as a tool with which to berate Sir Robert Walpole, the Prime Minister, for not fighting Spain and pressed for calling:

> Britannia's Glories back to view . . .
> triumphant on the Main . . .
> the Dread of Spain.

Westward Ho!: Raiding the Spanish Main

Westward Ho! (1855), by the Victorian clergyman and novelist Charles Kingsley, was based on the life of the privateer Amyas Preston (Amyas Leigh in the novel), who follows Francis Drake, a fellow Devonian, to sea. The novel focuses on a real expedition of 1595, the Preston–Somers raid on Caracas. The villainous Spaniards kidnap Leigh's love-interest, Rose Salterne, and the Inquisition burns both her and his brother as Protestants. Patriotism and sentiment coexist in the novel, with anti-Catholicism to the fore. The story became a film in 1919, and in 1925 was the first novel to be adapted for radio by the BBC. Kingsley, also a Devonian, became chaplain to Queen Victoria in 1859 and was Regius Professor of Modern History at Cambridge in 1860–9. In 1866, alongside Thomas Carlyle, Charles Dickens and Alfred Tennyson, he was on the committee defending Edward Eyre over his harsh suppression of the Morant Bay rebellion. Kingsley was also to extol English nationalism in his *Hereward the Wake* (1865). In *Westward Ho!* Kingsley offered descriptions of what hitherto he had not seen, but that reflected in part the already strong perception of the Caribbean. He went on, after he had been there, to publish *At Last: A Christmas in the West Indies* (1871).

At the end of the sixteenth century, the European Caribbean was very much Spanish and was particularly important due to its role as the route along which Central and South American bullion was shipped prior to the Atlantic crossing. The Spanish world included much of the Caribbean, notably the major islands and the Mexican, Panama and South American shores; but most of the shores of the modern United States were not under Spanish control, nor were all of the islands. Indeed, success on the more profitable mainland led to a slackening of interest in conquering, settling and developing the islands, particularly those not yet settled and where there was appreciable opposition from the Caribs. Moreover, in the context of a relatively small number of Spanish settlers in this large region, there was a decline in the commitment to some of the existing colonies, including Jamaica, Puerto Rico and, more significantly, Hispaniola once its gold was exhausted: it did not have the political or strategic significance of Cuba; and their cultivation in the late 1510s was hit hard by ants. Many Spaniards moved to Mexico and Peru.

CONCLUSIONS

'Atlantic history' became a term of scholarly debate and educational purpose in the late twentieth century, and therefore a way to locate the history of the Caribbean and its role in the world from the arrival of Europeans and (unwillingly) Africans. The value of the term has been debated and clearly varies: most of Africa, in particular, had no or few links to the Atlantic world, but, for the Caribbean, the impact was total, with the Atlantic the context and means for political, demographic, economic and technological revolutions, and for an exchange that was significant in terms of animals, plants and diseases. This transformative transaction was a relinking of parts of the world cast asunder when the super-continents of pre-history had been shattered by geological change, notably Pangaea, which existed about 335 to 175 million years ago, with what became Africa and the Americas then joined near the equator. At the same time, the process of linkage from the late fifteenth century, like that of globalisation as a whole, produced neither consistency nor homogeneity, but, rather, a series of different ecologies and societies. None had a 'true', 'original' or 'Ur' state, but, instead, were affected by the specific environments and dynamics of particular areas.

Comparison is again instructive with the East Indies where the European presence was headed by the Portuguese who expanded from India, capturing the major entrepôt of Malacca in modern Malaya in 1511. The military position and the geopolitical situation were very different to those in the Caribbean, which, again, provides an instructive contrast. Thus, there were numerous bronze cannon at Malacca. Moreover, the Portuguese presence in the Indian Ocean was affected by Arab,

Indian and Ottoman naval forces, for which there was no Caribbean counterpart, and, unlike with the New World, the Europeans in the sixteenth century did not dominate the nearby Asian landmass. In both the East Indies and the Asian landmass, there was a far greater native population than in the New World, and, in population terms, the Europeans were a minor factor.

Furthermore, unlike with the Spaniards in the Caribbean, the Portuguese in effect sought to insert themselves forcibly into a commercial system, creating a chain of fortresses protecting entrepôts and enforcing monopoly or near monopolistic trading terms. Especially beyond Malacca, the Portuguese emphasis was on trade, and, although there were fortified positions, notably Ternate (1522), Solor (1560) and Tidore (1578), the Portuguese did not acquire any significant military capability in the region. The English, when they arrived in the Caribbean, likewise sought to insert themselves into a commercial network, in this case that of Spain, and the sale of slaves depended on such an insertion as there were no English settlements at this stage. That trajectory for the Caribbean was to be pursued in periods of peace, but it was rendered problematic from the outset by the Spanish determination to maintain a monopoly, by the new animosities linked to the Reformation, which were crucial for the response to Huguenots, the Dutch and the English, and by the alternative profit and adventure offered by plunder and fighting.

The Spaniards were not universally successful against native opposition in the Caribbean, and were fearful of the Caribs; but the latter did not pose a challenge, in scale or capability, comparable to those confronting the Portuguese from local powers, particularly from the Sumatra-based state of Aceh and the Javanese one of Jepara. Indeed, an Aceh fleet of 300 ships with 15,000 troops attacked Malacca in 1553, while the Portuguese were driven from Ternate in 1575 as Islamic identity in the Moluccas increased. Again, there was nothing comparable in the Caribbean where the opponents of the Europeans lacked the resources, technology and organisation to counter them at sea, for example by building the big armed galleys with inshore manoeuvrability seen in the East Indies, notably with Aceh, Johor, Bantam and Brunei, while European warships suffered through their deep draught and lack of manoeuvrability; both of which exposed them also to Caribbean shoals.

Opposition to the Portuguese in the East Indies created opportunities for new arrivals that were greater than the still important ones offered in the Caribbean by natives and Maroons. Thus, the first English ships in the Indian Ocean arrived in 1591, and in 1602, reaching Aceh, the English found that they were seen as allies against the Portuguese. The first Dutch fleet reached Java in 1596.

The lack of further North American conquest by Spain in the seventeenth century was one of the most significant counterfactuals in Caribbean history, one comparable, to a degree, to the Portuguese and later Dutch failure to expand from the East Indies to Australia. In the case of Spain, the issue was not distance for there were bases in Florida, while the northern shores of the Caribbean were all within striking distance as was shown by the de Soto expedition. In part, native resistance was a factor for the Spaniards as it discouraged risk, altered the context, notably in northern Mexico, of opportunity, and made it difficult to accumulate relevant information. Operating in Venezuela, Colombia and Panama from the 1580s, Bernardo Vargas Machuca recorded both the dangers posed by traditional native weapons and tactics, such as poison arrows, rocks rolled down from on high, ambushes and pits, as well as native ability to respond to Spanish capability and limitations, such as profiting from the damaging impact of rain on gunpowder. In northern Mexico, the warriors of the Gran Chichimeca used their bows to deadly effect in terrain that was often difficult for the

Spanish cavalry. There was, moreover, the absence of local allies on the scale of those found when overthrowing the Aztecs. Opportunity factors were significant, but so also was the pursuit of advantage, which offered more in other regions.

4

The Seventeenth Century

....

Caribbean Cuisine

Drawing on a wide range of cultures and traditions, notably those of West Africa, Europe, and India, each of which is diverse, but also reflecting the development of distinctive styles and dishes, Caribbean cuisine relies on local products, particularly rice, plantains, beans and cassava, as well as leaf vegetables, fish and meat including goat. Local seasonings are important. Curried goat originated from India, a major source of immigrants in the nineteenth century, and is popular in Jamaica and Trinidad. In Haiti, there is French influence, but those from Africa, including plants introduced by slaves, have been more lasting.

The Caribbean remained preponderantly Spanish in this century, but the Dutch, English, French and Danes all established themselves, creating, as a result, a very different region politically; one in which the European presence was divided, and in which, for much of the century, the rival powers were formally at war, and for the rest ready to commit hostile acts. That focus helped ensure that the seventeenth century saw less expansion of control over native peoples than might otherwise have been the case. However, other factors also played a role, including the downturn in the world population and economy that century, as well as the extent to which the most desirable territory had already been seized, and also the strength of native resistance.

Nevertheless, the Spaniards continued to expand their control, while the conflict between Europeans also ensured that areas hitherto not occupied by them were seized, generally again with dire consequences for native people and the associated environment. Peace was agreed between France and Spain (1598), England and Spain (1604), and Spain and the Dutch (1609); but there was an exclusion for beyond 'the lines of amity' which were then seen as the meridian of the most westerly of the Azores Islands. Conflict certainly continued in the Caribbean, and piracy came to the fore in response to the combination of opportunity and need in the circumstances of shipowners and sailors.

THE CREATION OF THE ENGLISH CARIBBEAN

English settlements were established on islands that the Spaniards had not colonised; although this was not an easy process. Settlements were founded on St Lucia in 1605 and Grenada in 1609, but opposition from native Caribs helped lead to their failure. The example of a non-Caribbean island, Bermuda in the Atlantic, was important. Discovered by the English in 1609 and settled in 1612, it became a successful colony where tobacco cultivation was swiftly introduced. This settlement was followed by the establishment of lasting English colonies in the Caribbean: St Christopher (usually known as St Kitts, 1624), Barbados (1627), Nevis (1628), and Antigua and Montserrat (1632). As England was at war with both Spain and France in the 1620s, English schemes for new colonies were closely linked to bellicosity or, at least, to the likelihood of defending successfully against Spanish attack. This was a reason for the settlement of St Kitts, where the first crop was tobacco, albeit being hit hard by a hurricane. Initially friendly, the Caribs there turned against the colonists, while the English had to share their possession with the French under a treaty of 1627, only for fighting to break out in 1629. One colony proved the basis for another, Nevis being settled from St Kitts. Sir Thomas Warner, who was responsible for founding the first English colonies in the West Indies in the 1620s, was appointed king's lieutenant for St Kitts, Nevis, Barbados and Montserrat, and in 1629 governor of St Kitts. He died there in 1648, and his tomb in the churchyard of St Thomas, Middle Island, is inscribed 'General of y Caribee'.

Conflict did not always lead to success, as in 1626 when a British attempt upon the Spaniards in Trinidad failed. So also with the Puritan-run colony on Providence Island, off the coast of Nicaragua, which the Puritans saw in terms of their vision of a struggle between good and evil. Intended to enrich the godly at the expense of Spain, the colony, established in 1630, was presented as a means to support the struggle against Popery in Britain. Ironically, trade proved more lucrative than privateering, and the island's economy came to be founded on tobacco grown by African slaves.

That vulnerable colony did not last, and Spanish control was re-established in 1641; although an English role there was subsequently to recur. Moreover, that was not the sole colony to fail, as Carib attacks ended English attempts to settle on Tobago in 1639–40 and 1642–3. Nevertheless, the colonies that succeeded were to be important bases for subsequent expansion, and, without these, it would have been far more difficult to make later gains at the expense of Spain and France. Colonies also helped in a transfer of English energy in the Caribbean from buccaneering to a more regulated process of activity and expansion; although buccaneering remained very important to the established authorities in the second half of the century, notably so on Jamaica but also on other colonies.

Furthermore, the opportunities presented by colonies, and, more particularly, the profits derived from them, helped make their development, as well as the acquisition of new ones, normative. Moreover, although disease hit hard, with yellow fever first definitively occurring in the New World in Barbados in 1647 and then spreading rapidly, the presence of settlers permitted a process of acclimatisation and the development among survivors of a degree of immunity to tropical disease, an immunity that provided an important local resource for future aggression and development. Concern about water supplies has left a legacy in the shape of a seventeenth-century water filter from Spain that is still in use in a shop on the *Plaza de Armas* in Havana.

Separate to formal controls, there was also a process of long-standing continuity, as settlers often continued irrespective of changes in rule. Thus, in 1818, there were still white English-speaking Protestants and their slaves on Providence Island, which had been under the control of the English in 1630–41 and 1670–89. The descendants of the settlers remained there, while the population for long was largely Raizals, Protestant Afro-Caribbeans; only for that to be changed over the last half-century by large-scale immigration of mainland Colombians who are Spanish-speaking and Catholics, and when I visited the island, the mix of traditions was clear. The extent of continuity into periods of different rule was readily apparent in New Orleans and on many of the islands, and this remains the case, notably with continued French influence in St Lucia.

That Jamaica became English was a result of the extent to which conflict between European powers increasingly dominated the history of the Caribbean, a process encouraged by the loot it offered, in both reality and imagination, and the value of its plantation exports, and one facilitated by the development of navies. The 1650s saw the Parliamentarians overcome the Royalists in the English Civil War, taking Barbados in 1652 after a difficult struggle and holding off a Royalist squadron under Prince Rupert of the Rhine that year; but the key episode was the Western Design launched by Oliver Cromwell in 1654, after he had made peace with the Dutch, and intended to bring the earlier plans focused on Providence Island to fruition: God's elect nation was to over-throw Spain's Popish empire and seize its trade, beginning with the dispatch of the largest English fleet hitherto sent to the Caribbean and the seizure of Hispaniola. Cromwell brushed aside objections at a ministerial meeting that July: 'We consider this attempt because we think God has not brought us hither where we are but to consider the work that we may do in the world as well as at home ... Now Providence seemed to lead us thither, having 160 ships swimming ... this design would cost little more than laying by the ships, and that with hope of greater profit.'

Ten thousand troops were also sent, but the badly led expedition was mismanaged, notably with logistics, never an easy task, poorly planned. About 1000 troops died of hunger and thirst once landed, and about another 1500 were killed by the defenders, who had their own strong motivation. With disease hitting home, the expedition, its failure blamed by Cromwell on a lack of divine favour arising from sin at home, had to be content with less well-defended Spanish colonies: Jamaica, where the Spanish population was small, and Great Cayman, which was largely populated by privateers. Both were to be formally ceded to England under the Treaty of Madrid of 1670, which officially ended the war begun in 1654. The war had ended in Europe in 1659–60, with a formal treaty in 1667, but continued throughout the 1660s in the Caribbean as the issues there had not been settled.

The Caribbean islands were no mere adjunct to the English colonies in North America. Instead, they were more important, generated more wealth and, until the 1660s, attracted more settlers, readily accessible Barbados proving the most popular destination. These islands were rapidly focused on commercial agriculture, and the labour-intensive nature of the resulting plantation economies led to a need for more settlers. At this stage, they were largely white workers provided by contracts of indenture, a practice of labour provision and control transplanted from England. In addition, Cromwell sent Irish prisoners to Barbados.

Some imported crops did not work, particularly grapes, olives and wheat; but other transfers were successful, notably bananas, lemons, oranges and rice. Tobacco (also important on Cuba) and cotton were the major initial crops on the English colonies; but, from the 1640s, there was a shift to sugar, especially on Barbados. Sugar, which exhausts the soil less than tobacco, was to lead to slaves, but this was not the inevitable socio-economic trajectory for the European-ruled Caribbean or for the other islands. Instead, a more mixed economic pattern that was less capital intensive, and therefore possible for white settlers without much capital, was initially dominant; and this pattern continued to be important even after there was an emphasis on sugar. New settlers also provided the colonies with vital assistance against the serious inroads of war and, even more, disease.

The ecological impact, in part deliberate, in part unintended, of the Europeans was formidable. Their diseases ravaged native societies, while hunting, a necessary search for food as well as a practice from home, greatly eased by the availability of guns, affected the local wildlife. The deliberate or accidental introduction of new species, including horses, pigs, cattle, rats, wheat, grapes, apples, peaches and citrus fruit, harmed indigenous animals and plants, directly or indirectly. There was no sense of loss by the settlers, as these indigenous animals and plants did not play a role in Christianity as they did in native religions. In a major change, the natural cover was cleared to make way for cultivation, and water systems were altered, or at least disrupted, as new types of farming were introduced. Some animals proved easier to control than others: the feral hogs on Barbados and St Kitts were hunted to extinction; but the arrival of rats did much harm to other species, especially birds, iguanas and the indigenous tree rats. Marine life, including whales, was also affected by fishing.

While fortifications of a type offered protection for crops and food stores against animals, fortifications of a different type were rapidly erected by the English to protect bases against the Dutch, with which three wars were fought between 1652 and 1674, as well as against Spain and France. Thus, on Barbados, forts were located along the south-western and western coasts, for example Fort Needham in the 1650s to protect Carlisle Bay, whereas, on the eastern and northern coasts, the rough seas, towering cliffs and lack of harbours served as a deterrent. For many islands, shoals did the same. On French-ruled Grenada, Fort Royal, with its commanding view over the leading port, was designed by François Blondel in 1666, built in 1667, and improved in the early eighteenth century, becoming an effective Vauban-style masonry fortress.

Such fortresses could not be designed to be invulnerable but were intended to be able to resist for a long while and to require a strong attacking force. As a result, they should be able to see off assault by buccaneers who wanted rapid gains; while a conventional force of regular troops in attack would face major losses through disease. Other factors also played a role in deterring activity. In 1677, the Spanish Council of State decided that 'the Island of Trinidad defended itself by its bad climate and the barrenness of its soil, for which reason the French had not occupied it'. Indeed, that quarter of the Caribbean, like the islands off the shores of Central America, had attracted relatively little European settlement in the sixteenth century and continued in the seventeenth to be less settled.

DUTCH, FRENCH AND COURLANDERS

The establishment of Dutch colonies was also closely linked to military and economic opportunity. The Dutch, a major maritime power, and at war with Spain anew from 1621 to 1648, founded colonies from the late 1620s on Tobago, St Eustatius, Bonaire and Curaçao, adding Saba, St Martin and the Virgin Islands in the 1640s. In 1628, a settlement was established on

Tobago, but it was abandoned as a result of Carib action. The Spaniards played a role in this action and also ended Dutch settlements on Trinidad in 1636, but, in 1634, under Johannes van Walbeeck, the Dutch captured Curaçao from an outnumbered Spanish force, and then began Fort Amsterdam on the point of the eastern finger of land at the entrance to St Anna Bay, a natural harbour, in part using African slaves and local Arawaks for the work. A lack of drinking water, an issue on a number of the southern Caribbean islands, and food caused problems, but the fort, with its four bastions and 3-metre-thick walls, was completed in 1635 and became the headquarters of the administration by the Dutch West India Company, with the town of Willemstad growing up outside the fort, but protected by it. The grimness of conflict was shown in 1637 when the fifty-three Dutchmen captured when Tobago was seized by Spain the previous year were executed despite a promise made at the time of their surrender.

In a major blow, the Dutch captured the Spanish treasure fleet, long the dream of buccaneers, while Dutch privateers included Abraham Blauvelt who sought to establish a position on the Mosquito Coast, an area where there was scant Spanish presence. The Dutch, however, devoted far more effort to their, eventually unsuccessful, attempt to establish themselves in Brazil, which ended in 1654, than they did to the Caribbean.

Capturing the Spanish Treasure Fleet

Sixteen Spanish ships sailing from Mexico were attacked in 1628 by a Dutch fleet under Piet Hein, Vice-Admiral of the Dutch West India Company. All the ships were captured, several trapped in the Bay of Matanzas on the north Cuban coast. The booty of gold, silver and goods, notably indigo and cochineal, was worth 11.5 million guilders and enabled a massive cash dividend for the Dutch West India Company as well as providing funds that helped the European operations of the Dutch army against Spanish forces.

The French established bases on St Kitts in the 1620s, Guadeloupe, Dominica and Martinique in the 1630s, Tortuga and St Barthélemy in the 1640s, and Grenada in 1650. St Martin, settled by the Dutch in 1631, but then captured by the Spaniards in 1633, was of scant interest to the latter and was divided between France and the Dutch in 1648, the year of the Westphalian peace settlement that ended the long war between Spain and the Dutch. Separately that year, the French West India Company went bankrupt and the civil war of the *Fronde* began, a crisis of stability in France. Left, as a result, in large part to their own devices, the French colonists faced difficulties from the Caribs on St Lucia and Grenada, and could themselves be rebellious, as on Grenada.

There were others seeking advantage in the Caribbean. Duke Jacob of Courland (in modern western Latvia), who ruled from 1642 to 1682 and established a major fleet, also made an attempt to establish a colonial presence in the West Indies to match that attempted in West Africa. In 1634, a Courland settlement had been established in Tobago, but it had failed in 1639, in part due to the difficulties of developing agriculture there, although also thanks to Spanish hostility. In 1642, Courlanders made a second attempt there, only for it to end in 1650 as a result of attack by the Caribs, stirred up by Jesuits. A third and more significant attempt in 1654 to establish 'New Courland' was overcome by Dutch attack in 1658. The Duke regained Tobago after peace in 1660, holding it in theory until 1689, but pressure from buccaneers and from Spain led to the failure of the colony, which had only an intermittent presence.

The Knights of Malta and the Caribbean

Another unusual player in Caribbean power politics was the Order of St John (the Knights of Malta), which, in 1651, when the French West India Company was dissolved, purchased St Kitts, St Martin, St Barthélemy and St Croix. In 1653 it was agreed that the Order would govern the islands, which would remain under French sovereignty. In 1665, the Order sold its unprofitable interests to the new French West India Company.

The Dutch and French colonies had a similar trajectory to those of England, including the Spanish enmity that led to a successful raid on St Kitts in 1629; but also differences to the English colonies that reflected location, environment, warfare and demographics. Close to Venezuela, the Dutch colonies of Curaçao, Bonaire and Tobago relied heavily on their relations with Spain, both warlike and commercial, including supplying slaves, while their population also reflected the diversity of that of the Netherlands, including a significant number of Jews, many originally refugees from Portugal or Spain. The presence of the Jews on Curaçao was an aspect of the appeal of the Caribbean as a frontier zone for individuals and groups who lacked opportunity or even safety in Europe.

THE SLAVE ECONOMY

The European colonies were increasingly affected by the growth in plantation crops, especially sugar, tobacco and coffee, and by the related rise of slavery. These crops were designed to stimulate taste, appetite and consumption. Sugar had been a luxury, but came to be much more important to the response of many

Europeans to food and drink, partly replacing honey as a sweetener in cooking and drinks. Increasingly predictable as well as higher demand for sugar led to more investment and interacted with rapidly rising supply from the Caribbean, and during a century when the European population was not rising. As a consequence, the price of sugar fell considerably in the second half of the seventeenth century, which further encouraged demand for what had become addictive. Sugar was added to chocolate, jam, cakes, biscuits and medicine, and became important to alcohol consumption with rum.

Molasses and Rum

Molasses are the thick brown syrup made after the sugar crystals have been extracted from the juice produced by crushing sugar cane. Fermenting with yeast and water and then distilling molasses produced a liquor called rum from 1672. Production of rum began in Brazil and the Caribbean in the seventeenth century, and in this period the sugar-refining methods produced more molasses to sugar than today. Molasses were sold to rum producers in North America and rum was then exported to both Britain and Africa.

The production of sugar was intensive and very hard, notably hacking down the sugar cane, and required a large labour force. Slavery provided this more effectively than indentured European labour, which was not only less malleable, but also less attuned to the environment, particularly the climate. The impact in the late 1640s of yellow fever on the white settlers encouraged this process, and, as a result, there was much demand for slaves. Captain William Freeman (c. 1610–82), who, from 1670, in response to the French devastation of the family's St Kitts estate in 1666, developed a sugar plantation on the small island of Montserrat, and left nearly 700 letters written between 1678 and 1685, claimed that 'land without slaves is a dead stock'. By 1677, he had at least fifty-one slaves, and, from 1674, was one of the slave-trading Royal African Company's two agents in the Leeward Islands. As part of the range of activities typical of the settler class, including roles in both public service and private enterprise, Freeman also bought leases on Nevis plantations and acted as agent and banker for the Governor of the Leeward Islands, as well as advising London-based Lords Commissioners for Trade and Plantations. In 1678, 40 per cent of the 4500-strong population of Montserrat was non-white, but, by 1729, this was 80 per cent of the 7200.

A shift in cultivation was important as, after the 1640s, tobacco, the price of which slumped in response to competition from Virginia and Maryland, was replaced by sugar as the main crop. Whereas tobacco, a less arduous crop to cultivate, was grown on smallholdings and its cultivation relied heavily on indentured labour, sugar meant plantations and slaves and therefore more investment. Slaves suddenly appeared in Barbados's deeds in 1642 as a result of the first arrival of English slave ships there the previous year, and, by 1660, Barbados, which already in 1650 had exported 7000 tons of sugar, had a majority of black people. Although prices of slaves thereafter fluctuated annually, they fell over time, encouraging the demand and reflecting the increasingly sophisticated organisation of the trade, which was, at once, responsive to both sources and markets. While important, price was not the sole factor favouring the use of slaves, as they also ensured owners a longer labour availability than that provided by the indentured servants, many of whom died anyway.

Land-hungry Barbadians, unable to afford the capital requirements of plantations on Barbados, also settled elsewhere, including in South Carolina, but notably on Jamaica where they sought to subjugate the African slaves of the previous Spanish settlers, slaves who had used the English conquest in 1655 as an opportunity to win freedom. The escaped slaves had joined the natives who were willing to cooperate with the Spaniards against the English. Spanish resistance continued, but was overcome in 1660 as a result of the determined command of the talented Lieutenant-General Edward D'Oyley.

The spread of sugar production in Jamaica from the late 1660s was inextricably linked to the increase in slavery, both the hunting down of escaped slaves and the import of many new ones, including from Barbados. There were campaigns against escaped slaves in the 1670s and 1680s, and they withdrew further into the Blue Mountains. The population of Jamaica was transformed due to the import of many more slaves under English rule and, whereas, in 1662, there were about 3500 white people and 550 black people, by 1673 they were each about 7700, and, by 1681, there were 24,000 black people and 7500 white people. Over 1800 slaves were being brought to the island each year, in response to a clear demand, for, by 1675, there were 70 plantations able to produce 50 tons of sugar each year, and the black population rose to 43,000 in 1700, when there were only 7300 white people there. With this rise in the slave population, Jamaica largely switched from smallholdings to plantation monoculture, for, although slave-buying there was widespread among the white community, large purchasers dominated the market, which both reflected their access to credit and also accentuated social stratification. Furthermore, the market became more complex and was controlled by specialised traders.

The growing resale of slaves within Jamaica further increased the already harsh instability of the slaves' lives, and their experience of it as arbitrary, cruel and impersonal, notably in the destruction of personal links. In 1684, the Jamaica Assembly passed a new Slave Act that sought to codify slavery by regulating the control of runaways, the obligation to enforce slave law, and property rights in slaves, rights changed to increase those of creditors: if owners died in debt, slaves must be sold in order to satisfy their creditors, which pushed the interests of capital to the fore. This provision helped to liquefy slaves as property assets; but moving slaves from landed estates in this fashion added a further level of disruption to the fact that they were treated simply as property. Slavery was thus to be characterised by high labour mobility, rather than as part of a stable, albeit highly coercive, pattern of settled agriculture.

The greater ability of black people to adapt to the tropics was seen by Europeans, on a longstanding pattern, as justifying their use for hard labour. Indeed, the harshness and brutality involved were not solely a reflection of serious racism, which in part indeed was the result rather than the foundation of slavery, but instead also of an instrumentalism within the technology and opportunities of the age, although that instrumentalism was closely linked to racism. Slavery was justified by necessity and by reference back to the world of Classical Greece and Rome.

The growing imbalance of the numerical relationship between slaves and whites led to the need for garrisons; and the removal of troops for whatever reason alarmed the whites. The anxiety was communicated to European readers, creating an impression of the Caribbean, by publications such as *Great Newes from the Barbadoes, or, A True and Faithful Account of the Grand Conspiracy of the Negroes Against the English and the Happy Discovery of the Same* (1676). Government support, notably in the shape of troops, was therefore much in demand, a situation that looked towards the contrasting response to the fiscal policies of the British government: of the Thirteen Colonies (the basis of the modern United States) that rebelled in 1775, and of the colonies in the Caribbean, none of which did.

Sugar was not the sole plantation crop. For example, on Jamaica, aside from 246 sugar plantations in 1684, there were cacao, cotton, ginger, indigo and pimento ones. A more mixed economic pattern that was less capital intensive was initially dominant, and it continued to be important even after sugar dominated Jamaica, so that food crops and stock rearing were each significant there. Similarly, in Cuba, alongside sugar and tobacco plantations, there was stock rearing and food production. In the Spanish part of Hispaniola, there was economic decline in the seventeenth century and, linked to that, a fall in the number of slaves, while, instead of sugar, there was a production there of food for the French in neighbouring Saint-Domingue.

Linked to sugar, cacao, the main ingredient of chocolate, was another important Caribbean crop. Sugar made it a sweet drink not, as it had been for the local population, a bitter one; and the resulting popularity of hot chocolate in Europe greatly encouraged production which, in turn, as with sugar, led to falling prices and, thereby, to yet higher consumption, which helped drive the slave trade. Initially, much cacao was obtained by the Spaniards from the native population of the Americas via the *encomienda* system of tied labour. However, increasing demand, from Europe and from the Americas, encouraged plantation production, initially from the Venezuelan coast in the 1610s. In the 1630s and 1640s, rising cacao sales helped finance larger slave imports, and each adult slave annually earned on average about 40 per cent of their market value, which was a very high rate of return and one that made slaves valuable even if they died after only a few years of work. The slaves were initially provided by the Portuguese, but, from mid-century, the Dutch based on Curaçao became more important. The mobility of the slave gangs helped expand the frontier of production and, linked to that, the driving back of native wildlife and plants; and, by 1744, there were over 5 million cacao trees in the Caracas province. Cacao production also increased on the islands, the French establishing plantations on Martinique and Guadeloupe in the early 1660s, and the English, albeit with limited success, on Jamaica in the 1680s.

The difference between the requirements for particular crops interacted closely with environmental circumstances and entrepreneurial responses, such that individual islands developed specific economic profiles and the related social structures. In Barbuda, where English colonisers established cattle farming to supply meat to other islands, the open-range cattle herding appears to have drawn on Spanish and West African practices, as was also the case on Hispaniola. By the early eighteenth century, the majority of Barbuda's population was of black people and the island's cattle were controlled by using walled livestock wells during the dry season.

This utilisation of West African as well as European practices in cattle herding was yet another aspect of the diasporic character of the African presence in the Caribbean. This character in part drew on African roots, but was also a matter of transoceanic reshaping, in which brutality, coercion and alienation were only part of the equation. Instead, African Americans also helped greatly shape their new world; and from the original point of the Atlantic slave trade to its end, and then beyond to the present. Thus, the innovative agricultural role of the Africans was seen in the spread of rice to the Caribbean, for example to Louisiana where it proved crucial in feeding the colony, and is now cited as an instance of a shared colonial history.

The harsh slave regime included the total absence of slave rights and the ever-present possibility of brutal control, which encouraged flight and, less commonly, violent opposition, that, in turn, resulted in even stricter controls. Initially, the legislation largely treated servants and slaves in a similar fashion, but slaves were increasingly distinguished, being subject to a separate code from the Barbados Assembly in 1661, in contrast to the more piecemeal situation in 1652. The entire stance was far harsher: the preamble to the Barbados Slave Act described 'Negroes' as a 'heathenish, brutish and an uncertain dangerous pride of people' who required harsher punishment and laws accordingly. The word 'Negro' was used interchangeably with slave, while description as 'brutish', a word associated with beasts, further categorised and disparaged. 'Pride', a word employed to describe a band of lions, further treated slaves as animals with the additional sense of being brutish or fierce. As such, slaves could not possess rights, in contrast to the position taken in Portuguese and Spanish laws, and to be taken in the French *Code Noir*. A clear legal difference was established in the Barbados Slave Act, as slaves were not to receive a jury trial of twelve peers, but rather to be tried in a slave court, in which two justices of the peace and three freeholders, all five inevitably white men, were to pass judgment. Severe punishment was to be inflicted on any 'Negro' who struck a 'Christian'. The first offence was a severe whipping, while, for the second, the offender was to have their nose slit and face branded, a brutal disfigurement to demonstrate status and punishment. Even more ominously, the killing of a slave during punishment was not to be considered a crime. In contrast, the legislation of 1661 protected European indentured servants from such violence.

For slaves, life was totally disrupted, and more so than in the case of the widespread slavery within Africa. Alongside the extent to which slave buyers in Africa tended to buy from particular areas, and thus from specific tribes, and that plantation owners might want to maintain this in order to avoid conflict within their slave populations; there was also, in contrast, a widespread mixing of slaves from different backgrounds in a deliberate attempt to lessen their potential cohesiveness and rebelliousness, and this mixing helped ensure a lack of a common heritage, including language and religion. This was responsible, and notably so for the children born into slavery, for the development of creole languages and for the openness to Christian proselytism.

At the same time, Africans brought cultural practices with them and these contributed greatly to the establishment of their new society, one that was not destroyed by the greater adaptation with the children to a background that was New World as well as

African. The sources for the developing African American culture are varied, and the factors involved clearly differed, not least in terms of the response to European Africans. Some of the beliefs, moreover, proved more durable; while the repeated arrival of more slaves from Africa kept the cultural heritage alive, and diluted creole influences. Where spousal choices were possible, which was more the case for slaves in Spanish America than the British or French Caribbean, ethnic distinctions helped guide them. Monogamy became more common with Christian proselytism; and the bigamy trials that were a response to the polygamy seen in Africa became less common in Mexico by the early eighteenth century. Slave life and interaction both with white people and with other slaves tended to be freer in towns; and it was there that free black people, those freed by their masters, sometimes in wills and sometimes for payment from money earned, tended to congregate and define and develop their own 'spaces' and culture. The role of ethnic boundaries, or at least cohesion, was also seen in religious brotherhoods organised by African Americans in Latin America.

Empire Building

The 1660s saw further English expansion, as a product of the Second Anglo-Dutch War (1665–7), with Tobago, St Eustatius and Saba captured from the Dutch in 1666, and a Dutch position established in the Virgin Islands seized; although, in 1666, a hurricane destroyed most of an English fleet en route from Barbados to attack the French in the Leeward Islands. Active privateering at the expense also of Spain and France was part of the situation; the English likewise suffering from such attention. For England, the Bahamas, which had been granted by Charles I (1629) and then Parliament (1649), leading to a small settlement at New Providence, were granted anew in 1670 with more credibility; and the colony developed, albeit with a reliance on piracy that led to destructive Spanish attacks in 1684.

The French, more significantly, founded the colony of Saint-Domingue in the western portion of Hispaniola, whereas the Spaniards had focused their settlement of the island on its eastern part, a process encouraged in 1606 when the colonists, in part to ensure protection against pirates, were instructed to move to the area round the capital, Santo Domingo. The pirates established bases in the west, notably the French on the offshore island of Tortuga in 1625. Alongside piracy, there were on the nearby mainland food and hides from wild cattle and pigs, as well as plentiful water and wood. From the 1660s, there was also a greater reliance by the French on Hispaniola on the products of slave-based plantations, particularly tobacco and coffee, and, from the 1680s, indigo and sugar, a process helped by settlers from Guadeloupe and Martinique where land was in shorter supply. The same process, later seen, less successfully, with the French settlement of Louisiana, also took British settlers from Barbados to South Carolina, which, indeed, was founded as part of what was in effect a greater Caribbean, thus underlining the mistake of restricting Caribbean history to the islands.

The 1670s saw the Danes, in part with convicts, create a base at St Thomas in 1672, but the decade was dominated by the Franco-Dutch War of 1672–8. Although this conflict, which was bitterly fought in Europe, appears to have left scant lasting impact on the territorial situation in the Caribbean, that is only because expeditions were unsuccessful or their impact not permanent; the Dutch notably failing in 1674 to capture Martinique, a key target. The French recaptured St Martin (1676) after Jean, Count of Estrées defeated a Dutch squadron off Tobago, which they also captured; but a French expedition sent to Curaçao in 1678 ran aground on the Isle of Aves off the coast of Venezuela with the loss of seven ships of the line. In the Peace of Nijmegen negotiated in 1678–9, French possession of Tobago, which had frequently changed hands, was confirmed, although Spain refused then to acknowledge French claims to Hispaniola, claims that it was feared might be followed up by French attacks else-where, notably on nearby Cuba.

Important in mercantile circles, and aided by improved maps such as John Thornton's *A Chart of the Caribe Islands* (1689), the value of Caribbean trade was further enhanced, in a period of only limited economic growth in Europe, as government loans could be raised on the basis of anticipated customs revenue on the goods imported and re-exported from there. Thus, naval power could be regarded, more particularly by government, as part of a benign administrative cycle, securing colonial trade that produced tax revenues that, in turn, could be invested in naval strength that offered not only protection, but a means of harming the rival systems of opposing states, and thus transferring revenues. 'Taxing' these revenues, via piracy, privateering and smuggling, was another, somewhat different, aspect of the situation, one from which all powers suffered as part of what was at once poli-tics (international and domestic), economics and social practice.

Prior to 1688 when the Nine Years War began, the largely peaceful 1680s were only peaceful in terms of formal war between the major powers. There was, in practice, large-scale piracy and privateering in the Caribbean. For example, the new Danish colony in the West Indies on St Thomas became a base for priva-teering. Separately, in 1683, Cartagena had resisted a pirate block-ade by Laurens de Graaf.

In the Nine Years War (1688–97), England, the Dutch and Spain fought France, although the Caribbean proved a dangerous area for operations due to disease, storms and shoals, and a small English squadron under Vice-Admiral John Neville sent there in 1697 lost Neville, all his captains and half of the sailors to disease. Fighting was largely a matter of local initiatives, combined with occasional interventions by metropolitan forces. Thus, St Kitts and St Eustatius, taken by the French in 1689, could not be retaken until English reinforcements arrived in 1690. Only eight small ships of the line under Commodore Lawrence Wright, this expedition was a contrast to the large English forces deployed in home waters. In 1691, Wright and Christopher Codrington, the effective governor of the Leeward Islands and commander of the troops there, successfully landed troops on Guadeloupe; but the strength of the fortifications, the arrival of a French squadron, and disease among both troops and sailors led to the abandonment of an expedition that was plagued by poor relations between the two commanders.

Seeking to protect Jamaica, Wright's replacement, Ralph Wrenn, fought off, and successfully withdrew from, a much larger French fleet off La Désirade, near Guadeloupe, on 22 February 1692, before falling victim to disease at Barbados; although the year was overshadowed by the earthquake that largely destroyed Port Royal. Yellow fever and poor leadership helped cause the failure of an English invasion of Martinique in 1693, and, in 1694, the English naval focus was on the Mediterranean. In 1695, a squadron cooperated with the Spaniards in raiding the French in Saint-Domingue, the western half of Hispaniola, acquiring lots of booty, but there were again serious differences between army and naval commanders, as well as disease. French expeditions to the Caribbean, meanwhile, made the English anxious, and renewed threats to Jamaica, which was raided by privateers, and in 1694 briefly invaded, encouraged the English to send fleets to the Caribbean in 1694 and 1696, a process eased by the major defeat inflicted on the French navy at Barfleur in 1692, which ended plans for a French invasion of England in support of the exiled James II. As so often, the content and pace of Caribbean history were being set in Europe.

The fleets the English sent were both defensive and offensive in their function. Although concern focused on rival Europeans, the war also made slave risings, such as on Jamaica in 1694, more worrying. As in 1673–8, Spain benefited from being part of an alliance system directed against France, because the English and Dutch (allied after William of Orange became William III of

England in 1689) focused their energies on attacking France, which lacked the strength to focus on Spanish America and concentrated its naval operations in European waters: in support of a rebellion in Sicily against Spanish rule in 1675–6 and in seeking the overthrow of William in 1690–2. In contrast, Franco-Spanish alliances in the eighteenth century spread vulnerability to attack from Britain.

Operations in the Caribbean did not determine the outcome of the war, and conflict there still bore many of the characteristics of buccaneering, as when the French, with over ten ships carrying near 2000 soldiers and buccaneers, captured and looted Cartagena in 1697, with the buccaneers, who felt cheated of their loot by the French, returning to cause fresh mayhem. Force and intimidation were also to the fore in relations between supposedly friendly powers, as when the Danish Governor of St Thomas clashed with the attempt by Brandenburg (Prussia) to develop a position, not least thwarting an attempt by the latter in 1692 to establish control of Crab Island.

English and French forces were able to launch major attacks, but found it more difficult to sustain operations in the face of opposition and the logistical and ecological problems of campaigning there, so that French operations on Hispaniola were cut short in 1690 as a result of illness and the onset of the wet season. Naval action alone was inadequate because of its dependence on wind and current, the need for bases in order to prepare expeditions and support naval operations, and the inherently transient nature of blockades. Instead, it was necessary to capture the bases of other powers in order to limit their options, but that was a task that involved a very different capability to that of naval action alone. These bases were protected with fortifications with European-style features; there could be adaptation to local circumstances, but it was less prominent than an attempt to reproduce the standard formula which was aided by the ubiquity of the basic building materials, stone, earth and timber.

In 1697, the French claim to Saint-Domingue, the western part of Hispaniola, was recognised in the peace treaty, the Treaty of Ryswick, that brought the war to an end. That was not the sole area of French expansion, for, albeit in very small numbers, the French had established themselves in Louisiana, a key episode in a developing competition on the northern shore of the Gulf which, in turn, led the Spaniards to extend their presence in Florida westward by founding Pensacola in 1696. Earlier, they had no real incentive to establish posts along the northern shore. René-Robert Cavelier, Sieur de la Salle, who had founded a series of trading posts on the Illinois River, canoed down the Mississippi to its mouth and, on 9 April 1682, raised the arms of France and claimed the river basin for Louis XIV. The King, in turn, criticised these discoveries as worthless; but his opinion on the latter was changed by clerics eager to extend Christianity, and because Louis, who also presented himself as a champion of the Church, came to see an opportunity to challenge the Spanish position in the Caribbean. Moreover, he was interested in travellers, their books and overseas expansion in general.

La Salle, accordingly, was sent in 1684 to the Gulf of Mexico with four ships and 300 settlers but, attacked by pirates and missing the Mississippi delta, landed 650 kilometres (400 miles) to the desolate west at Matagorda Bay, where he founded Fort St Louis. This, however, fell foul to disease, the barrenness of the coast, recriminations and the mutiny that cost him his life in 1687, and the hostility of the Karankawa who wiped out the surviving colonists at the close of 1688.

Nevertheless, La Salle's initiative bore fruit with the foundation of a colony named Louisiana in honour of the King. In 1698, Jérôme, Count of Pontchartrain, the active Minister of the Marine, a key expansionist who supported the development of Saint-Domingue, organised the expedition to found the colony, and Fort Maurepas in Biloxi Bay was built in 1699. In his *Description de la Louisiane* (Paris, 1683), part of a longstanding tradition of

Caribbean boosterism, Louis Hennepin, a missionary who had accompanied La Salle, had described Louisiana as the future breadbasket for the French empire, a fertile area able to produce wine and foodstuffs for the French West Indies; but reality proved otherwise. This was an issue for all the French islands, but particularly for Louisiana which, in practice, was initially an island-style colony in the midst of difficulty.

By the end of the seventeenth century, native control of the Caribbean had been greatly further restricted. Whereas, for example, the early settlers of north-west Venezuela had faced major opposition, such that the city of Maracaibo was founded three times, it had a continuous history from 1574. Moreover, the establishment of a colony in Louisiana was not the sole important development in the following century. In 1697, Nojpetén, the capital of the people known as Itza' and the last unconquered Maya kingdom, fell to Spanish attack. Located on an island in Lake Péten Itzá (now in northern Guatemala), it was taken with very heavy losses among the defenders, a marked contrast with the defeat of the previous Spanish attempt in 1622. Martín de Ursúa, the acting Governor of Yucatán, ordered his men in 1697 to plant the flag with the royal arms of Spain and religious standards among the Itza' temples 'in which the majesty of God had been offended by idolatries'. Thanking God for his victory, he then joined soldiers and Franciscans in destroying a large number of 'idols' in what was a religious war against opponents presented as guilty of human sacrifice, cannibalism and killing priests.

This was no easy conquest, for the Spaniards found it difficult to support their new position and the thick forests limited their control. They were helped, however, by the rapid decline of the Itza' under the pressure of Spanish seizures of food, terrible epidemics, probably influenza and, later, smallpox, the capture of much of their leadership by the Spaniards, and subsequent disputes among the Itza'. Rebellions in 1704, 1746 and 1761 were ultimately unsuccessful, as was other resistance, and the

Spaniards were able to impose a measure of control thanks to moving the population into new colonial towns, such as San José, and to proselytisation by Christian missions, although this was hampered by a difficulty in speaking the language. Those Maya who evaded control lived in isolated forest areas, and were no longer able to challenge Spanish dominance. At the same time, this contrast in control underlined a more general one in presence, authority and power; a contrast that is not readily perceived if the focus instead is on formal claims to control, not least as depicted with the clear lines and bold colours with which rule is recorded in modern historical atlases.

BUCCANEERING

Piracy was an essential part of the lifestyle of the sea: the sea was both less policeable than land, and it spanned claims to state authority. The inherent attraction of piracy as a means, however precarious, to adventure, livelihood and wealth was enhanced by the role of war in the definition of English, French and Dutch views of the Caribbean. Overlapping with this came the economic rationale: piracy could be a rejection of society, but also part of the varied processes of creating and mediating economic links, and in a governmental and legal contest where the established official position did not meet the varied needs and expectations of much of the population. Alongside plundering others, not least by seizing slaves who could be readily resold, pirates provided fledgling communities with supplies, protection, loot, and commercial and fiscal opportunities. Maritime predation became a means to safety and financial viability, which helped make it acceptable, and notably so in colonies where there was a shortage of both force and liquidity, which was generally the case.

Thus, pirates became privateers in acceptance, if not law, and this was the case for all of the powers. Just as imperial forces were inserted into local patterns of opportunity and need, both exploiting them and being exploited by them, so also with piracy. Local politicians were calculating pragmatists, willing to turn a blind eye to criminal behaviour, while popular support rested in similar patterns, as well as traditions of self-reliance and autonomy that rejected metropolitan attempts to control the situation. Rulers and officials were willing to have peace in Europe but war 'beyond the line', as with the English at the expense of Spain in the 1660s. This practice, orally agreed between the French and Spanish negotiators of the Treaty of Cateau-Cambrésis in 1559, meant that whatever happened in the Caribbean would not lead to war in Europe.

Moreover, that ambiguity was the practice for many in the region. Pirates were not a counter-culture or criminal culture in their home territories, but part of a continuum with privateering and one that was highly fluid in its context, contours and circumstances, again contributing to the nature of the Caribbean as a frontier zone. Thus, pirates could be integral members of coastal communities that were more than simply lawless or at least disorderly. Indeed, piracy, like privateering, was a product of liquidity in the shape of investment, and in turn enhanced by it.

Nearly everyone who plundered in the Caribbean during these decades had paperwork of some sort, for example from the Danes in St Thomas or the French in Petit Goâve, Saint-Domingue, and the degree to which these men called themselves privateers, a term coined in 1661, is instructive, not least because it underlines the fluid nature of war, commerce and sovereignty in the Caribbean. Buccaneers were initially French cattle rustlers who turned to plunder on occasion. The English soon anglicised *boucanier* into buccaneer, and simply forgot or ignored the original meaning of the term.

Most European men made their way to the Caribbean with few prospects or by force, for example criminals sent there to make up numbers, or Irish compelled to go to Barbados as a result of the Cromwellian conquest of Ireland (1649–53). These men had no means of purchasing a plantation or slaves to work those plantations, and did not intend to toil like slaves. This was the origin of logwood cutting, cattle raiding and raising and, eventually, piracy. Henry Morgan was one of the few who actually obtained enough capital from his plunder to purchase plantations and settle down. Thus, the Caribbean was not only a region that was difficult to police, but also a place of limited potential for those without capital to plant and grow sugar.

While the establishment of colonies, therefore, helped in a transfer of energy from buccaneering to a more regulated process of activity and expansion, for example for the French buccaneers based at Tortuga establishing themselves in Saint-Domingue, this was, in fact, a gradual process. Indeed, encouraged by international rivalry, buccaneering continued to be important to the established colonial authorities in the second half of the century. Christopher Myngs, the energetic commander of English warships in Jamaica in 1656–7 and 1658–60, had mounted destructive, privateering raids on the Caribbean coast of South America. He returned in 1662 as a commander cum privateer, and captured and destroyed Santiago de Cuba that year, following with San Francisco de Campeche in 1663 when he commanded fourteen ships and 1400 men, a formidable force for any coastal community.

Henry Morgan (c. 1635–88), a ruthless Jamaican-based privateer, achieved particularly great and notorious success, being used from 1667 by Sir Thomas Modyford, the Governor of Jamaica, to try to force Spain by privateering to recognise the English control of Jamaica and the Caymans, which was not done until 1670. Morgan sacked Puerto del Principe (Cuba), which was an inland town, Portobello (Panama) and Maracaibo (Venezuela), in each case with great brutality. Torture was a standard means to force prisoners to reveal their money, and rape was frequent. Despite the 1670 treaty, Morgan seized and destroyed Panama City in 1671. He bought three sugar plantations on Jamaica, was knighted in 1674, and became lieutenant-general the same year, in that capacity supporting privateers, including at times against Spain in cooperation with the French Governor of Tortuga. Morgan invested in privateers/pirates, and also built up the defences of Port Royal from the late 1670s against the risk of French attack, as well as seizing Providence Island from Spain and using it as a privateering base.

With their concentration of wealth, cities proved especially attractive targets. Thus in 1683, Laurens de Graaf, a Dutchman who had been a privateer for the French, after successes over Spanish warships in 1679 and 1682, captured Veracruz, which was attacked by several pirate chiefs who deployed thirteen ships and about 1300 pirates. Campeche fell to him in 1685. Graaf had a plantation on Saint-Domingue and in effect fought the English and Spaniards on behalf of France, raiding Jamaica, as in 1693. Another privateer, Michel de Grammont, found Spanish coastal towns of great value as targets, capturing in 1678 Maracaibo. It had already been plundered by Henrik de Gerard (Dutch) in 1614, William Jackson (English) in 1642, François l'Olonnais (French) in 1666 and Morgan in 1669. As a reminder that pirates did not have to fear only conflict, Grammont's ship was lost in a storm in 1686.

The scale of privateer activity reflected both a response to opportunity and the product of the gains made. As scale and cooperation increased, cooperation both between pirates, and between them and at least some of the 'authorities', as well as the merchants who resold ships and goods seized by the pirates, so piracy became more effective and profitable. Cooperation with state officials meant that to a degree the pirates were a mercenary navy, part of the sharing of resources and tasks necessary for imperial activity. In response to the threat of attack, governments relied on convoying, on fortresses, such as the *Castillo de Jagua* near Cienfuegos in Cuba, and the city walls of Havana built between 1663 and 1746, and on buying over pirate support. In the absence of fortresses, vulnerable settlements sought protection from attack by moving inland, as at Remedios in Cuba.

Conclusions

Again, comparisons with the East Indies are highly instructive to show the different ways in which European power could develop. Whereas, in the seventeenth century, the Europeans had expanded and consolidated their control of the Caribbean at the expense of the native population, both on the islands and on the continental littoral, the situation was different in the East Indies, although in the latter there were both adventurers, notably Portuguese *feringhi*, and states, especially in the shape of authorised trading companies with military power, of which the Dutch East India Company was the major force. The Dutch made major inroads, particularly in Java, where they had a trading base in Jayak rta (Jakarta) from 1603. Becoming the centre of their power from 1619, after the forces of Bantam were defeated, it was renamed Batavia.

Yet, alongside the Europeans, in a contrast to the Caribbean, there were also mighty regional powers, notably Aceh and Mataram, each of which had significant navies, while the Dutch were heavily dependent on cooperation with local powers, such as the Sultan of Ternate in the Moluccas, the Bugi in Sulawesi and Mataram in Java. In the Caribbean, a key element was the search for support from other European powers, with Spain, France, England and the Dutch all manoeuvring accordingly, but in the Moluccas, the Dutch were reliant on local support against the Portuguese; and to a degree greater than that of any European cooperation with Caribs, however important that was on individual islands.

If there was 'no peace beyond the line' in the Caribbean, the situation was much more the case in the East Indies due to the semi-independent role of the trading companies, as well as the far greater distance from Europe. Indeed, although a surprising point, it was the proximity of the Caribbean to Europe and, later, to the United States, that emerges as crucial in this respect; and notably so when compared to the distance of the East Indies from both. This closeness aided settlement (from both Europe and, involuntarily, Africa), the movement of plants, animals and diseases, and transatlantic economic integration; and also intervention, both in the case of the dispatch of military forces and that of government. These factors were all challenged by constraints and frictions, notably disease, climate, ocean currents and the frontier character of illegality; but there was nothing like the far greater constraints and frictions posed by the East Indies. The major continental power that could have intervened there in a manner comparable to the Europeans in the Caribbean was China, but, after the Ming's overseas visits of the early fifteenth century ended in 1433, it focused, instead, on landward challenges and, eventually, from the 1690s, expansion. As so often, what did not happen was crucial in history; another prime instance being the lack of American expansion onto the Caribbean islands prior to 1898 and, related to that, a peaceful transition as great powers between Britain and the United States.

The Spaniards remained the dominant power in the Caribbean in the seventeenth century, notably so on the landmass, where the wealth of Cartagena, the leading port of the Caribbean coast of South America, amazed Philippe de Villette-Mursay, a French naval captain, in 1678; but also on the largest island, Cuba, as well as Santo Domingo and Puerto Rico. Nevertheless, although there was no comparison in the Caribbean to Brazil, which was Portuguese, or to the Guianas, where the Dutch, English and French all had colonies, the Spanish continental position around the Caribbean was challenged by the English in what became Belize (from 1638) and on the Mosquito Coast (from 1655); and, from the 1680s, by the French in Louisiana. Separately, settlements near the Spanish coastal bases of Pensacola and St

Augustine had been converted to Christianity; but much of Florida, and notably the south, was outside the Spanish sphere of influence, let alone control. These bases were the outlier of a Spanish Caribbean in which attention was strongly focused on the continental landmass, especially Mexico and the Panama isthmus, with, in addition, Havana a key naval base. On the islands, the English benefited from a freer economy than that of France, and from surpassing France in overall naval strength from the early 1690s, although such strength did not necessarily make for superiority in Caribbean waters or, more specifically, particular waters.

The Dutch devoted most of their attention in the New World to an unsuccessful effort from 1630 to drive the Portuguese from Brazil, a highly profitable sugar/slave economy, but they surrendered there in 1654; and, although the Dutch West Indies benefited from the transfer of resources and skills from Dutch Brazil, nevertheless, there had been no comparable transfer of military resources. The Dutch, who had also failed, in the face of three Anglo-Dutch wars in 1652–74, to sustain their position in what became the United States, were, by the late 1670s, very much second-rank players in the New World; which had not been the case in the early 1650s and, again, serves as a reminder of the unpredictabilities of Caribbean history. More generally, the linkage of activity and resources between the different spheres in the New World meant that weakness in one rapidly affected the situation in the others; with the same being the case across the Atlantic. Despite the failure of the Dutch, the Danes were far weaker. In turn, Brandenburg (later Prussia), which had established a position in the slave trade and had what proved a precarious position on Danish-ruled St Thomas in 1685, failed in attempts to purchase Tobago, St Eustatius and Tortola, and, eventually, ceased operations on St Thomas in 1718.

In the English case, there were key linkages between the Caribbean and North America. These were enhanced when settlers on Barbados played a major role in the development of South Carolina, where, in accordance with a charter of 1663, the first settlers arrived in 1670. This development paved the way to English efforts in the early eighteenth century to seize Florida and, more successfully, establish a colony in Georgia, founding Savannah in 1733, which, again, underlined the linkage of the Caribbean with North America. The North American colonies provided manpower for the unsuccessful attack on Cartagena in 1741. More consistently, they provided the crucial food for the British Caribbean colonies, as substantial populations, notably of slaves, had to be fed; and it was more economic to use tropical plantations for cash crops, and to import food. Thus, in many respects, the Caribbean's linkages ensured that its history was wide ranging. At any rate, the Caribbean was entering the eighteenth century, with England increasingly dominant at sea and also determined to use that dominance in order to enhance control and strengthen its imperial economy.

5

Competing to Run an
Economy of Misery, 1700–50

Mr Thomas Inkle, an ambitious young English trader cast ashore in the Americas, is saved from violent death at the hands of savages by the endearments of Yarico, a beautiful Indian maiden. Their romantic intimacy in the forest moves Inkle to pledge that, were his life to be preserved, he would return with her to England, supposedly as his wife. The lovers' tender liaison progresses over several months until she succeeds in signalling a passing English ship. They are rescued by the crew, and with vows to each other intact, they embark for Barbados. Yet when they reach the island Inkle's former mercantile instincts are callously revived, for he sells her into slavery, at once raising the price he demands when he learns that Yarico is carrying his child.

Published in the *Spectator*, the leading English periodical, on 13 March 1711, this version was but a stage in a tale that had surfaced in Richard Ligon's *True and Exact History of the Island of Barbardoes* (1657), but it was the most influential one, and was taken up by a number of prominent writers in Europe, an adaptation being staged at the *Comédie-Française* in Paris in 1764. A Royalist, Ligon left for Barbados in 1647, buying into a sugar plantation, but, affected by fever, he returned to England in 1650.

The profitability of the Caribbean to Europeans was indicated by the Danish purchase from France for 750,000 livres, of St Croix, a small island, in 1733 as a base for the Danish West India and Guinea Company. It was followed by the revival of the Company, which provided sugar and cotton not only to Denmark but also for re-export to Danzig (Gdansk), Königsberg, Lübeck and Kiel. One hundred and forty-two plantations were listed in 1742 and by 1754 there were 7566 slaves. Fifteen million pounds of sugar and 616,000 pounds of cotton were imported by the Company from the Caribbean in 1730–45. This was little compared to the British imports, 1,494 million pounds and 29 million respectively; but there was margin for future growth, as well as suspicion that the Danish company was reliant on British investment.

THE BRITISH AND SLAVERY

The British were the leading participants in the transatlantic slave trade during the eighteenth century, selling slaves to others, notably Spain, but mostly to their own colonies. Most slaves bought and transported by the British went to the West Indies rather than the North American colonies, as, although Virginia, Maryland and South Carolina had many plantations, the Caribbean was the centre of the British slave economy and its colonies were the most profitable and therefore best able to afford purchases. The slave economy ensured in particular that a number of British ports had close links to the Caribbean, notably London, Bristol, Liverpool and Glasgow, with Bristol and Liverpool particularly important for the slave trade itself. Sugar was the prime import from the Caribbean, but other goods were also transported, so that, when Lancaster's merchants found sugar harder to obtain from the Caribbean, there were other imports in which to invest their proceeds from slave sales, especially mahogany, rum and dyewoods.

The British Atlantic stood out from the Atlantics of the other European states in the eighteenth century in terms of the combined degree and intensity of the processes of exchange and linkage; although it would not have benefited the slaves to know that they were part of a dynamic economic system in which consumerism, capital accumulation and investment in industrialisation were all linked. Investment became less risky and more profitable for the British as successful moves were made against pirates, which increased the significance of the navy, and thus of the state, as the guarantor of trade; a situation that was different to that for much of the seventeenth century when both the navy and the state were less powerful. Conversely, by the more peaceful late nineteenth century, this role, because essentially implicit, was less significant.

Imperial linkages included the shipping of food to the West Indies from British America, not least Newfoundland cod, the salting of which encouraged preservation. Herring for the slaves was also shipped from Britain. Molasses for rum was exported in return and was a major aspect of the sugar economy. There was also much trade within the Spanish New World, including cacao from Venezuela, notably to Mexico, sugar from Mexico and Cuba, and textiles from Mexico. This trade challenged the dominance of exports to Spain itself, while the dynamism of the Spanish Caribbean had an impact on social structures there, not least with the rise of regional élites that were to play a major role in striving for independence. Yet, the limited disposable income of the bulk of the population of the Spanish Caribbean, a point even more apparent for slaves, was a barrier to economic development, as were technological, environmental and organisational limitations.

Developing commercial links in the Caribbean reflected the extent of wealth in the colonies, the role of regional specialisation within a series of protected free-trade zones, the opportunities for shipping, and the degree to which the new links that were to follow colonial independence from 1775 onwards were already prefigured during the colonial era. Moreover, these trades provided yet more opportunities for privateers and pirates, not least because the primitive nature of communications on land where there were few bridges or reasonable roads meant that the reliance was necessarily on shipping.

At the same time, the key trade was with Europe, which very much was the Caribbean's connection with the global economy. Exports from the Caribbean brought profit and greater liquidity to some of the states of Atlantic Europe, but for Britain were less important than coal, a point that it is too easy to overlook today due to the understandable focus on slavery. In turn, imports to the Caribbean brought prosperity to European manufacturers. Thus, Catalan calicos, known as indianas, found an important market.

The most important sources of profit from the Caribbean were goods produced by slave labour, which was arduous and under the control of often harsh owners and overseers. Sugar cane was grown in wet conditions, which exposed workers to trench foot, and to wildlife, notably snakes including cottonmouths (water-moccasins), and, in Louisiana, alligators. The cane could lacerate the skin, and – as I discovered when, for a television programme, I, well-nourished of course, cut sugar cane on Antigua – working long hours in the fields under a hot sun was very tiring and indeed disorientating. In addition, cane cultivation required constant weeding, which was hard work. Moreover, milling work involved grinding the cane, which was dangerous, with arms or legs caught in the grinders, and also boiling the cane juice to remove water and impurities and granulate/crystallise the sugar: the fires under the open cane kettles posed a risk, while smoke from the fires led to respiratory illnesses. Ladling the cane juice from kettle to kettle, a dangerous process, caused injuries, not least if the hot juice spat onto the skin. The series of kettles was known as the Jamaica Train. Boiling time was especially arduous as work needed to be swift for crystallisation. Indeed, sometimes slaves worked throughout the night.

Slaves could be treated harshly, indeed very harshly, with brutality, callousness and cruelty all taking a role, although, as with so much, the situation needs to be put in the context of often arduous labour control elsewhere in the world, while, in the Caribbean, the situation varied by island. Thus, in Barbados, a key producer of sugar, the insurrectionist attitudes that had led to plans for revolt in 1649, 1675 and 1692 were replaced by an emphasis on limited protest designed to secure the amelioration of circumstances. In other islands, such as Jamaica, which exported 248,000 cwt (hundredweight) of sugar and 523,216 gallons of rum to London in 1750, and 513,581 and 911,480 respectively in 1770, circumstances were harsher and, in general, the situation was less favourable than on Barbados. Within each island there were significant differences in behaviour, but, at the same time, the settlers on individual islands had their own overall culture of behaviour, a point, like that of contrasting slave experiences, that is of more lasting significance in helping to explain differences between the islands.

The diaries of Thomas Thistlewood, the overseer of the Egypt plantation in Jamaica from 1750 to 1786, indicate clearly that he treated his slaves cruelly, not least abusing his female slaves sexually. Similarly, on Sir William Stapleton's profitable sugar estate on Nevis there were very exploitative working arrangements, and in the 1730s the black population fell by nearly 25 per cent. In Dominica, Grenada, St Vincent and Tobago, in the 1760s and early 1770s, there was harsh treatment that did not encourage family life and reproduction, in large part because it was easier to buy new slaves than to raise children to working age. The resulting regime led to high mortality and low fertility, with far too little food provided to slaves. Sir William Young, whose father owned land there, wrote of Tobago in the early 1770s that slaves newly arrived from Africa: 'had the laborious task of cutting down woods hanging on steep declivities, and of smoothing paths for intercourse and conveyance over or through hard and pointed rocks; scanty food, a food they were unaccustomed to, accompanied with the severities attending first coercion aggravated the grievances of their toil. Hence a sullen and refractory spirit had shown itself in the deportment of the Negroes.'

From Tobago, the British exported sugar, cotton and indigo. The harshness of sugar-cane cultivation contributed to the high rates of slave mortality, including infant and child mortality; and the latter helped lead slave-owners to treat slaves like animals in their assessment of how best to improve survival rates.

The widespread severity of treatment contributed to flight, suicide and slave risings or plots accordingly, including the risings on Jamaica in 1746, 1760, 1765 and 1776, Montserrat in 1768, and Tobago in 1770, 1771 and 1775, and this is not an exhaustive list. In 1733, a slave rising in St John seized most of the island, but in 1734 French troops arrived and put down the rebellion. There were also conspiracies discovered by the authorities before they could be launched, including on Nevis in 1725 and Antigua in 1736. Circumstances did not favour slave risings, as the whites limited the availability of firearms and made efforts to prevent plotting. When Pensacola, the capital of West Florida, was under British rule (1763–81), no slave was allowed out without his owner's written permission, and meetings of more than six slaves were forbidden after 9 p.m. Frequent declarations of martial law served as a means of control in the British West Indies, while slaves were unable to coordinate action, except in very small areas.

Flight was a more common form of resistance and led, in Jamaica, to unsuccessful expeditions against the Maroons, the runaway slaves who controlled much of the mountainous interior, a situation, there and elsewhere, that helps to lessen the value of maps of imperial control. Conflict between the Maroons and the settlers became more serious from the late 1720s and led to fears that they would help launch a slave revolt or cooperate with Spain. Expeditions had mixed success in the early 1730s. Colonel Edward Trelawny, the Governor of Jamaica, reported in 1738, 'Here the great difficulty is not to beat, but to see the enemy – nothing can be done in strict conformity to usual military preparations, and according to a regular manner; bush-fighting as they call it being a thing peculiar by itself.' Burning crops proved more successful. The failure of expeditions was followed in 1738 and 1739 by agreements that granted the Maroons land and autonomy. In return, the Maroons agreed to return any runaways that made it to the Maroon lands, making the runaway option more difficult for slaves. These treaties were necessary because Britain was moving to war with Spain and it would have been hazardous to provide an opportunity for Spanish subversion. In this respect, the Maroons had inherited the earlier position of the Caribs.

So also in 1785 on Saint-Domingue, when the French recognised the Maroon community at Le Maniel. In Trinidad, slaves took refuge in the forests, while in Louisiana, slaves could take refuge with Native Americans, the combination of the two being of particular concern to the French authorities. Part of the complex nomenclature of Louisiana society was reflected in the term Grif for those who were the children of Native Americans and black people.

THE BRITISH CARIBBEAN

A high rate of migration from the British Isles was facilitated by an Act of Parliament of 1697 which allowed people to seek work outside their own parish if they carried a certificate, thus encouraging the emigration of indentured servants who bound themselves to service for a number of years in return for their passage. Benefiting from more predictable and rapid transatlantic crossings, with a significant change in both occurring in the period from 1675 to 1740, between 30,000 and 50,000 white migrants arrived in Jamaica in the first half of the eighteenth century, and the cultivated area there increased greatly; although, tellingly again, this information refers to the land under imperial control, not that tilled by escaped slaves. But for disease, this migration would have led to a British New World dominated by the West Indies: with nearly 3 million people in 1760, compared to only 1.7 million in British North America; but disease prevented that outcome. Similarly, the African-descended population of the United States equals that of the Caribbean, although nearly ten times as many African migrants went to the Caribbean.

The willingness to accept non-British European migrants was seen with the Plantation Act of 1740, under which it was possible for all bar Catholics to become eligible for naturalisation after seven years in a British colony, a measure that threw them open to all European Protestants and that was only fully ended in 1773. The French and Spanish empires conspicuously lacked that tolerance, although that did not prevent people evading regulations.

Alongside the racial oppression that understandably attracts so much modern attention, there were serious social tensions within the settler community, many of whom were poor indentured servants or wage labourers. Racial issues were frequently affected by these social tensions, with poorer white people often resentful of free black people and harsh to black slaves. Meanwhile, opportunities within the white community varied greatly, for, in contrast to the poor white people, élite families were able to seek not only to exploit the local resources, but also to control the institutions of local government and to become representatives of their state; an always shifting, but generally prosperous, combination. At the same time, there was a strong sense of local rights and privileges, leading to frequent disputes over the power and pretensions of governors. Thus, in 1710, Daniel Parke, the Governor of the Leeward Islands, was lynched by colonists in Antigua when he sought to overawe complaints with a display of military strength. More significantly, no one was punished.

The surveying of the British colonies, which was very much to the benefit of the élite, readily displayed economic, social and racial landscapes. The utilitarian origins of the plans that were produced ensured that a premium was placed on accuracy of representation and measurement; and successfully so as recent tests for Jamaica suggest error of less than 2 per cent for the gross dimensions of plantations. Planters there wanted precise information for land-use management, and fields planted with major export crops were plotted more carefully than areas of woodland or than land planted with provision crops in what were known as 'Negro grounds'. In about 1745, Michael Hay, a surveyor on behalf of Edward Trelawny, Governor of Jamaica, produced a map of Kingston, with property ownership identified and the upper sides of the map showing prominent homes. Hay's survey was based on a layout in 1702 by John Goffe and the military engineer Christian Lilly who devised Kingston as a parallelo-gram with a rational grid of streets, at the centre of which was a 4-acre square known as Parade (used initially as the military camp), at the junction of King and Queen streets. Mention of the active Trelawny, already discussed in terms of the campaigns against the Maroons, serves as a reminder that individuals, such as Henry Morgan earlier, show up in different contexts; which, of course, was part of the history of the Caribbean, as of other regions.

Another aspect of change was provided by the development of newspapers, although these were very much for the white settlers. The pattern of this development replicated the situation in Britain. Caribbean newspapers began on Jamaica, with the *Weekly Jamaica Courant* (1718). The number of towns on the island supporting a newspaper increased with the *St Jago Intelligencer* (1756) and the *Cornwall Chronicle* from Montego Bay (1773), and with the foun-dation of newspapers at Savanna-la-Mar (1788) and Falmouth (1791). Elsewhere, the *Barbados Gazette* (1738) was followed by the *Barbados Mercury* (1762), the *St Christopher Gazette* (1765), the *Bahama Gazette* (1784) and the *St George's Chronicle and New Grenada Gazette* (1789). Newspapers were also launched in newly conquered colonies, as with the *St Lucia Gazette* (1780) and the *Trinidad Weekly Courant* (1800). The tradition continued and, founded in Kingston in 1834, the *Daily Gleaner* was later to survive the transition from colonial times to independence. Progress on non-British colonies was slower and the first Cuban newspaper, the *Papel Periódico de La Habana*, did not follow until 1790.

Newspapers provided news of the wider world for the Caribbean, and vice versa. The publication elsewhere of reports about the Caribbean reflected greater outside interest in the region, interest that in large part was a reflection of the strong and growing European and North American awareness of its importance. Thus, maps of the Caribbean and, more generally, of the New World came to play a greater role in atlases published in Europe. At the same time, there could also be gains in information. Thus, at a time of Anglo-French disputes over the island, the *St James's Chronicle* of 13 September 1764 prefaced its own account with the remark: 'many inaccurate descriptions having been given of Turks Island'.

THE FRENCH CARIBBEAN

Alongside the expansion of the British Caribbean, there was also major growth in the French West Indies, as well as the development of Louisiana. Bordeaux's imports of sugar, indigo and cocoa from the Caribbean tripled in 1717–20, the beginning of a massive increase in re-exports to northern Europe, which competed directly with those of Britain in key markets such as Hamburg. French sugar was cheaper, in part because its plantations were newer, and the soil therefore less denuded of nutrients. French sugar exports grew especially strongly from 1736, until cut short in 1743 by conflict with Britain, which affected trade and hit the ability to finance imports from France. In 1749, in turn, peace ensured that large quantities of sugar and coffee from the French Caribbean reached Hamburg, while insurance rates for French shipping fell. There was another revival after the Seven Years War ended with the Peace of Paris of 1763: war had begun formally in

1756, but hostilities had started in 1754, with many attacks on shipping in 1755.

Precarious in the face of Native American opposition and economic difficulties, Louisiana, in contrast to prosperous Saint-Domingue, Martinique and Guadeloupe, remained a sparsely populated colony, and hopes that it would serve as a base for trade with the Pacific or, at any rate, New Mexico proved abortive, as did the search for bullion deposits. Nevertheless, the colony served as the basis for a wider-ranging trading system in the hinterland. Its beginnings were difficult, not least due to the environment. In 1710, the wood of the fortress at Fort Louis (later Mobile), which had been built in 1702, was so rotted by humidity and decay that it could not support the weight of the cannon. The garrison suffered from an absence of fresh meat, from an insufficient supply of swords, cartridge boxes, nails, guns and powder, from demoralisation and desertion, and from the lack of a hospital. The survival of Louisiana at this stage rested on its acceptance by the native population, with trade the key element of mutual benefit. Relocation led first to a temporary fort and then to the greater commitment of a new brick fort with a stone foundation, which was begun in 1723 and renamed Fort Condé. Founded in 1715, New Orleans was named after Philip, Duke of Orleans, the regent for the infant Louis XV.

The commitment to the colony was to be given dramatic form in the financial speculation of the Mississippi Company, which became a proposal to refinance the French state, only for its greatly over-inflated share value to collapse at the close of 1720. As with the South Sea Company, a British company that established a position in trade to the Spanish Caribbean, the Mississippi Company reflected the bold hopes placed on the Caribbean, hopes that represented a high point in outside interest.

Efforts to encourage immigration to Louisiana had scant success. In 1717, there were 700 Europeans in the colony, but the Mississippi Company led to an increase, not least by arranging the dispatch of freed prisoners and prostitutes. Voluntary settlers were promised a benign environment, but, once there, did not find it easy and faced a high death rate. Alongside French settlers, others, including Germans, were given land, in order to provide food; but all had to be Catholic. Initial hopes that Native Americans would provide a ductile labour force proved naive and this encouraged a reliance on African slaves. The cultivation of tobacco was not a great success, but these slaves brought knowledge of rice growing and that helped to feed the colony, although that did not provide the necessary revenue stream. Free black people became an important part of the population of New Orleans and offered valuable skills. They were a key element of the nuances and adaptability of a frontier society, their skills both pushed to the fore by the resulting needs and providing the ability to meet them.

The population of Louisiana, however, remained small. By 1763 there were only about 4000 white people and 5000 black people in the colony, which was associated by the French with savage natives. Meanwhile, the *Code Noir* (1724) sought to define a racial hierarchy. There were also the results of relationships between groups, such as quadroons, who were a quarter black, and such categories became more common with time. The earliest map of New Orleans, that of 1744 by Jacques-Nicholas Bellin, showed only about a hundred buildings, most of which were not to survive a series of fires that hit hard at the close-packed wooden buildings. Founded in 1718, the city had a grid structure radiating from the riverfront *Place d'Armes*, now Jackson Square.

Conflict, 1702–13

The wealth of the Indies attracted governmental attention, more particularly when the stakes were high in wartime. The accessibility of the Caribbean coasts to amphibious operations, and the extent to which warships provided firepower, troop-carrying capacity and logistics, made this focus a matter of opportunity as well as need. Warships were able to fulfil their operational role, the decisive test of a naval administration. An account of the wars serves to underline the particularly bloody nature of Caribbean history and to explain the importance of fortifications for this period. The resources used were formidable, so that, on Barbados in 1748, Charles Fort, originally known as Fort Needham, whose remains are now in the grounds of a Hilton resort, had a complement of thirty-five pieces of artillery, with another fourteen in nearby batteries, and 'in time of alarm there are two field officers and three companies posted here, and a proportional number at all the other forts, and batteries through the island'. However, they were often not maintained. Gun carriages rotted and the weather honeycombed the iron cannon, which made the defences less formidable in practice.

Far from being a list without consequence, the wars explained the fate of the islands and of the region as a whole, and also underlined the unpredictability of both. In the War of the Spanish Succession (1702–13), a war triggered by the end of the Spanish Habsburg line, the Mediterranean, where it was easier to support major fleets, took precedence for Britain and France, and naval weakness in the Caribbean meant that the French, although they could now use Havana as a base, generally did not take the initiative except to try to escort the Spanish treasure ships home. However, in addition to devastating privateering attacks on English shipping mounted from Martinique and Guadeloupe, the French were able to conduct damaging raids, as when they raided the Bahamas in 1703 and 1704, and sacked both St Kitts and Nevis in 1706 (with great gain of plunder including slaves), Montserrat and Barbuda in 1710, and Montserrat in 1712. The English had captured St Kitts in 1702, but, helped by the sickness that affected the attackers, Guadeloupe successfully resisted invasion in 1703, although much damage was inflicted by the English troops who landed. Caribbean campaigning was seen as deadly, Lieutenant-Colonel James Rivers writing in 1703 of his wish to leave Jamaica:

'to get out of this unhealthy climate as soon as possible which diminishes the forces both sea and land very considerably every day . . . for fear of this service several of the officers quitted their commission'.

In 1701, England sent twenty-one warships under Vice-Admiral John Benbow to the Caribbean for Spain was no longer an ally and seizure of her treasure offered gain and the dislocation of the Bourbon financial system. Although hit hard by disease, French warships that arrived in 1702 safely convoyed the treasure ships. Others fought Benbow off Santa Marta in a running action that began on 29 August. Before Benbow was seriously injured by a chain shot, he had lost control of his captains, and most failed to give him sufficient support in the battle. As a result, two were later court martialled and shot. In 1708, the far stronger Spanish treasure fleet was attacked off Cartagena. The flagship, the *San José*, blew up after its powder magazine was hit and most of its crew were killed, and, despite damage to the *Expedition*, Rear-Admiral Charles Wager pushed on to bombard another ship into surrender. The captains of two other warships were court martialled for failing to help Wager sufficiently. Most of the Spanish treasure went down with the *San José*, which became allegedly the world's richest shipwreck with cargo valued in 2018 at about £15 ($17) billion; but Wager still gained considerable spoils. Gain of a different sort was pursued in 1713, when a French privateering force intimidated Curaçao into paying money to avoid being looted: the Dutch were at war with France.

The war left England (from 1707 Britain) victorious, largely due to the campaigning of John, Duke of Marlborough on the Continent. The French claimant, Philip, Duke of Anjou, beat his Austrian rival to the Spanish throne, becoming Philip V and beginning a Bourbon dynasty in the Spanish empire, but part of that empire in Europe went to Austria. Under the Peace of Utrecht (1713), Britain also made gains, including Gibraltar and Minorca. There were benefits in the New World, notably a limited breach, by means of an annual 'permission ship' to the commercial fair at Porto Bello, a means into the protected trade of the Spanish Caribbean. The British also gained for thirty years the *Asiento* contract to transport slaves from West Africa to Spanish America. This had been awarded to the French Guinea Company in 1701, while France had also been granted permission to sell goods in Spanish American ports, which was a major challenge to the British contraband trade there. Indeed, in 1705, Queen Anne told Parliament, 'Nothing can be more evident than if the French king continues master of the Spanish monarchy, the balance of trade in Europe is utterly destroyed; and he will be able in a short time to engross the trade and wealth of the world.'

In contrast to the *Asiento* and the permission ship, there were not territorial gains of note in the Caribbean, with the exception of recognition of St Kitts as British in 1713. Certainly, there was nothing to match the situation in North America where the British position in Nova Scotia, Newfoundland and Hudson Bay was recognised by France. Nevertheless, there had been a major transition since 1688 in the relative strength of those European powers with Caribbean colonies.

Set in the Eighteenth Century: **Pirates of the Caribbean**

The Disney film franchise, which began in 2003, was based on a theme ride of that name that had opened at Disneyland, California, in 1967 and been copied elsewhere in Disney parks and products. The five films – *The Curse of the Black Pearl* (2003), *Dead Man's Chest* (2006), *At World's End* (2007), *On Stranger Tides* (2011) and *Dead Men Tell No Tales* (2017) – had grossed over $4.5 billion by March 2019. Video games, board and online games, and books have brought further publicity and profit. In the first film, the pirate hero, Jack Sparrow, played by Johnny Depp, fights it

---

out in the early eighteenth century with a crew who, as a result of an Aztec curse, are all-too-lively skeletons at night. The action sequences and Depp's frenetic acting as a comic action hero with madly active eyes made a great impact; which was just as well as the plot was at once horribly complicated and very silly. The British navy, in the person of Commodore James Norrington, is villainous. The plots do not improve. In *Dead Man's Chest*, the fastest film to gross over £1 billion, a magic compass, cannibals and a vodou priestess all play a role; as does the deadly Kraken, a mighty and devouring sea monster that returns.

PRIVATEERING AND PIRACY

War had encouraged privateering but, with peace, privateers and pirates had to manage a difficult transition to fewer opportunities, as indeed did the Royal Navy which had benefited greatly from prize money as well as from taking part in shipping goods. The Peace of Utrecht of 1713 proved particularly difficult as it followed a period dominated by war (for Britain 1689–97, 1702–13), when trade had been heavily disrupted by commerce and opportunities for piracy plentiful. From 1713, Britain was at peace with France until 1743; and with Spain until 1739, with the exception of a brief war in 1718–20. This meant far fewer men employed in the navy. The harsh and hazardous life of ordinary service in warships or merchantmen was not at all appealing, and it is understandable that many were unwilling to abandon their wartime activity. Sailors, often recruited from the polyglot Caribbean, had floating loyalties, and the population of illegals was fed by new recruitment, which included desertion and mutiny. Opportunism was important as it was fairly easy for privateers, or indeed mutinous crews, to reach an enemy-held island or coast for refuge, and seamen who could abscond with a ship stood a good chance of getting away with it.

Piracy was also part of a far-flung system. In the late seventeenth century, pirates from the Caribbean, such as William Kidd, some also logwood cutters on the Central American coast, very much a frontier area, had turned to the opportunities of the Indian Ocean, establishing bases in Madagascar in the 1690s. St Mary's Madagascar sold their captures, including purchased slaves, to New York, whence they received goods, all with the connivance of Benjamin Fletcher, Governor of New York, who provided privateering commissions. In the early eighteenth century, however, they turned back to the Caribbean, in part in response to greater anti-piracy activity by the English East India Company in the Indian Ocean.

After peace in 1713, the threat from buccaneering to British trade in the Caribbean and also wider afield helped lead the Royal Navy to try to stamp it out in the 1710s and 1720s, while peace freed the navy for that role. The pirate base in New Providence, Bahamas, was brought under control in 1718 by Woodes Rogers, a former privateer, and by mass executions of pirates in 1718 and 1723. Women pirates included Anne Bonny and Mary Read, both captured in 1720 but not executed because they were pregnant. In contrast, Bonny's pirate lover, later husband, John 'Calico Jack' Rackham, was hanged. Aside from British pirates there were others, with Spanish pirates being a particular problem for Jamaica in 1720.

The British anti-piracy effort was part of the process by which the colonies established civil societies with differently sustainable political and economic structures. The changing nature of British governance was important, for the 'Revolution Settlement' that followed the 'Glorious Revolution' of 1688–9 saw more limited authority for central government, and this meant that colonial leaders could accept governmental anti-piracy measures knowing that they would not infringe on their position. As a result, the supporting land/sea connection of the pirate *ancien régime* was transformed.

Moreover, as another aspect of modernisation, merchants were able to hand over most of the cost of protection to the state, and thereby to increase the profitability of their trade and of plantation societies, which thus encouraged further expansion. Furthermore, greater commercial profits lessened the appeal of cooperating with pirates, and this appeal diminished for merchants and officials alike, while, in addition, peace and profit ensured that employment was available for ship owners and sailors, thus lessening the appeal of piracy. However, circumstances varied by island: in the 1720s and 1730s, the British Virgin Islands were scarcely under control, which provided an opportunity for pirates; a situation that was totally different to that on Antigua where there was a naval base. The Royal Navy's effort against piracy could be lax and spotty. This was an aspect of the continuum of piracy and suppression overlapping with the earlier one between piracy and privateering, yet again providing a frontier that was zonal rather than linear, one in particular with much local variety.

'Blackbeard'

Edward Thatch (his name was erroneously spelled Teach in a newspaper of the day), a Bristol-born privateer during the War of Spanish Succession, turned to piracy, basing himself, like many others, in the Bahamas. In command of the *Queen Anne's Revenge*, he was a successful pirate in 1717–18, but was killed off the North Carolina coast in 1718 during a vigorous governmental campaign against piracy. Discovered in 1996, the remains of his ship included a syringe filled with mercury, which was a means to treat venereal disease.

CONFLICT FROM 1719 TO 1748

War between Spain and the Quadruple Alliance, notably Britain and France, in 1718–20 led, in May 1719, to the French capture of Pensacola and eastern Texas, both surprise attacks. Pensacola was then recaptured in August by an expedition of 1400 troops from Havana, underlining the hierarchy of bases and the important role of forces available in the colonies as opposed to having to face the lengthy voyage from Europe. Pensacola was next retaken in September by the French and their local allies, the Choctaw. Colonial conflict, however, was generally dependent on European peace politics, and Spain regained Pensacola as part of the peace. In 1720, a Spanish force from Cuba launched a damaging raid on Nassau, but it was driven off by the local militia.

In 1726–7, when the British came close to war with Spain, a fleet of twenty warships blockaded Porto Bello, a key port on the isthmus of Panama for the transhipment of South American bullion en route to Spain. The British fleet lost heavily to yellow fever, with the commander, Rear-Admiral Francis Hosier, dying, as did his replacements in 1728 and 1729, but the blockade served to put acute pressure on the Spanish system, notably the ability of its government to subsidise allies and that of Spanish merchants to pay debts. The latter affected the French economy, encouraging France to seek a solution to Anglo-Spanish differences. France traded with the Spanish New World via Spain, thus supporting its monopoly.

The British, meanwhile, developed their Caribbean naval capacity. There were two bases on Jamaica – Kingston, which was able to careen the larger ships of the line sent there, and Port Antonio where Fort George was built from 1729 – as well as, to the leeward, English Harbour on Antigua begun in 1728 and still an impressive site, not least with a mango tree providing its luscious fruit to the visitor. These British bases were able to mask the Spanish one at Havana where durable tropical hardwoods – cedar and mahogany – were used to build particularly good ships, some of which served at Trafalgar.

Even in periods of alliance, there were tensions in the Caribbean, as when the French expelled British settlers from St Lucia in 1723, and, in 1730, seized British ships loading timber at St Croix which the French sold to the Danish West India Company in 1733. That year, French troops from Martinique helped suppress a slave revolt on St John, which the Danes had occupied from 1716. There was frequent conflict between the British logwood cutters based at Belize on the Bay of Honduras and the Spaniards who claimed the coast.

The Spaniards' determination to protect and increase the profitability of their American empire conflicted with the interests of British merchants determined to exploit these markets and to secure Spanish bullion, but, as ever, there is the danger of taking one issue and making it all powerful, a point that is also relevant as far as the role of sugar in the British economy is concerned. Rather than trade and empire being responsible for poor diplomatic relations, instead relations that were naturally bad as a result of Spanish anger over the European provisions of the Utrecht peace settlement of 1713 were further harmed by the issue of Caribbean trade. So also with Anglo-French relations. Representations to the French government, for example from the Bayonne Chamber of Commerce in 1728, that British possession of the *Asiento* limited the markets for French industry were frequent, but they were far from the key issue in relations.

Nevertheless, the seizure of ships and the ill treatment of sailors provided a vivid and easily grasped issue, and it was from this that the fame of Captain Jenkins's ear, severed in 1731, derived. These issues could be readily grasped, they provided good copy for the press and, as an issue of national pride and honour, they were most effective in Parliament. Compared to such issues as St Lucia, confused at the Board of Trade and in Parliament with St

Vincent, Spanish depredations on British commerce had a very wide emotional appeal, and it was this that the opposition exploited, for the actual merits of the case were confused and difficult to grasp. Indeed, the ministry, although frequently pressing Spain for redress over grievances, were nevertheless unhappy about mercantile claims. Horatio Walpole commented in 1739, 'ambition, avarice, distress, disappointment, and all the complicated views that tend to render the minds of men uneasy, are got out of Pandora's box, and fill all places and all hearts in the nation'. The crucial element was not simply the widespread agitation, but rather its relationship to strains within the ministry and doubts within ministerial ranks in Parliament. Trade with the Spanish empire was the successful political issue because it could be used to focus widespread dissatisfaction in Britain. Indeed, the move to war with Spain in 1739 revealed not the importance of commercial considerations in the conduct of foreign policy but, rather, somewhat differently, the strength of defending trade as a political issue.

The opposition, however, was advocating a foolish policy. War with Spain wrecked the trade with that country and did not produce the expected collapse of the Spanish empire. Moreover, Anglo-Spanish commercial differences were not settled to Britain's satisfaction in the Treaty of Aix-la-Chapelle that ended the war in 1748, and Britain lost a lot of its trade during the war to other powers. Many British ships were taken by privateers, insurance premiums rose, and convoying proved difficult to arrange. The war was bad for commerce, as well as being a disaster politically and fiscally. Sir Robert Walpole, the Prime Minister, told Parliament in 1739 with regard to mercantile pressure for war with Spain: 'However some private persons might suffer, with whatever reason they might call out for justice upon Spain, yet our pacific forbearance was the safest and wisest conduct for the general interest of a trading people', in which view he was justified by the succeeding war.

In the long term, Britain benefited but, in the short term, the challenge from France, Spain and the Jacobites was serious. The opposition, with its boasts of national glory, underplayed the challenge, while trade suffered from its ideology of gaining trade and empire through conflict. It was easy to applaud such sentiments as

> Rule Britannia, rule the waves:
> Britons never will be slaves.

The reality, instead, was to be British sailors rotting off Cartagena in 1741. The Spanish empire was far more resilient than was appreciated in Britain, where notions of Spanish decadence and the vulnerability of the Spanish Caribbean were well-established.

Initially, the government sought a spectacular victory in the Caribbean in order to build on the hopes created in 1739 by Edward Vernon's bold seizure of the port of Porto Bello, a victory that was to be much celebrated in Britain. The British warships were becalmed alongside one of the three defending forts, but, with a heavy fire, silenced it before landing sailors and marines who, climbing through the embrasures, took the surrender of the position. The other forts and the town then surrendered, which encouraged jingoistic hopes of fresh gains. These, however, were undercut by the difficulties of the situation including concern about possible French intervention on the side of Spain. Indeed, the French sent a watching fleet to the Caribbean in 1740, although it did not intervene.

At any event, Vernon, who in this respect was in a situation not greatly different from that of earlier privateers, was in no position to retain Porto Bello, which he only wanted to make indefensible for future refuge by Spanish galleons. Moreover, he achieved little in 1740. In 1741, the situation appeared to change with the arrival of a substantial force that was launched against Cartagena, but, helped by the heavy losses caused among the British by disease, its impressive defences held out. Subsequent British operations that year suffered from the impact of failure, and the consequent loss of impetus, morale and confidence. Operations against Santiago in Cuba, from which Jamaica could be threatened, and against Panama were seriously mishandled; and the army was ordered back to Britain in late 1742. This was not the world of Francis Drake or Henry Morgan. Relying on charismatic leadership for forces that were smaller and less complex, they had faced command difficulties but nothing matching the differences between army and navy in this conflict. Later moves in the War of Jenkins's Ear were smaller scale. In 1743, a British squadron sent to act against La Guayra and Porto Cabello, the ports on the Caracas coast, was beaten off.

On the Mosquito Coast of Nicaragua, the British supported native people well-attuned to fighting on the coast, not least to moving by canoe, against Spanish authority, and, in 1747, the natives surprised and captured the fort of San Fernando de Matina, only for the Spaniards to destroy an English settlement at the mouth of the San Juan River in Guatemala. Although Spanish naval weakness tended to leave the initiative in the Caribbean to the British, tropical diseases and the Spanish defensive system helped to compensate for the naval inferiority of the Bourbons and for their decision to devote most of their resources to ambitions and conflict in Europe. In parallel, the environmental issues of the Mosquito Coast also helped thwart the Spaniards.

The Anglo-Spanish War of Jenkins's Ear had been subsumed into the Anglo-French conflict that began in 1743 as part of the War of the Austrian Succession, with Spain an ally of France. In this, Britain did not really win naval mastery until after the battle of Toulon (1744) and the two off Cape Finisterre (1747); and this delay left only limited naval resources available for the Caribbean, a point underlined by French invasion attempts or at least preparations against Britain in 1744-6. Despite the size of the British navy, there were often too few ships to spare for the many tasks for which the fleet was required. Moreover, the nature of communications ensured that, once detached, ships were difficult to recall speedily, which was an increasing problem as more ships were sent to transoceanic stations. In the Caribbean, with wooden ships very much affected by the constraints of the tide and wind, it was hard to maintain all-weather stations, and thus effective blockades. In 1748, British warships captured Port Saint Louis on Saint-Domingue by sailing close in to the defending fort and bombarding it into ruins. However, after the fort was demolished the position was not retained, while a boom across the passage to the harbour led to the abandonment of the subsequent attack on Santiago in Cuba. Nevertheless, the British proved successful in using trade for warfare, the navy capturing many French and Spanish merchant vessels, while, in addition, Martinique was successfully blockaded. Yet, it was not until the next war, the Seven Years War (1756–63), when the French invasion attempt of 1759 was crushed with two major British naval victories at Lagos (Portugal) and Quiberon Bay, that Britain would be able to seek to transform the situation in the Caribbean.

CONCLUSIONS

The comparison with the East Indies again is instructive, for, with the exception of India, the Europeans were most effective on islands rather than on the mainland of South Asia. The Dutch East India Company played an important role in Java, intervening in disputes in the kingdom of Mataram in the First and Second Javanese Wars of Succession (1704–8, 1719–23), but the company's small army was weak, and its ability to operate successfully away from coastal areas was limited, as was shown in the Third War in 1746–57, and in operations against Bantam in 1750. A 1749 treaty gave the Dutch sovereignty over Mataram, but this amounted to little in practice. Indeed, the Dutch had little interest in conquering the interior, instead seeking to ensure that the rulers there did not contest their coastal positions and trade. The situation in the Caribbean was totally different.

While the emphasis for the Caribbean is often on the activities of states, imperial systems and governments, it is important to appreciate the significance of creole societies and their ability to absorb and transform the demands of the metropole and its governmental structure. At the same time, that very process helped ensure that the imperial systems worked and could do so by drawing on the networks of these societies and their ability to adapt to circumstances. Such adaptation was of the essence of creole society, and was seen with the response to environmental contexts and events, and with relations between, as well as within, races and genders. The imperial systems cooperated with this adaptation because they deployed limited resources and worked on accepting restricted, even episodic, control, and in part, indeed, by giving the local élites the instructions they were willing to observe. Thus, creole societies sustained their own version of the imperial order.

Familiarity with local circumstances was not really possible for distant imperial governments, and, instead, it was best to adopt a policy of 'salutary neglect', while maintaining the military support necessary for protection. This protection became most important in wartime, but it was then that states were under greatest pressure across their range of commitments, not least in the currency most vital for the Caribbean, warships, and therefore had to rely on local support, not least volunteer militias. At the same time, the local response could include an accommodation with threats and invaders, accommodation ranging from accepting the terms of blockade and other aspects of offshore 'protection costs', to paying ransoms to attackers or readily yielding to conquest. The course of each eighteenth-century war left the British successful by the close, but attention to detail indicates that the balance among the powers was up for grabs in every conflict and could easily have yielded a different configuration.

6

Britain to the Fore, 1750–90

Your Lordship is doubtless too well acquainted with the natural and uncommon strength of this island to doubt that a vigorous opposition may be expected. The fatality attending the climate at this season particularly joined with the numbers of the savages, present difficulties only to be overcome by our outmost diligence and perseverance.

Major-General William Dalrymple was in no doubt about the difficulties of his task on St Vincent in 1772; both task and difficulties very different to when he had been in command of two regiments sent to Boston in 1768 in what turned out to be a failed attempt to preserve royal authority. Operating against the Caribs on St Vincent, Dalrymple was part of a Caribbean world that it is all-too-easy to overlook with the standard focus on sugar, slaves, and conflict between Britain and France or Spain. Instead, native independence continued to be a reality in some areas, for example in most of Florida, although, even there, the European presence remained a factor.

Campaigning on St Vincent, the British benefited from taking the initiative and from the safety of their crucial Caribbean military bases, notably Antigua and Jamaica, for the Caribs were not able to attack other islands, and the war, therefore, was in part a matter of the build-up of the British ability to deploy resources on the island. The British did not have slave soldiers at this point, but could move troops from elsewhere in the Caribbean and from North America. By the end of 1772, Dalrymple had reached a clear frontier with the end of the existing road: 'no white man has ever been in their [the Caribs] concealed places of retirement ... neither guides nor intelligence can be procured ... this fatal climate'.

Despite losses, through ambushes, and by 'the neglect of a villainous set of surgeons', Dalrymple obtained in February 1773 what he was able to present as a satisfactory treaty. This entailed a recognition of British sovereignty; but, in return, the guarantee of much land to the Caribs in perpetuity, a guarantee, however, that subsequent conflict was to put aside. In practice, the army, as so often in its history, was manoeuvring in a situation made complex by contradictory pressures: from the settlers, who wanted Carib land and 'strong' measures; the Caribs; and the government in London, which wanted peace, stability and economy, and, moreover, was willing to support the Caribs and to protect their land. In many respects, there was a parallel with the same government angering settlers in North America by its protection of Native Americans and their land.

In the Caribbean, there were also multiple tensions between European settlers and government, but the racial balance, in the shape of the far larger percentage of slaves, acted as a dampener on settler activism. However, that situation changed in revolutionary scenarios, as the 1790s to the 1820s in Saint-Domingue and continental Latin America, and the 1870s in Cuba, were to show. The Caribs went on being an independent force until defeated in 1796 and then deported, first to the Grenadines, and subsequently to Roatán in 1797, becoming important to the ethnic mix on the latter.

The British had 636 casualties in the 1772 campaign, 394 of them 'sick', but what was striking was their ability to deploy over 2000 troops, which was a clear sign of imperial power, albeit while Britain was not at war in Europe or the Americas. Native resistance could check, not reverse, the tide of European and European-American advance; although it did impose important checks, as by the Caribs for the British on Grenada, and also with Spain in the case of the Guajira peninsula in Colombia in the

1770s, and on the Mosquito Coast. The Guajira peninsula only started being converted to Christianity from the 1880s.

More generally, a sense of fellow humanity, to imperial enemies, subordinated peoples and the lives of troops sent into battle, was generally absent; and this period saw the slave trade, the value of the Caribbean and the struggle over its control all at a height. In his futuristic novel *L'An 2440* (1770), the radical French writer Louis Sébastien Mercier described a monument in Paris depicting a black man, his arms extended, rather than in chains, and a proud look in his eye, surrounded by the pieces of twenty broken sceptres, and atop a pedestal with the inscription *Au Vengeur du nouveau monde*: 'To the avenger of the New World'. This idea would have seemed totally fanciful as well as radical, for, in these decades, the slave trade increased to an unprecedented extent, and its profitability encouraged the longstanding competition to control it.

Britain Triumphant, 1756–63

Titling this chapter 'Britain to the Fore' may seem mistaken as it was France in Saint-Domingue that was advancing economically, much to the discomfort of Britain. However, Britain was the naval superpower, and even in the war she lost, that of American Independence, eventually beat the French at sea, going on to affirm her dominance anew in the Dutch Crisis of 1787.

Peace in 1748 had scarcely brought British disputes with France and Spain to a close. The former continued to be particularly important in the case of St Lucia and Tobago, which were far from being the neutral islands that they were termed. British newspapers, furthermore, emphasised a more general threat, *Old England*, on 18 May 1751, one to Barbados. However, conflict when it came in 1754 was over competing claims in the Ohio River valley in North America. In the Seven Years War, known in the United States as the French and American War, the British achieved unprecedented success, against first France and then Spain, in attacks on other European-ruled islands in the Caribbean, indicating a potential that was only to be matched by the United States in the twentieth century. The British benefited from nearby bases, from considerable experience in amphibious operations, and from an administration able to ensure that warships fulfilled their operational role on distant stations. The major French possessions were tough targets, not least because, like Spanish-held Cartagena, in 1741, they were strongly fortified and well-garrisoned. Indeed, an attack on Martinique in 1759 failed in the face of strong resistance from the largely mulatto militia that fought in a dispersed fashion and took advantage of the natural cover, thus denying the British easy targets for their firepower. Arguing that there were insufficient troops, both to besiege the citadel and to maintain the lines of communication to the landing base, the British commander withdrew; instead, landing that year on Guadeloupe and heavily bombarding the French position at Basseterre. After the defending batteries had been silenced, troops landed and occupied the town; while, driven into the mountains where they could not really take shelter, the French on the island soon surrendered. 'The affluence of money from East and West Indies, from Spain and Portugal' was cited that October by the Duke of Newcastle, the First Lord of the Treasury, in order to explain why Britain could fight on.

In 1761, as a reminder of the dependence of Caribbean history on wider international currents, a large British force, freed by the fall of Canada with the surrender of Montreal to Britain the previous year, conquered Dominica and then, in 1762, landed on Martinique. The British tried to do the same in 1814–15: following the fall of Napoleon for the first time in 1814 by dispatching an expedition to the New World, the force that was defeated at New Orleans the following year. In 1762, supported by sailors and Marines, the British troops on Martinique rapidly cleared the fortified hills behind Fort Royal, built a battery on the Morne

Garnier from which they could bombard the fort, and cut it off, so that, with no hope of relief, the French surrendered. This led to the surrender of the island, and to the collapse of the French position in the Windward Islands, with Grenada, St Lucia and St Vincent all rapidly falling. Aside from Louisiana, the French were left with only Saint-Domingue, a far larger target and one that was not attacked; a lesson the British would have done well to heed in 1794.

THE CONQUEST OF CUBA, 1762

The British, instead, then moved against Havana, for the war had broadened out to include Spain. Anglo-Spanish relations were embittered by a number of disputes, including that over the Mosquito Coast whence logwood was exported, which was an aspect of the longstanding Spanish concern over breaches of their commercial and territorial position. However, again as a reminder of the significance of European affairs, Spain's alliance with France was the key element in leading to war, and the crucial Spanish move was the invasion of Portugal to whose assistance a British force was sent. British commentators welcomed the war, the *London Evening Post* of 2 January 1762 declaring 'it will in a little time bring us in large quantities of dollars'.

There was unwonted optimism in Britain about the prospects, the *Monitor* announcing on 1 May 1762: 'A war with Spain is purely maritime. She must submit to the power which commands the ocean. Her strength depends upon her American treasure; and her American colonies are at the mercy of the sovereigns of the seas.'

For Britain, there was, crucially, to be no repetition of the failure at Cartagena in 1741, and the contrast marked the growing sophistication of the British in the joint operations that had been continuous practice since 1757. A force of 12,000 troops, much of which had left Spithead on 6 March, landed at Cojímar to the east of Havana on 7 June, covered by twenty-two ships of the line, a formidable fleet. Operations were concentrated against Morro Castle, which commanded the channel from the sea to the harbour of Havana, was protected by a very deep landward ditch, and is still an impressive site. On 1 July, the British batteries opened fire, supported by three warships, but damage from Spanish fire forced the latter to abandon the bombardment. The summer passed in siegeworks, which were hindered by the bare rock in front of the fortress, and by artillery duds. A third of the British force was lost to malaria and yellow fever (which also hit the defenders), but the Spanish batteries were silenced by heavier British fire. On 30 July, the British exploded two mines on either side of the fortress's ditch, creating an earth ramp across it and a breach in the wall, both still clearly visible. Having stormed the breach, the British captured the fort, from where cannon could dominate the city, which surrendered on 13 August.

The fleet in the harbour, which included twelve ships of the line, also surrendered: by attacking Havana, the British had wrecked Spanish naval power in the Caribbean and captured Cuba, for the seizure of major bases was sufficient to cause the collapse of imperial control. The news was received in Britain with joy, the *Salisbury Journal* on 4 October 1762 reporting that the news arrived during a choral concert in the annual music festival: to shouts of applause, the choir at once burst into the song 'Britons, Strike Home'. There was optimism about pressing on to make more gains, but the government wanted peace, and was also aware of practicalities, the cautious Lord Chancellor Hardwicke pointing out that, although Britain could stop the Spanish treasure fleet, it could not conquer Mexico.

THE PEACE OF PARIS, 1763

The British, in exchange for returning conquered Cuba to Spain, received unconquered Florida, which was extended, at the expense of Louisiana, as far as the Mississippi, creating, for the British, the separate colonies of East Florida and West Florida; the latter being the modern 'Panhandle' of Florida extended over to the Mississippi. As a result, Fort Condé in Mobile was renamed Fort Charlotte in honour of George III's new wife. The right to cut wood in Belize was also gained from Spain. The British, in turn, returned their conquests of Guadeloupe, Martinique and St Lucia to France; but kept Dominica, Grenada, St Vincent and Tobago (none leading sugar-producing colonies), Fort Royal on Grenada being renamed Fort George. In exchange for responding to French pressure for peace, including accepting the return of Minorca to Britain (captured from the latter in 1756), Spain, under an agreement of 1762, received from France the rest of Louisiana, which was seen by the French government as a costly incumbrance.

The return of Guadeloupe and Martinique to France was controversial in Britain; the *St James's Chronicle* of 27 September 1764 discussing whether Britain should have continued the Seven Years War in order to retain them, commented: 'even our tinkers and cobblers are politicians and the first to roar'. The *Monitor* of 6 September 1760 had wanted Louisiana in exchange for the return of Guadeloupe. However, in part by their not being islands run by Britain, this return lessened competition in sugar production within the British empire, and there was also much support in Britain for the retention, in contrast, of the conquest of Canada. Similarly, Jamaica had been worried about competition from a conquered Cuba. As wars usually ended with a compromise peace, Canada and Guadeloupe/Martinique were treated as alternatives. In France, the loss of Louisiana was criticised in mercantile circles in the Atlantic ports, but had only limited impact elsewhere, due to the lack of élite commitment to the colony, and regaining Guadeloupe and Martinique was regarded as more important.

The Sense of Opportunity

On 28 April 1762, the *Monitor* presented the British capture of Martinique as a mark of Providential support. Somewhat differently, the *St James's Chronicle* of 24 July 1766 printed a letter from Mobile in newly acquired West Florida by Thomas Miller who was developing a rice plantation. He stressed the quantity of wood available and:

> Those swamps appear to me to be good lands, capable of producing either rice, hemp, flax, indigo, or cotton; indeed, indigo and cotton I have seen succeed in them very well. The whole face of the country is covered with grass of so good a kind, that cattle fat to good beef on it . . . The woods abound with deer, turkeys, quails, rabbits, etc . . . I never saw a place so full of fine fish as this Bay of Mobile.

Such an enterprise would have required many slaves, and their treatment in West Florida, by new masters seeking a rapid return, tended to be even harsher than those in older-established colonies.

AFTER THE WAR

The post-war 1760s saw the development by the European powers of their Caribbean colonies, as part of a deliberate imperial position so as best to cope with what was likely to be another war, with military and economic preparedness seen as linked. Thus, the British sought to chart the waters of the American coastline of the Caribbean in order to assess navigable routes: George Gauld did so for the Admiralty from 1764 to 1781. There were also improvements to fortifications, with Fort Shirley begun in 1765 to defend northern Dominica.

There were disputes between the recent combatants. These tended to arise from the actions of local colonial and military officials whom it was frequently difficult to control from Europe, as with the dispute with France over Turks Island in 1764. The *St James's Chronicle* of 9 January 1766 carried a London coffee-house dialogue in which this island, as well as Belize, were among the items discussed. However, the future of Corsica, purchased by France from Genoa in 1768, proved a more serious cause of concern.

The period also saw growing criticism of imperial rule by European settlers. In Britain's Caribbean colonies, there was considerable opposition to the Stamp Act of 1765, notably on St Kitts and Nevis; although the trajectory of opposition did not match that in the Thirteen Colonies in North America that rebelled from 1775. It is always difficult to explain something that did not happen. Material factors in the shape of self-interest tend to come to the fore, and this would lead to an emphasis on the need by the settlers for imperial support in the face of the more numerous slaves, but ideological, cultural, social and religious elements, some of which were shaped by the slave economies, were also important, not least in the shape of the absence of a culture and society similar to that of New England. Instead, Caribbean white culture was more similar to that of the southern colonies in North America and, alongside opposition, loyalism was strong there.

The attempt to raise revenue and improve governance seen in the British world with the Stamp Act was matched by Spanish policy under Charles III (r. 1759–88), who greatly favoured *peninsulares* as officials rather than *criollos* (creoles; in this case, American-born descendants of Spanish settlers). The fall of Havana in 1762 had come as a major shock and there was an attempt to increase defensive precautions, as on Puerto

Rico, and strengthen the government accordingly, as with the dispatch of more troops for garrison duty, for example to Venezuela, and the raising of militia. In order to help the economy, restrictions on slave imports were lifted, and in Cuba the number of slaves approximately doubled between 1774 and 1792, with sugar and coffee production also growing rapidly as well as the development of snuff mills to process tobacco. To prevent a recurrence of the failure in 1762, large new fortresses to protect Havana were built: *San Carlos de la Cabaña* in 1763–74 and *Castillo del Príncipe* in 1767–79. The latter was to be used as a political prison, both in the nineteenth century by Spain and in the twentieth by Fidel Castro. Wealth and governmental power came together in the Palace of the Captain General that was inaugurated in 1791 and is now Havana's *Museo de la Ciudad*.

The number of slaves in Puerto Rico also increased greatly, as did sugar and coffee production, although a major portion of the growth followed the revolution in Saint-Domingue in 1791 and owed much to the French planters who then moved in with their expertise and slaves, which was one of the many diasporas of Caribbean history. These diasporas both complicate the idea of specific frontiers but also contributed to the idea of the Caribbean as a frontier zone.

In New Orleans, opposition to Spanish rule, after trade outside the Spanish imperial system or in non-Spanish ships was banned, and enslaved Native Americans freed, led to a rebellion in New Orleans in 1768, one that prefigured later hostility there after takeover by America (1803) and capture by Union forces (1862). Mindful of its ally Spain's determination to restore authority, France rejected this attempt to return to its rule, and Spanish forces sent from Havana reimposed control in 1769, with the rebellious ringleaders executed. This was atypical, as Spanish rule in Louisiana in large part was a matter of the nuances of power, with what was to be called enlightened despotism in practice a matter of the negotiation of concessions to local interests, needs and circumstances, in order to ensure internal tranquillity and a degree of local economic satisfaction; a process that included the free blacks, but not the slaves.

At the same time, slave agency emerged, notably in the informal economies linking slaves and poor whites. Participation in the informal economy, an interdependence of consumption and criminality, provided slaves with a way to earn money and also a degree of continuity with the hucstering and peddling activities familiar from West Africa. Spain, moreover, permitted subjects to marry across colour lines, whereas France had forbidden such marriage in the *Code Noir*. In the event, social practice and prejudice ensured that there were few such marriages (as opposed to less formal relationships), but there were many gifts in wills, legacies that endowed relationships across lines of colour and legal status with a degree of formal recognition and protection that had been previously denied to them.

As allies for most of the eighteenth century until 1792, France and Spain largely cooperated, for example in 1777 by the Treaty of Aranjuez settling their differences over boundaries on Hispaniola which, despite the Treaty of Ryswick of 1697, had been a vexed issue from the seventeenth century with the French trying to expand their territorial presence. Whatever their differences in the Caribbean, France sought the maintenance of Spain's empire, not least as a market for French goods, but also as a way to offset British power. This situation changed under the French Revolutionaries and, even more, Napoleon.

So also with British views. On 1 December 1770 when war had seemed imminent, the *Westminster Journal* printed a piece attacking popular prejudice: 'We know very well that Jack Helter-Skelter says "damn the Spaniards, we shall soon give them a belly-full, and bring home their ship-load after ship-load." Better to cultivate their friendship, and supply them with the manufactures of Great Britain.' The latter view was to be to the fore after the Spanish empire collapsed in the early nineteenth century.

THE WAR OF AMERICAN INDEPENDENCE

The War of American Independence (1775–83) initially did not trouble the British in the Caribbean, as the Americans, although making inroads through privateering, lacked a significant fleet while the British seized or blockaded the major American harbours. The war also brought benefits, as the British troops deployed in America provided a major market for Jamaican rum, with the leading contractor, Richard Atkinson, being expected to provide 350,000 gallons a year. His Jamaican plantation supplied part of the demand, and Atkinson may have fathered three children with a slave named Betty, while his nephew Matt abused slave women.

Britain faced a major crisis in the Caribbean from 1778, with France entering the war, followed by Spain in 1779, and the Dutch in 1780. The British could neither ensure a close blockade of France's naval bases, and thus stop warships sailing to the Caribbean, nor, until 1782, achieve victory in Caribbean waters. Earlier, a British squadron was outnumbered and roughly handled by the French off Grenada in 1779, and naval engagements in 1780 proved fruitless. This situation enabled the French to secure many of the sugar islands, taking inadequately garrisoned Dominica (1778), Grenada (1779), despite the British having begun Fort Matthew the previous year, St Vincent (1779), Tobago (1781), Nevis, St Kitts and Montserrat (all 1782), and Turks Island (1783). In Dominica, the French benefited from the support of much of the largely French white population. The islands that were not attacked suffered from privateers, including American ones, food shortages, higher insurance costs and the need for defensive precautions.

In contrast, France lost St Lucia in 1778; and failed to reconquer it that year and in 1781. Of the island's population of 19,230 in 1779, 16,003 slaves worked forty-four sugar plantations. The British captured St Eustatius, a major commercial entrepôt, from the Dutch in 1781; but the French regained it that year. Meanwhile, in the early 1780s, General Sir Henry Clinton, the British commander in North America, reportedly warned that the focus of British naval activity on the Caribbean was a major threat to the position in America; a view that was vindicated by the British defeat at Yorktown, Virginia, in 1781, as too many British warships had been retained in the Caribbean rather than being sent into American waters to match the French.

In one of the more impressive campaigns of the war, the Spaniards conquered West Florida, Mobile falling in 1780 after its walls were breached by cannon in a two-week siege. The British relief attempt, from Pensacola, held up by difficult river crossings, did not arrive in time. In turn, Pensacola fell in 1781: a 2000-strong garrison successfully resisted a siege by 7800 troops until a Spanish shell hit one of the magazines and blew up part of the fort. The significance of combined capability in defence was underlined when the British commander attributed his defeat 'to the notorious omission or neglect, in affording Pensacola a sufficient naval protection and aid'. Indeed, Spain's Havana-based Caribbean fleet played a key role, both in moving troops from Cuba and in supporting amphibious operations. The complaint was a reminder of the range of commitments facing the British.

In Central America, the Spaniards, in 1779, captured St George's Caye, the principal port of the British loggers at Belize. In turn, a British expedition in 1780 against Fort San Juan in modern Nicaragua took it, but withdrew with the loss of 77 per cent of the force, mostly to yellow fever. Horatio Nelson thereafter was to be greatly troubled by a recurrence of the malaria he contracted on this expedition.

Nelson in the Caribbean

The Caribbean was formative for the career of Horatio Nelson. As for so many, its waters offered career opportunities as well as the risk of death. There were also key personal events, notably his courtship and marriage with Frances Nisbet and his significant friendship with William, Duke of Clarence, George's III's naval son. Born in 1758, Nelson sailed first to the West Indies in 1771–2, on a merchantman to Jamaica and Tobago. After seeing naval service in Indian waters in 1775–6, Nelson was promoted to lieutenant in 1777, and then made several cruises to the Caribbean. The hunt for prize money was a key goal, but he had time in 1777 to make notes on the wildlife of the Caicos Islands. Promoted to captain in 1779, he was placed in command of Fort Charles, Kingston, in the face of a French attack that did not in the event happen. Later that year, Nelson took American prizes in the Caribbean, but in 1780 fell seriously ill on an expedition to Central America. After recovery, a failed attack on a French position in the Turks Islands in 1783 was followed by the capture of French and Spanish prizes. Sent to the Caribbean in 1784 to enforce the Navigation Acts, Nelson married Frances 'Fanny' Nisbet, a Nevis widow, in 1787, the year in which he returned to Britain. He had met Clarence in 1782, and the latter served in the Caribbean in 1782–3 and 1786–9, giving away Fanny at Nelson's wedding, which took place in the grounds of Montpelier House (now the Montpelier Plantation Inn), the property of John Herbert, President of Nevis and Fanny's uncle. A copy of the marriage licence is preserved at the nearby Fig Tree Church. In 1805, Nelson visited the Caribbean anew in an abortive pursuit of the French fleet he was subsequently to defeat at Trafalgar.

A decisive British naval victory on 12 April 1782 saved the situation in the Caribbean, ending the threat of an invasion of Jamaica, which was a goal Spain was pressing on France. Off the Îles des Saintes, south of Guadeloupe, François, Comte de Grasse, the outnumbered French commander, was soundly defeated by Admiral George Rodney who broke through the French line, capturing five ships of the line, including the flagship, the *Ville de Paris*, with de Grasse himself, after a long fight. Thanks in part to the use of the carronade, a new, light, short-barrelled gun, and to innovations introduced by Captain Sir Charles Douglas of Rodney's flagship, the *Formidable*, that increased the ease of serving cannon, of firing them instantaneously and the possible angles of training them, including improvements in flintlocks, tin tubes, flannel cartridges, wedges to absorb recoil, and steel compression springs, British cannon fire was particularly effective; although Rodney, who could be apt not to capture the wider strategic picture, failed to pursue his defeated foe. Relief in Jamaica led to the erection there of a statue of Rodney.

The Treaty of Versailles of 1783 was very different to that of Paris in 1763. Alongside Spain retaining Louisiana, Florida (both the conquered West and the unconquered East) was ceded to it by Britain, Fort Charlotte in Mobile being renamed Fort Carlota; while Tobago was ceded to France and St Lucia returned to it by Britain. However, Jamaica had not been captured, or even invaded, by Spain, while France returned most of its gains from Britain. The return of gains was normal after war, but, in addition, France, defeated at sea in 1782, had also been abandoned by the Americans in the negotiations, was financially exhausted, and wished to refocus on the challenge posed by Russian expansionism. In 1783, Crimea was seized, posing a threat to France's ally Turkey: as so often, purposes and events outside the Caribbean were influential there. The French also did not want to fight on for the sake of Spain.

At the same time, the negotiations reflected the degree to which different fates for the Caribbean were on offer, a point that helps explain the significance of the wars and treaties discussed at length in this book. Far from being an 'old-fashioned' treatment of history, this approach underlines the 'unfixed' character of the Caribbean, a character that reflects its role as a frontier zone for competing powers, and one that was to be demonstrated anew in 1791–1815, notably with the revolution in Saint-Domingue.

Contrasts today between islands in large part reflect the consequences of past conflict and negotiations. At the end of 1782, Spain proposed that it regain Gibraltar, with, in return, Minorca restored to Britain, and France allowing Guadeloupe and Dominica to become British. The French acquisition of Santo Domingo was also a possibility. In the event, Britain kept Gibraltar, to which both ministers and the public were committed, and surrendered the Floridas and Minorca. Cabinet preferences as regards British possession of West Indian islands varied, partly swayed by the King's own views. Dominica was always the first choice with the majority, who were willing to cede Tobago in exchange. In 1786, Charles, 3rd Duke of Richmond, an influential member of the government, opposed the idea of acquiring Puerto Rico in exchange for ceding Gibraltar to Spain, arguing that there was no need for more sugar islands as they would be 'more . . . than our number of people or riches could afford to cultivate . . . The protection of such distant possessions is always difficult for this country which has so few troops to spare.'

The Importance of the Caribbean

In 1782, Sir Charles Middleton, the Comptroller of the Royal Navy who had served in the Caribbean during the Seven Years War, notably against French privateers in 1761, pressed the Prime Minister, the Earl of Shelburne, against concessions in the peace:

> immense sums of private property have been expended in the cultivation of them. Grenada in particular . . . St Christophers is in more than metaphor a mine of gold. The West India trade is not only a great nursery for seamen but, by the immense revenue arising from its produce, a great support of the navy . . . Concession in these quarters therefore will ruin thousands of our most opulent citizens, occasion a great reduction of our public revenues, and cause great and well-founded clamour.

Indeed, Middleton favoured using Loyalist refugees from North America to conquer Hispaniola.

1783–90

The war's aftermath saw a Caribbean of mixed control, with Britain, France and Spain still the key players, and certainly not America: the situation was totally different to after the Spanish–American War of 1898. Alongside the resumption of exports to European markets came attempts to alleviate the damage of the recent war. The revival of trade with the now-independent United States ensured the resumption of the food supplies needed by the British Caribbean.

Yet, tensions remained. Spain 'meditates an attack upon Jamaica', reported Ivan Simolin, the Russian Ambassador in London in 1784; and there was an anxiety in Britain that the peace of 1783 would only be a brief lull. In 1785, the Spanish envoy in London demanded from the British government: 'strict orders must be sent immediately to Jamaica to retire those adventurers lately situated on different parts of the coast of Spain (not speaking now here on Mosquito Shore) and to put a stop to the villainous behaviour of furnishing arms to all Nations of Indians besides offering them the protection from England'. Playing a cautious role, the government provided no support to the East Florida Loyalists who wished to thwart its cession to Spain, and in 1787, under a convention of the previous year that was criticised by the British settlers and in the London press, evacuated the Mosquito Coast, moving 2214 settlers (mostly slaves) to Belize. Crises with France in 1787 (the Dutch Crisis) and with France and Spain in 1790 (the Nootka Sound Crisis) led to military moves, including the dispatch of British warships to the Caribbean, and indeed a quarrel between civilian and military control on Barbados; but there was no conflict with the Bourbon powers.

THE FRENCH CARIBBEAN

As after previous wars, so after the War of American Independence, exports from the French Caribbean boomed, and the economist Adam Smith favourably compared the production of sugar there to the British islands. French sugar imports from the French Caribbean rose from about 20 million pounds in 1670 to about 60 million in 1730, and 215 by the eve of the French Revolution. In 1788, Saint-Domingue exported 1,634,032 quintaux of sugar (100 kilograms to a quintal), which was more than that from all the British sugar islands combined; most of the latter were small and had little cultivated land. In what was to be a sequence in Caribbean history from the sixteenth century to the nineteenth, plantation production drove a slavery-fed population growth. Whereas, in 1687, Saint-Domingue contained 4500 white people and 3500 slaves, by 1789, when there were about 800 sugar plantations, the numbers were 28,000 white people, 30,000 free black people and 406,000 slaves. The free black people themselves owned about 100,000 of the slaves, which was an aspect of the effectiveness of hierarchy in controlling slave resistance, hier-archy in this case including highly privileged slaves, slave drivers, slave overseers, and the free black planters and slave-owners. Racial categories, indeed, while important, were not the only ones of relevance, a point also very true of the colonies of other European powers. Only white people owning at least 25 slaves could be in the colonial assemblies of the French island colonies, which excluded the *petits blancs*.

Saint-Domingue continued to benefit from the use of fresher, less exhausted, soils than those of the rival sugar colonies, such as Barbados; and its profitability encouraged the importing of more slaves: nearly 30,000 annually to the French Caribbean, mostly to Saint-Domingue, so that, in 1788, there were 594,000 in the French West Indies. Louisiana imported its first African slaves in 1719, but never became a major slave society.

Introduced to Martinique and Guadeloupe in 1725 and to Saint-Domingue in 1730, French West Indian coffee swiftly became the principal global source, while also fostering rising demand in Europe. In 1770, 350,000 quintaux were produced by the French in the Americas and in 1789, by which time Saint-Domingue was probably supplying more than half the world's coffee, over 950,000. Its wealth made the French Caribbean a major market for France's exports, notably of wine and textiles, which helped finance the French economy. However, investment and profitability at the level of individual traders and companies were frequently low and, in the 1780s, many of the Bordeaux merchant firms trading with the Caribbean colonies were finan-cially weak, with a limited margin of security and little liquid money.

The significance of the slave trade explained the foundation in August 1789 of the Club Massiac to resist the Abolitionism (of the slave trade) advanced by the *Société des Amis des Noirs*, founded in February 1788, and the club had branches in major ports, includ-ing Nantes, Bayonne and Bordeaux. It was to be dissolved after the Saint-Domingue revolution in 1791. Of the extant 536 *cahiers de doléances*, or petitions of grievance, presented to the government in 1789 in preparation for the Estates General, fewer than 50 pressed for Abolition.

SWEDES, DANES AND DUTCH

The Swedes gained St Barthélemy from France in 1784, which reflected their desire to enter Caribbean trade, France's wish to woo Gustavus III, and an exchange, with the French being able to establish a presence in Swedish trade at Gothenburg. The Swedes declared the island a place of free trade, which facilitated contraband commerce.

The Danish and Dutch islands were developed for plantation exports, which encouraged mapping, as by the Danes of St Croix in 1754, such maps being important for land speculators as, alongside government support, the relevant information was important to success.

Curaçao was a major Dutch entrepôt in the slave trade to Venezuela that increased from mid-century, in part in response to the expansion there of cacao production. The island indicated the extent to which nodal points within the Atlantic system not only played a key role in the development and texture of this system, but were also shaped by it because Curaçao's commercial role, notably through illicit trade with Spanish America, created opportunities for other types of intercolonial exchanges, from architecture to ideas, and the resulting activity and profitability encouraged immigration into Curaçao, both voluntary and involuntary. Creolisation and contraband underlined the role of locals in defining the parameters of colonies and empires; in this case in resisting the monopolistic practices of the Caracas Company on the Venezuelan coast.

The development of creole languages was an important aspect of local agency, as in Curaçao where Papiamentu developed as a means for communication between the ethnic groups and as a fundamental marker of local identity. The language came originally from the Dutch usage of Afro-Portuguese, and Portuguese creoles and their languages in West Africa, but, in the Caribbean context, drew heavily for its vocabulary on Spanish words.

The Beginnings of Tourism

The overwhelming majority of those who travelled to or within the Caribbean did so for work reasons, and that included élite figures going there on government business or in pursuit of other forms of profit. However, tourism also developed, and, as in Europe, health was a major reason, notably the pursuit of warmer climes particularly in order to fight tuberculosis. That took Lawrence Washington to Barbados in 1751, accompanied by his half-brother George, later first President of the United States. Lawrence had served in military operations in the Caribbean in 1741–2. The 1751 trip did not work: George contracted smallpox while Lawrence died the following year at Mount Vernon, the house named after Edward Vernon, the British naval commander in 1741. With its mineral hot springs, Nevis also offered health benefits, and the Bath House, opened there in 1778, was visited by William, 2nd Earl of Clarence and his friend Horatio Nelson.

CONCLUSIONS

'A set of buccaneers merely subsisting by smuggling, and hitherto uninterrupted rather by connivance than authority.' That was how Edward, Lord Thurlow, the Lord Chancellor, speaking in the House of Lords in 1787, dismissed the British settlers on the

Mosquito Coast. He also 'reprobated any shadow of right to our settlements . . . at any time' there. Francis, Marquis of Carmarthen, the Foreign Secretary, was unhappy about the latter point, instead arguing that in any future war the British should re-establish themselves and not give their position up; but he felt that the description of the settlers was made 'perhaps with justice at least'. This was still a frontier world in many respects, and certainly one with an uncertain destiny.

It is indeed unclear what would have happened in the Caribbean had external events not intervened in the shape of the French Revolution, which began in 1789. Rebellion in Latin America would have transformed the situation, but the extent to which that was also heavily dependent on crisis in Europe is suggested by its linkage to the Napoleonic Wars in the shape of France's takeover of Spain in 1808. But for that takeover and the resulting long-term disruption, Spain might well have suppressed any rebellion.

Separately, newly independent America had become an important market, for example for Cuban sugar; but was in no position to challenge European dominance of the Caribbean, and did not seek to. The universal propositions offered in the Declaration of Independence in 1776 were not for export, other than the failed attempts to conquer Canada in 1775–6, 1812, 1813 and 1814. Moreover, the Americans were not in a state to seek to do so. Their naval strength during the war had been poor, and their strategic situation dependent on France, and in an alliance that did not survive the war. The last was crucial to Caribbean geopolitics, indeed one of the many 'non-happenings' that was important to its history, as also to that of other countries. So also with the failure of America to maintain its wartime military or to develop strong replacements, a failure arising from it being a federal state long organised on the basis of a weak central government. Nor were any of the individual American states to do so in the pursuit of their own foreign policies, notably South Carolina, the wealthiest of those in the south and the one that had produced volunteers for fighting in the Caribbean during previous conflicts. This left the option for action essentially reliant on adventurous individuals and groups who were to seek a buccaneering state-making in a process known as filibustering.

Meanwhile, the slave trade had partly Africanised the Caribbean, although, in an important contrast, far more the islands than the continental shores: by 1800, about 15 per cent of the 800,000-strong population of Venezuela were slaves working in the plantations, and the percentages were lower in Colombia, Central America and Mexico. The slaves used their African culture to adapt to the Caribbean, but pre-existing ethnic ties and identities were seriously eroded when the percentage of those born in Africa decreased in slave communities, although that situation varied by colony and, even more, plantation. New and vibrant ties between slaves, however, developed, and, in the second half of the century, the influences of Evangelical Christianity and the American Revolution helped lead to more widely based notions of black identity.

The impact of African nationhood within the colonial context was to be powerfully revealed by the rebellion in Saint-Domingue in 1791; but, prior to that, there was (and is) little reason to believe that the slave economies and European imperial rule of the Caribbean would have succumbed. The situation, however, was to change radically in the 1790s.

7

The End of Slavery, 1790–1850

Jane Austen and the West Indies

The Caribbean played a role in Jane Austen's fiction, with the family wealth of the Bertrams in *Mansfield Park* (1814) dependent on a plantation in Antigua, while Miss Lambe, a wealthy 'half mulatto' from the Caribbean, plays a part in the economy of matrimonial choice in *Sanditon* (1817). In that unfinished novel, Lady Denham notes the money offered the embryonic resort of Sanditon by visiting white plantation owners, adding: 'Because they have full purses, fancy themselves equal, may be, to your old country families. But then, they who scatter their money so freely, never think of whether they may not be doing mischief of raising the price of things – and I have heard that's very much the case with your West-injines.' Austen, who disapproved of slavery, had two brothers in the Royal Navy: Francis escorted the expedition to the Caribbean in 1795, pursued the French fleet to the West Indies in 1805, fought at the Battle of San Domingo in 1806, and protected British shipping during the Mexican–American war of 1846–8. Charles was second in command on the Jamaica station from 1826, intercepting slavers until late 1828.

The European impact in the Caribbean had been a destructive nightmare for native societies, and the subsequent treatment of African slaves was horrendous. To refer then to Saint-Domingue as a nightmare in the 1790s and early 1800s might seem in some respects to seek unfairly to shift the blame onto the slaves who rebelled, as well as to extenuate both the previous slave economy and the more widespread Caribbean practice of control. That is not the intention, although that was certainly the response of many white people, and notably so as atrocity stories of killing, rape, mutilation and devastation were spread across the white societies of the Caribbean and then kept alive as a warning and as a product of the white diaspora from Saint-Domingue that followed the rebellion. That, however, was a nightmare and for everybody, because the slaughter was widespread: white people were killed by black people but also by other white people, while black people, both slaves and free, were killed by white people and by other black people. Cruelty knew no ethnic barrier and devastation was the experience of all as it proved easier to destroy an uncivil society than to make a civil one. Arguably, the black people suffered far more, as the white people could and did flee from the island, and that was not an option for most black people other than slaves.

Saint-Domingue, the epicentre of Caribbean change in the 1790s, was a very prosperous slave society that was totally destabilised by the French Revolution that began in 1789. Initially, the crisis was handled without too much difficulty in the French Caribbean. Furthermore, in Paris, proposals for change were stalled, including the rejection in March 1790 of the proposal that free men of colour be given the franchise. The measure did not pass until May 1791 and then only if they were born of free parents, with full equality not until April 1792.

Growing hostility between steadily more radical revolutionaries in Paris and conservative whites in the colony provided opportunities for a slave rebellion that broke out in August 1791. The complex situation there included the fighting between two other elements in the crisis, free blacks and *petits blancs*, that helped lead to the burning down of much of Port-au-Prince in November 1791. There were dynamic factors in both Saint-Domingue and Paris that led toward crisis in the former. Despite persistent reports that Britain would seek to gain the colony and appeals for intervention by white colonists, the British government adopted a very cautious response, ignoring the appeals. The Foreign Secretary, William, Lord Grenville, observed that there was no intention of retaliating in the West Indies for French intervention in the War of American Independence, 'and that we are fully persuaded that all the islands in the West Indies are not worth to us one year of that invaluable tranquillity which we are now enjoying'.

Increasing radicalism in Paris led in April 1792 to the abolition of the colonial assemblies and their replacement by new assemblies that included the free black people, and, after France became a republic and executed Louis XVI, was followed by the widening out of the French Revolutionary War to include conflict with Britain and Spain from 1793. That year, slavery was abolished in the colony by the local representatives of the increasingly radical Revolution, who, having in 1792 sought the help of the free black people, were now also seeking the support of the slaves against the conservative white people. The National Convention in Paris followed suit for all French colonies in February 1794; an abolition that was possibly less solely the result of ideological conviction than a recognition of a step already taken by France's representatives in the colony.

Meanwhile, in Saint-Domingue, alongside bitter and violent rivalry between, and within, the white and black populations, there were also cross currents in relations with Paris and with other powers. Spain, which was at war with France until 1795, provided aid to the rebels, while British troops also intervened in 1794 on behalf of the conservative white people, only, having faced major difficulties including in particular from yellow fever, to withdraw in 1797. This left the colony divided between black forces under Toussaint L'Ouverture, who controlled the north and claimed to be acting for France, and mulattoes under André Rigaud who controlled the south: the mulatto planters feared the former slaves and kept a plantation economy going. In an instance of the geographical-political division also very much to be seen in Cuba, Haiti was long to have a division politically between north and south, with the west often also forming a separate area of control.

Having defeated Rigaud in 1799–1800, Toussaint, who, like so many, was an ambivalent figure, part liberator, part harsh dictator, overran the neighbouring formerly Spanish Santo Domingo in 1801, which had been ceded to France in 1795. He also declared himself Supreme Head of the Island, although insisting that the island was still part of the French empire. Toussaint's seizure of power was not too different to that of Napoleon, a general in France in 1799, not that the latter, a racist, would have accepted the comparison.

In turn, peace with Britain in 1802 gave Napoleon an opportunity to counterattack, sending an army of 40,000 men, many Swiss conscripts or Poles, under his brother-in-law Charles Leclerc, to regain Saint-Domingue. Rigaud accompanied the expedition. Treacherously seized on 7 June 1802 during negotiations, Toussaint died in prison in France in 1803, his only visit to the country. With his characteristic ambitious impracticability already seen in the plans to exploit his invasion of Egypt in 1798 in order to overthrow the British in India, Napoleon hoped that Saint-Domingue would be part of a French empire in the west. This would include Louisiana, Florida, Cayenne, Martinique and Guadeloupe. In the last, in 1802, thanks in part to amphibious capability, French authority was rapidly reasserted against the resistance of former slaves: the French killed about 10,000 people, a tenth of the population, including all the black soldiers captured. Slavery was re-established.

Although effective on Guadeloupe, a relatively small island, this policy of re-establishing slavery, as well as the brutality of French occupation, made it impossible to reach a compromise in Saint-Domingue where, indeed, resistance continued and became much stronger from October 1802. Terrible brutality, with Leclerc pressing for a war of extermination, compromised French success, but so also did poor leadership and planning, distance from France, a lack of troops, money and supplies, and the resumption of war with Britain in 1803, which led to a British blockade that both cut supplies and destroyed the basis for any French empire in the West. In turn, the Haitians benefited from their ability to work with the environment, from their use of irregular operations, and from the deadly impact of yellow fever not only on the locals but even more on the French, including Leclerc who died in November 1802.

As so often in analysis, it is helpful to emphasise more than one approach to causation, in this case stressing both Haitian resistance and British naval power. At present, it is more fashionable to emphasise the former, but that does not necessarily make that account more accurate. Driven back to Le Cap, and crucially defeated at Vertières on 18 November 1803, the French force agreed a truce with Toussaint's successor, Jean-Jacques Dessalines, a former slave who had fought under Toussaint from the north, and, that month, he was transported by British warships to Jamaica. The surviving white settlers fled, to Cuba, New Orleans, Philadelphia and other destinations, and the independence of Haiti was proclaimed on 1 January 1804. However, all the commodity production on the island and therefore its exports had declined steeply, which had enormous consequences for markets, notably in Europe, and for production elsewhere in the Caribbean.

Vodou

Part of the strangeness and menaces that many whites found in black life in the Caribbean was focused on vodou, which was to be a source of exotic description and melodramatic speculation to the present, with particular interest in the late twentieth century as reflected in particular in discussion of the Duvalier regime in Haiti and seen in the James Bond film *Live and Let Die* (1973).

A major problem for discussing the origins of Caribbean vodou is provided by the sources which are those of outsiders, notably Moreau de Saint-Mery's *Description topographique, physique, civile, politique et historique de Saint-Domingue* (1797), in which the cast includes divine spirits, an intermediary, priests and trances. There appear to have been cults closer to African origins, and others that were more distinctly creole, the latter including red-eyed witches or devils who favoured violent rites. African languages were used for the ritual incantations which included hostility to slavery and whites.

There were overlaps between vodou and the Saint-Domingue revolution, including the experience of secret activity, the extent to which vodou was a rejection of Christian authority and the role of vodou priests, such as Boukman Dutty, in the leadership of the revolution. Practices that were described included drinking the blood of a sacrificial pig and beliefs included Africa as a holy place that could be re-entered after death. On 14 August 1791, a vodou ceremony at Bolis Caiman (Alligator Forest) in which the mambo priestess Cécile Fatiman, a slave, played a crucial role, was a key prelude to the revolution, with an oath made during the ceremony to kill all white people.

Haitian vodou is not the same as Louisiana voodoo, which began in the eighteenth century; though they share roots in West African vodou. The Louisiana version for example has a greater role for women. There is a variable degree of combination with Christianity. In Haiti, the spirits were disguised as Catholic saints in part because the *Code Noir* insisted that slaves become Catholics and not practise African religions. Vodou represented both resistance and adaptation, separateness and linkage.

More generally across the Caribbean, white fear centred on concern about a second Saint-Domingue, which, for the British, was accentuated by the killing of many settlers in Julien Fédon's rebellion on Grenada in 1795. Using revolutionary ideology to build up their military strength, the French had conscripted freed slaves and recaptured St Lucia in 1795 in what was to be called the First Brigand War, as well as stirring up rebellion on Grenada, St Vincent and Dominica, in part by means of a black-manned privateer squadron, and driving the British back in Saint-Domingue. The white royalist slave-owners fled St Lucia with the British. Slavery was abolished on the island and several planters guillotined.

The British, in turn, harshly suppressed slave risings. On St Lucia, notably in 1796–7, they tortured and shot prisoners and attacked the subsistence fields that supported the guerrillas in what was termed the Second Brigand War. On Grenada, Fédon's rebellion was crushed in 1796 after reinforcements had arrived. On St Vincent, where in 1795 the Caribs rose in response to encouragement from the French and overran most of the island bar the capital Kingstown, they were defeated in 1796, after bush fighting and the destruction of their homes and provision grounds, and then forcibly expelled from the island, being sent first to the Grenadines and then to Roatán. A Maroon rising in Jamaica in 1795 did not extend to the slaves. The Maroons successfully ambushed militia forces but the combination of military action, which included cutting the Maroons off from their provision grounds, and the threat of using Cuban hunting dogs helped persuade the Maroons to submit, after which many were sent in 1796 to Nova Scotia and thereafter to Sierra Leone.

In Curaçao, the Dutch faced a rebellion by about 2000 slaves and free blacks in 1795, a rebellion encouraged by the Haitian example, but defeated by the local militia, some of whom were black. Across the Caribbean, indeed, the use of black soldiers became more significant in the 1790s. In 1790 George III of Britain had responded to the prospect of war with Spain and attacks on the Spanish Caribbean (a war that did not break out) by suggesting that 'the measure of raising Blacks is much improved by attaching ten men to each company'. In 1794, in the West Indies, the British used specially raised units of slaves under white commanders, units capable of moving rapidly and acting as light infantry, which was an aspect of the flexibility of the imperial slave system. These became eight West India regiments in 1795, a number raised to twelve by 1798; but a practice opposed by the local settlers and legislatures, notably on Jamaica.

About 13,400 slaves were purchased to fight in the regiments between 1795 and 1808. The Eighth West India Regiment fought bravely in the capture of St Martin from the French in 1801, but mutinied in Dominica in 1802 fearing they would be sent to work in the cane fields, a mutiny, in which white officers were killed, that led to a bloody response by other military units. As a reward for service, all of the slaves serving in the army were freed in the Mutiny Act of 1807, thus increasing the number of free blacks.

Despite the significance of the suppression of slave risings, military effort generally focused on conflict between the European powers, and notably so after 1803. The key naval clashes occurred in European waters, with its ports the easiest place to intercept ships going to or from the Caribbean, where the major naval battle occurred in the battle of San Domingo on 6 February 1806, with superior British gunnery overcoming a French squadron of five of the line, all of which were captured or destroyed, while no

British ships were lost. In the Caribbean, most naval action was on a smaller scale, as in October 1799, when the *Surprise* frigate, itself the French ship *Unité* captured in 1796, having taken numerous French and Spanish privateers in the Caribbean in 1798–9, stormed and cut out the *Hermione*. The latter was a British warship whose mutinous crew had handed it over to Spaniards in 1797, and was then moored by the Spaniards between the shore defences at Puerto Cabello, Venezuela. The *Surprise*'s daring action was much celebrated in Britain and Jamaica. In 1806, the Spanish frigate *Pomona*, anchored off Havana close to a shore battery, was captured by a British frigate. Naval power was crucial in the struggle with hostile privateers as in April 1797 when boats from a British frigate squadron attacked the town of Jean-Rabel on the northern coast of Saint-Domingue, recapturing nine merchantmen seized by the privateers based there and inflicting damage and deterrence to help protect the northern Caribbean sea lanes. Earlier that month, a French frigate had been destroyed near there.

Naval predominance provided the crucial basis for attacks on Caribbean positions, which to Britain seemed the most possible, profitable and appropriate way to strike at France. Such operations would make effective use of the striking power of the navy, and, by taking French colonial bases, would lessen the likelihood of successful French attack on nearby British colonies, not least by denying the French bases where they could shelter and resupply any fleet sent to the Caribbean. It was necessary to convince actual and potential allies that Britain, despite her defeats in Europe, was weakening France, and to demonstrate to domestic opinion that the war was not without point and profit. In 1793, after war began, Tobago was rapidly captured by troops from the local British garrisons, an unsuccessful attack was mounted on Martinique, and a position established on Saint-Domingue. In 1794, with 6000 troops arrived from Britain, and good use of the winter campaigning season, Martinique, St Lucia and Guadeloupe were captured, the British being welcomed by the white planters. However, with disease hitting hard, impetus was lost. A French force landed on Guadeloupe, and, backed by free blacks and rebel slaves, defeated the British and local royalists, in street fighting on Points-à-Pitre, and drove them from the island.

This was a crisis for the British Caribbean, and therefore the British imperial system, and was seen in that light. The Caribbean was important to British trade, public finances and credit worthiness: but now even more so after the loss of the Thirteen Colonies in 1783, and because Britain had failed to break into the Chinese market and had been militarily driven from the European continent, was at war with Spain from 1796, and the Dutch, under French control from 1795 until 1814, had followed France into war with Britain.

Interest in China was a prime instance of the 'Turn to the East' that became more significant in British imperial planning after the crisis in the North American colonies, and this, in the longer term, when combined with the impact of Abolitionism, was to lessen the significance of the Caribbean. There was the foundation of a trading base at Penang in Malaya (1786) and a convict colony at Botany Bay in Australia (1788), a greater British military commitment in support of expansionism in India, interest in the Bay of Bengal and the East Indies, and growing speculation about prospects in the Pacific which led, in the Nootka Sound Crisis of 1790, to the prospect of war with Spain over what became British Columbia.

In response to the crisis in the Caribbean, 33,000 troops were sent in late 1795 under the talented Major-General Sir Ralph Abercromby, the navy providing crucial 'lift' and mobility, not least matching supplies to troops. Thus, the mighty East Indiamen, the big ships that usually sailed to India, carried 300 tons of provisions each, while the total carried by the fleet was deemed sufficient to sustain 40,000 men for eight months, and amounted to 5824 tons of pork, beef, butter and flour, and

52,031 bushels of pease. These figures indicated the importance of Britain's Agricultural Revolution and organisational capability to its military action in the Caribbean. So also with the Industrial Revolution. Thus, in 1780, when the British had many other commitments as well, Lieutenant-General Sir John Vaughan's force on recently captured St Lucia submitted a request for 1800 spades, 800 pickaxes, 800 hand hatchets, 500 wheelbarrows, 600,000 musket cartridges, 200,000 flints, 2400 cannon shot, 12,000 barrels of powder, 50 tons of musket balls, 366 reams of musket cartridge cases, and 4 light 6-pounders on travelling carriages. In five days in 1809, 46 British cannon fired a large number of shot and shells at Fort Desaix on Martinique.

Acting with great energy, Abercromby captured St Lucia and crushed rebellions in Grenada and St Vincent in 1796, pressing on in 1797 to capture vulnerable Trinidad from Spain, although failing when he attacked San Juan, the well-prepared key position in Puerto Rico. The pace of British conquest continued. Curaçao was captured in 1800, and St Martin, the Danish West Indian islands and the Swedish island of St Barthélemy all in 1801.

However, aside from the death of sailors, 45,000 British troops were lost in the West Indies in 1793–1801, over 96 per cent to disease, principally malaria and yellow fever, about 14,000 of them on Saint-Domingue, and these casualty rates affected morale, leading to desertion. If the British had not deployed troops for conquest, they would have had to send them there to protect the colonies against both the French and slave risings, but the losses were savage given the high death rate they represented, one about seven times that of the British garrison in Canada, the overall size of the entire army, the absence of conscription, and the need to provide men for the navy. The 'opportunity cost' was also high in terms of what else could have been done with these men. There was an equivalent in the very heavy losses of troops in the capture of Havana in 1762 and the argument that this loss of skilled men compromised the military response to the American rebellion in 1775. To remind us of the rippling effects of these losses, Jane Austen's sister Cassandra became engaged to the Reverend Thomas Fowle in 1795, but he accompanied his patron, the libidinous William, 7th Lord Craven, to the West Indies as a regimental chaplain and died there in 1797 from yellow fever.

The Peace of Amiens in 1802 meant the restoration of all these British gains, bar Trinidad, from a Spain that was not in a position to complain; so that the islands had to be captured anew after war resumed in 1803. That year, St Lucia and Tobago were easily taken and the French plan for an attack on Antigua thwarted, but, after a failed British attempt in 1803, Curaçao was not captured until 1807, a year after the last French squadron in the Caribbean to risk combat was destroyed in the battle of San Domingo. When war was declared against Denmark in 1807, St Croix was quickly taken. In turn, French squadrons arrived in the Caribbean, most prominently in 1805 when ransoms to be spared devastation were obtained from Dominica, St Kitts, Nevis and Montserrat, but to no lasting effect.

The year 1809 was one of major success for the British. Martinique fell when a shell from the besiegers detonated the principal magazine in Fort Desaix, the major French position, Thomas Browne recording next day: 'The inside of the work presented a shocking spectacle of ruins, and blood, and half buried bodies, and was literally ploughed up, by the shells we had thrown into it.' The French in Santo Domingo, an area of complex competing interests, surrendered that year to an Anglo-Spanish besieging force, with British naval support playing an important role, Captain William Cumby writing of:

> the unremitting perseverance with which the vessels main-
> tained the stations assigned to them, through all the vari-
> ety of weather incident to the season, on a steep and
> dangerous shore, where no anchorage was to be obtained,
> as well as to the vigilance and alacrity of those officers and

men who were employed in the night guard-boats, by whose united exertions the enemy's accustomed supply by sea was entirely cut off, and the surrender of the city greatly accelerated.

The navy also provided crucial cannon. With concern about disease leading to instructions to avoid a lengthy campaign, the British then turned against Guadeloupe, first instituting a close blockade in order to encourage the garrison to surrender, while the use of a smallpox vaccine also helped the British forces cope with the challenge of disease. Guadeloupe, St Eustatius, St Martin and Saba, the last three without a fight, were rapidly taken in February 1810; a marked contrast with the total disaster that awaited the British near New Orleans in January 1815.

Handed back to France in 1814, the French islands were swiftly captured anew in 1815 after Napoleon seized power again. The rapid British success indicated the strength and dominance in the Caribbean of a military system that prefigured that of America. Lieutenant-General Sir James Leith, a veteran of the Peninsular War, Governor and Captain-General of the Leeward Islands, moved rapidly, sending troops to Martinique from nearby St Lucia. They landed on 5 June 1815 and occupied all the strong positions, helping to stop a revolution in favour of Napoleon. There was similar success on Marie-Galante, but on Guadeloupe the situation was more difficult, and an insurrection, mounted ironically on 18 June, the day of Waterloo, succeeded with the support of the local authorities. Napoleon was proclaimed emperor there the next day, replacing Louis XVIII.

In response, Leith, covered by Rear-Admiral Sir Philip Charles Dunham, the commander-in-chief of the Leeward Islands station, landed his men on 8 August. Advancing rapidly in columns the next day, the British prevented the French from concentrating, and, on the tenth, the French surrendered, the last French flag being struck to Dunham as the first of the war had been on

13 February 1793 when, in command of HMS *Spitfire*, he had captured the French privateer *Afrique*. Leith had been helped in his task by bringing the news of Waterloo to Guadeloupe. Some French soldiers, however, deserted, refused to surrender, and took refuge in the woods on the island where, as a result, low-level guerrilla opposition continued. This, however, had no future, the crisis was over, and relief at victory was indicated by the subsequent awards: for Leith, a sword worth 2000 guineas from the British government, and the Grand Cordon of the Royal Order of Military Merit from Louis XVIII, to whom the islands were returned, while Dunham was created a Knight Grand Cross of the Order. Leith, however, died of yellow fever on Barbados in 1816.

During the war and at other times, the relatively low cost of protection afforded British shipping by British naval power helped ensure that, despite French privateering, British trade was safest and most profitable, and certainly compared to that of other powers. This situation further encouraged those under British control to see this control as an acceptable protection cost. In practice, the fear of slave risings ensured that no British colonies were going to follow the American route.

AMERICA TO THE GULF

Far from taking America to the Caribbean, the War of American Independence had left Spain in control of the entire northern shoreline of the Gulf of Mexico, a situation it had never previously enjoyed. The lack of naval strength further limited America, which had nothing to match the durable ships built using tropical hardwoods at Havana. Prefiguring early twentieth-century worry about Germany, in 1805, to the concern of President Thomas Jefferson, the French, then allies of Spain, were able to concentrate European warships at Martinique before sailing back to Europe. America, indeed, appeared a bystander of possible action by Britain, France and Spain, whether a British seizure of New Orleans from Spain

in 1790 during the Nootka Sound Crisis, or French interest in seizing Florida and Louisiana from Spain in the 1790s. Moreover, the
political, religious and, especially, racial radicalism seen in France
and Haiti was not welcome in America, particularly, but not only,
in the South. In addition, in 1798–1800, the 'Quasi War' saw very
damaging French privateering attacks on American merchantmen
in the eastern Caribbean, while, in response, the Americans under
the Federalists had to build a navy, turned to Britain for help
against French privateers, and, in 1799, considered conquering
Louisiana and Florida from Spain, which had allied with France
three years earlier and thus become an enemy. In 1800, an
American warship spiked the guns of a Spanish fort at Puerta
Plata, Santo Domingo, where a French privateer had taken shelter.
American ships took French prizes, although far fewer than they
lost.

A SEPARATE LOUISIANA?

In the event, Louisiana, gained by France from Spain by treaty in
1800, was to be acquired by the Americans by purchase in 1803.
As a result of French failure in Saint-Domingue, and the collapse
therefore of Napoleon's Caribbean plans, Louisiana, an outlier,
became apparently worthless to the French. Napoleon sold it to
Thomas Jefferson in order both to stop it, and more particularly
New Orleans, being a target for British attack, which had indeed
been considered in 1800 by Henry Dundas, British Secretary of
State, and to gain crucial money for operations in Europe. As yet,
France's triumphs in 1805–7 in the War of the Third Coalition
were in the future.

There was no certainty in developments, a situation repeatedly
the case in the history of the Caribbean. The Americans did not
need the force assembled at Natchez in order to overcome any
resistance in Louisiana on behalf of Spain, and Jefferson was
eventually correct in his view that common values would bind

Louisiana and America together. In particular, slaveholding was continued. Even anti-slavery Federalist officials in the south-west recognised this political reality, such that any challenge to slavery, it was feared, would prompt secession by Louisiana or, at least, disunion.

While most of the 1803 purchase was not turned into states for many decades, Louisiana was organised as a territory in 1804, and was admitted as a state in 1812. However, in the short-term the situation was far less propitious for the Americans and notably so in New Orleans. Whether previously loyal to France or to Spain, the population had been Catholic and looked across the Caribbean. This was true for personal and family social and economic links, while Louisiana's sugar and cotton was shipped thence to Europe.

Prefiguring the situation from 1862 when Union troops occupied the city, and that in Cuba towards Americans after 1898, the population did not take kindly to the American incomers, and, indeed, on a pattern more commonly seen in the Caribbean, there was a large-scale evasion of the regulations and requirements of the new state and of the officials sent down. Officials generally responded by accepting local views, as with William Claiborne, the Virginia-born Governor of the Territory of Orleans from 1803 to 1812 and the Governor of Louisiana from 1812 to 1816, who learned French and, as a result of the successive death of two wives from yellow fever, married local women, his second and third wives. Part of the evasion of regulations was provided by large-scale smuggling and privateering, both of which represented ways to continue Caribbean trade links. Indeed, from 1809, as part of the process by which some French people resettled from Saint-Domingue, Jean Lafitte (c. 1780–1823), who had a 'fleet' of around four schooners, became more active as both smuggler and pirate.

Jefferson's first-term vice president, Aaron Burr, sought, in 1804–6, British naval and financial backing for his plans for an independent Louisiana, which he claimed would be followed by independence for Florida and parts of Latin America. In the event, although he gained support in New Orleans, Burr failed because he exaggerated his strength and was unable to maintain secrecy, the latter leading to his arrest. So also with the failure of the separatist plans of the self-serving American fixture Brigadier-General James Wilkinson, who had betrayed Burr in 1806, although Wilkinson was exonerated by the court martial that tried him and went on to military and then diplomatic service. Meanwhile, the varied dynamic character of the black world, both slave and free, could be seen in the 1810s when Africans in Louisiana met with the challenge of coexisting with a massive influx of American slaves.

AMERICAN EXPANSION AND SPANISH AMERICAN INDEPENDENCE

The American gain of Louisiana challenged the Spanish position to the east and west: in Florida and Texas. Jefferson at once sought gains at the expense of the more vulnerable former, although, however, reversing the attitude of President Adams, he was unwilling to recognise Haiti. Friendly relations with France were more important to him, but there was also a racist dynamic. A black country proved too much for the influential slaveholding interests in the United States, for black independence was perceived as a threat to the racial order in America: Jefferson was far closer to these interests than Adams. Haiti itself was highly unstable, with Dessalines assassinated in 1806, and Haiti then divided between north and south for many years. The independence of Haiti was not recognised by the Americans until 1862, and that of the Dominican Republic until 1866.

Mobile was to be seized by the Americans in 1813, indeed by Wilkinson, who had bobbed up anew. By then, the Spanish empire had been totally transformed as a result of Napoleon's seizure of power in Spain itself in 1808 and the subsequent turmoil in the Spanish empire as structures of authority and practices of power collapsed in the face of rebellion and civil war. In the empire, there was a complex pattern of power and authority, with Napoleon's brother, Joseph, the new king of Spain, enjoying scant power, but division between those at least ostensibly following the Spanish Bourbons, now prisoners of France, and those increasingly seeking independence. Initial risings for independence, as in Mexico in 1810 and Texas in 1812, were to be suppressed by royalists loyal to Ferdinand VII. On the pattern of the Haitian rising, although not on the same violent scale, racial tension played a major and lasting role in the Caribbean, with *criollos* often most concerned not about rule, welcome or unwelcome, from imperial centres, but about the *mestizos* (mixed blood) and natives who were more likely to rebel.

In the event, despite the Bourbons regaining power in Spain in 1813–14, and making a major effort in the late 1810s and early 1820s to re-establish their position in the New World, Spanish imperial control ended on the continental landmass after a long struggle. Spain repeatedly suffered from the willingness of Britain to provide assistance to the rebels, including shelter for Simon Bolívar in Jamaica, as well as volunteers and diplomatic support, not least in dissuading possible French intervention on behalf of Spain. In 1825, Spain lost its last stronghold in Mexico, San Juan de Ulúa, 'the Gibraltar of the Indies', albeit with a garrison that proved less successful. Spanish rule continued in Cuba and Puerto Rico, but not in Santo Domingo which declared independence in 1821, briefly becoming part of Colombia before, with the support particularly of black people and mulattoes, part of Haiti from 1822 to 1844.

The continental Spanish Caribbean, for a while two states on the basis of the Spanish vice-royalties, Mexico and Greater Colombia, splintered, with Central America becoming a separate state in 1823, only to fragment in 1838, meanwhile recognising the boundaries of British Honduras (now Belize) in 1834, while Venezuela separated from Colombia in 1830; although the latter retained what subsequently became Panama. After a short and highly successful war, Texas won independence from Mexico in 1836. Again, there was nothing inevitable about these developments, and notably so with Mexico's independence from Spain in 1821. In part, as with France in the 1790s, political rivalries and changes by Spain interacted with those in the colonies.

THE WAR OF 1812

The War of 1812 (which continued until 1815), a war essentially about trade, Canada and relations with Native Americans, and not about the Caribbean, nevertheless had consequences in the latter with American privateers causing problems, notably in the Bahamas and off Jamaica. In turn, American concern about the Gulf Coast, and in particular Britain establishing control in West Florida, increased in response to fears about British intentions and mores. Lastly, Britain's intervention in the region led to a total failure in battle near New Orleans on 8 January 1815. This had not seemed at all inevitable, and the Americans were worried about cooperation between the British and the Creek Confederation, the local Native American power. In 1813, Benjamin Hawkins, an American agent with the Creek, had warned of 'an invasion of British and West Indian Blacks, several regiments of which are actually concentrated at Jamaica'. However, in what turned out to be an important battle in Caribbean history, the Caribbean being understood as being affected by its hinterland, the Creeks were heavily defeated by Andrew Jackson at Horseshoe Bend on 27 March 1814.

Admiral Thomas Cochrane, nevertheless, counted on support in the New Orleans expedition from 'some thousand Indians and by their assistance after the fall of the city to drive the Americans out of Louisiana'. In 1814, furthermore, he set up a corps of colonial Marines composed of escaped slaves. Such plans and provisions offered the prospect of a very different Caribbean, in terms of state control and of racial politics. They also underline the extent to which, whatever the view of American triumphalists, progress was not necessarily a matter of success for America which, indeed, in large part remained, like the rest of the Caribbean, a deeply racist society.

The British, however, found success elusive despite their naval strength. In 1814, they failed to capture Fort Bowyer at the mouth of Mobile Bay, the fort's robust gunnery, instead, inflicting damage. In general, shore artillery, which had a stable fire platform, was more accurate than that from ships, while the latter presented a more vulnerable target than gun embrasures. The focus in 1814–15 was on New Orleans, but the expeditionary force from Britain was delayed by contrary winds. Alerted to the British build-up, and to the news that it was intended for New Orleans, Jackson, who had initially thought that the British were aiming for Mobile, then purposefully and rapidly marched to the city, arriving there on 1 December 1814. This was a key step as the loyalty of the city's population, much of which was used to French or Spanish rule, rather than American, was unsettled (giving rise to British hopes); while there was a lack of troops and materiel there. Despite American claims, the British did not wish to annex New Orleans for themselves: instead, its return to Spain was seen as in Britain's interests.

With the forceful Jackson present with troops, and declaring and harshly enforcing martial law, as Wilkinson, also controversially, had done in New Orleans during Burr's trial, the population did not rebel. As in the case of Virginia during the War of American Independence, Cochrane's encouragement to slaves to take refuge with the British alienated Louisiana opinion. Moreover, the British failed to win over Lafitte's Baratarian pirates, one of the many local forces that played a role in Caribbean power politics, only to be weakened or squeezed out after peace was negotiated. Instead, Lafitte, who had earlier been attacked by American forces, provided Jackson with crucial flints for his army's firearms.

Defeat at New Orleans

On 8 January 1815, Major-General Sir Edward Pakenham launched what he saw as the decisive attack on the strong American fieldworks protecting New Orleans. Although he sent up the signal rocket before the British troops on the opposing west bank of the Mississippi were ready, they seized the American covering position on the bank. The weak defence of this position led to subsequent recriminations among the Americans.

In contrast, the British had no success on the main front. There, they were organised in four columns, but key units had not taken up their positions before the advance was launched, and the sugar-cane bundles and ladders designed to allow the troops to cross the American defences were not brought to the fore, which later led to the court martial and cashiering of Lieutenant-Colonel Thomas Mullins. Moreover, the main column was directed against what was the strongest part of the American defences in the mistaken belief that it was the weakest. In addition, whereas the British cannon focused on the American artillery, the latter, many manned by French veterans, fired on the British infantry, causing heavy casualties with their grape and canister shot on the tightly packed formations moving forward over the cane stubble on a narrow front.

In the face of this fire, the British slackened, losing impetus and the initiative, and one regiment broke and fled. Peter Bowlby, one of the British participants in the battle of New Orleans, recalled 'a tremendous fire' from the Americans, while Joseph Hutchison's company of eighty-five troops had 'only fifteen men serviceable' after an hour.

Having galloped up to stop the rout, Pakenham was shot and his horse killed. In the act of mounting his aide-de-camp's horse, he was shot again, and as he lay dying proclaimed that the battle was lost 'from want of courage'. British officers struck wavering troops with the flat of their swords, but to no effect; although doggedness led other troops to stand under fire, rather than flee.

Pakenham's replacement, Major-General John Lambert, argued that a delay in the assault was crucial in its failure, a delay, due to a fall in the river, that affected the arrival of the boats intended to help cover the attack on the American artillery on the other bank of the Mississippi, and that meant that the attack was launched after it became light, helping the aim of the defenders. He continued: 'As they advanced, a continued and most galling fire was opened from every part of the line, and from the battery on the right bank.' Lambert claimed that the death of the commanders and 'the preparations to act in crossing the ditch not being so forward as they ought to have been . . . caused a wavering in the column, which in such a situation became irreparable' and therefore led to the troops falling back. The *Annual Register* complained of 'an enterprise which appears to have been undertaken with more courage than judgement'.

The battle showed that Louisiana was willing to fight for America; or, at least, could be presented in that light, which was important to local public myth. The modern presenta-tion of the Chalmette battlefield at the Jean Lafitte National Historical Park underlines the diverse nature of Jackson's army and, in particular, the creole role.

The American leaders knew how close they had come to disaster, as they realised that, had British troops taken the city, it would have been difficult to dislodge them short of accepting British terms; and that whoever controlled New Orleans ultimately controlled all the states of the Ohio and Mississippi valleys. Indeed, the strategic significance of New Orleans in the pre-railway age helped explain why what was then Florida (West and East) was so important, as any power that controlled one of its ports, notably Mobile, would have a good base from which either to blockade the mouth of the Mississippi or to mount an attack on New Orleans. In contrast, without a port, mounting a sustained attack on New Orleans would have been a lot more difficult. The British could have withdrawn to Mobile and regrouped for another effort, as they had done in Halifax, Nova Scotia, in 1776 after failure at Boston before attacking New York. Or, possibly, there would have been no need for an amphibious assault as a squadron in Mobile would have been just as effective at shutting down the port of New Orleans, and thereby throttling the trans-Appalachian west, as a direct attack. Thus, New Orleans, whose population had been expanded by about 10,000 as a result of flight from Saint-Domingue, was the key to West Florida, but New Orleans's vulnerability to maritime attack made Florida, or, indeed, Cuba, appear the key to New Orleans. That the war finished soon after the conclusion of the battle ended the prospect of renewed British maritime pressure.

Instead, economic links helped join Britain and the United States, as with Barings Bank backing the cotton exporting business of Vincent Nolte, a German immigrant, responsible for transporting about a quarter of the cotton that passed through New Orleans. The city was no longer a French backwater and very much peripheral to Saint-Domingue; it was now the central place in the prosperous and developing cotton-slave economy.

American Expansionism Renewed

British failure in 1815, and the lack of a continued British post-war presence, provided the opportunity for America to advance its power. Negro Fort on Prospect Bluff, overlooking the Apalachicola River in West Florida, was destroyed on 27 July 1816, with some of those blacks not killed by the blowing up of the power magazine, or enslaved, taking refuge in the Bahamas. In turn, Florida was invaded in 1818, ostensibly to overcome the Native American Seminole. Their towns were destroyed, while the Spanish fort at San Marcos was seized. Andrew Jackson, the American commander, had two British subjects with the Seminole, one a Bahamas-based merchant, executed. He also seized Pensacola. The rest of Spanish Florida was taken by America in 1819 and it successfully pressurised Spain into ceding it the following year. The Native Americans, of course, were not consulted.

However, American filibusters initially proved less successful in Texas. From 1817, Lafitte developed Galveston, the base of Louis-Michel Aury (1788–1821), a French privateer, as his own smuggling and privateering base and called it Campeche. Capturing slave ships, he resold the slaves in the American South. In Galveston Bay in 1820, independence was declared at the significantly named Bolivar Point, only to be crushed by Mexican forces in 1821, while, under pressure from an American warship, Lafitte left Galveston Island. He continued as a pirate, soon after establishing a base in Cuba, only to fall foul of the Cuban government and the American navy. Lafitte died in 1823 as a result of wounds when attacking Spanish ships as a privateer with authority from the Colombian insurgents/government. Aury, who established himself on Providence Island in 1818, had allied with the Colombian insurgents in an unsuccessful attack on the Honduras coast in 1820, but failed to capture the ports of Omoa and Trujillo.

American ambition was seen with the Monroe Doctrine of 1823 which sought to thwart attempts by European powers, notably France and Spain, to establish or re-establish colonies in the New World, as well as with treaties of commerce with Latin American countries from 1825, and with discussion from the mid-1820s about building a canal across the isthmus of Panama. At the same time, the Americans also tried to protect their coast-line from possible attack, which essentially meant British naval power. Thus, intended to protect Mobile Bay, Fort Morgan was designed by Simon Bernard, a military engineer for Napoleon who had been banished from France. Contracted in 1818, the fort was completed, with slave labour, in 1834, but was to be bombarded into surrender by Union forces in 1864. Fort Pickens in Pensacola Bay was similarly built, largely by slaves, in 1829–34. Fort Gadsden was built in 1818 to secure Prospect Bluff, although it was poorly constructed and abandoned in 1821. Forts were criticised by Brigadier-General Edmund Gaines, who had arrested Burr in 1807 and had been in command when Negro Fort was destroyed in 1816. He pressed instead, from 1826, for a rail and canal system financed by the federal government, able to move militia from the hinterland to oppose any invasion and thus counter Britain's oceanic power.

Gaines was thinking of American geopolitics as a whole, but his point was highly relevant to the pivotal quality of the relation-ship between the two powers for the Caribbean, and indeed to the importance of the Caribbean for this relationship. Britain was unlikely to be able to prevail by military means on the continent, a point dramatised by total failure against Buenos Aires in 1807 and New Orleans in 1815, and this was even more the case because it was no longer up against rival imperial systems similarly dependent on vulnerable maritime links. In contrast, Britain's opponents in the New World, although developing naval forces, did not have the capacity to employ them to seize the islands of the Caribbean. This situation was not to change until, in 1898, a far more powerful America became clearly able to seize Cuba from a Spain that did not enjoy British support.

The marked reduction in Spanish power in the 1810s and 1820s was not accompanied by the other European powers seizing its Caribbean territories. Britain, which was pursuing postwar retrenchment, did not seek such gains from other European empires. Moreover, France did not, as was feared, a fear expressed in the Monroe Doctrine, come to the aid of Spain in the New World or pursue Aury's 1820 idea for the conquest of Panama; although it was determined to punish Haiti. Indeed, in 1825, France deployed twelve warships in support of its harsh and nonnegotiable terms for the recognition of Haitian independence: an indemnity of 150 million francs, later reduced to 90 million, which compared to the 60 million for which Louisiana was sold. The debt swallowed up much of the country's limited budget, and was only paid off in 1947. Moreover, in response to the imprisonment of the French Consul who had been arrested at the behest of a drunk magistrate, two French warships from Martinique blockaded Cartagena, Colombia's major port, in 1833 until the matter was settled with the Consul's release; all again without any reference to the Monroe Doctrine.

Into the Future

The Monroe Doctrine had also not been to the fore in 1829 when Spain sought to reconquer Mexico with an expedition from Cuba that landed near Tampico, only to be defeated at Pueblo Viejo. Only in 1836 did Spain recognise Mexican independence. So also for the ineffective Monroe Doctrine in 1837–8, when a dispute between France and Mexico that reflected demands arising from the mistreatment of French citizens, including the pillaging of the stock of a pastry chef, led to a French squadron blockading Veracruz and seizing merchantmen. In late 1838, a second, stronger French squadron using shell guns bombarded the fort of San Juan de Ulúa off Veracruz into surrender. There was also a successful raid of the city, forcing the Mexican army to evacuate it.

In 1839, Mexico paid compensation to France, but the discredited government was overthrown soon after.

Far more significantly, American power increased when Mexico totally failed to suppress Texan independence in 1836, and when, after successful campaigning in 1838–42, American forces overcame the resistance of the Seminole natives in Florida. Texas could have become an independent empire and, indeed, the base for expansion in the Caribbean and Central America, and Britain and France favoured its continued independence, but, instead, it joined the United States in 1845. Mexico's major defeat by the United States in 1846–8 consolidated this position. Although France had been significant in the background from the 1820s, Mexico and the United States were, only in the 1860s, to be brought into a power politics in which France played a key role.

PIRACY

The ability of the Caribbean to suggest very different outcomes increased from the 1790s as the French Revolution spawned new possibilities, international, political, social and ethnic, a process taken further with the Latin American wars of independence and during their aftermath. Thus, Sir Gregor MacGregor, a free-moving Scottish warrior and adroit confidence trickster, became a Venezuelan general, tried to conquer Florida from Spain, and in the 1820s and 1830s attempted to establish a principality in Poyais near the Black River at the northern end of the Mosquito Coast, a fraud designed to attract investment, only for settlers to discover that they had been duped.

Privateers and pirate ships were regarded as particularly troubling because many had black sailors, whether former slaves or free men. Indeed, from the 1790s, and notably with the situation on Saint-Domingue, there had been a revival in the extent to which privateering was an aspect of such social mobility as well as freedom for African Americans, a situation that had underlined the wider instability represented in piracy and threatened by it. In rebellion from Spain from 1811, Cartagena became a major centre of piracy.

In the aftermath of the War of 1812, however, the Americans became more forceful against piracy, turning against the Baratarian pirates, based on the coastal islands of Louisiana, who had decided to continue piracy and smuggling: several were hanged in New Orleans in 1819. The campaign against piracy reflected part of the more general pressure to contain and control the Caribbean.

With the West Indies Squadron deployed from 1821 in response to President James Monroe's determination to establish order and demonstrate an American presence, there was also extensive American activity against pirates and slavers in the Caribbean, with operations offshore and onshore at Cuba, Puerto Rico, Santo Domingo and Yucatán, operations that were politically significant given well-justified concern that the Spanish colonial authorities in Cuba and Puerto Rico were not being cooperative. Fourteen ships were deployed in 1822; David Farragut, the leading American admiral in the Caribbean during the American Civil War, won notice in command of a shore party in Cuba while on anti-slavery duties; and, in 1824, David Porter, the commander of the West Indies Squadron and a veteran of the War of 1812, landed armed sailors, spiked Spanish cannon and, without sanction from the American government, threatened to destroy the port of Fajardo, Puerto Rico, unless local authorities apologised for arresting Charles Platt, one of his lieutenants, who had made representations on behalf of an American merchant in the Virgin Islands. The goods of the latter had been taken, probably to Fajardo where the local government had links to pirates. This action resulted in an apology, but was regarded as too blunt by the American government of the day, which court martialled Porter. He resigned in 1826, and went on, from 1826 to 1829, to command the small Mexican navy, but the attempt to use this to put pressure on the

Spaniards in Cuba led to failure in the battle of Mariel in 1828. At that stage, both America and Britain were willing to back the Spanish retention of Cuba, rather than see it go to Mexico.

Piracy from and off Colombia was only suppressed in the 1830s: by the new Colombian navy, as well as by that of the United States. The Colombian navy also tried to impose its authority on offshore islands; and both Colombia and Venezuela ended up in control of islands, albeit Venezuela being limited by the extent to which those in the southern Caribbean were held by the British and Dutch.

With time, technology enhanced naval capability in the perpetual struggle with piracy, notably in the introduction of steam-powered gunboats that were able to come close inshore when attacking pirate bases. Artillery firing shells, rather than round shot, also enhanced naval firepower, leading observers to be impressed by French success against Mexico in 1838; being followed in this by rifled cannon.

American Expansionism, Again

Alongside the attempt to police instability, there was a separate sectional interest in American expansionism, one linked to the maintenance of slavery in both political and economic terms. Fear of soil exhaustion played a part, but so did a concern that slaves, as well as poor white people, with the radicalism they could offer, would become too numerous for the stability of the South unless it could gain new territories, and therefore opportunities, in Mexico and the West Indies. The mental space of the South expanded to include Cuba, Haiti and Mexico, an expansion accompanied by ethnic contempt for Hispanic society. Separately, in a dangerous sign of independence, William Worth, an able and ambitious general, was ready in 1848 to resign and to command an invasion of Cuba, having accepted an offer by the Havana Club of prominent Cuban liberal whites to invade at the head of 5000

American veterans in return for $3 million. He abandoned the idea under presidential pressure, being transferred to command in Texas where he soon died of cholera.

The potential of American power was well to the fore, with interest in 1848, as part of the peace with Mexico, in an Atlantic–Pacific communication through the isthmus of Tehuantepec, where Mexico was at its narrowest, a route that would rival the overland routes across Nicaragua and Panama. Moreover, American naval strength was on display in the war with Mexico (1846–8), as with the capture of Tampico in November 1846, and in the heavy bombardment of Veracruz in March 1847 including by the eighty-four-gun *Ohio*. American amphibious capability served to make the entire Mexican littoral, which could be overawed, blockaded, interdicted and bombarded, feel threatened. American forces landed along the Caribbean coast across a broad front, and were better supplied than the Mexicans, notably in food and weaponry. To Mexicans, the Mexican–American War, which led to major American territorial gains, was the 'War of American Intervention' or 'Aggression'; and this interpretation and naming remain the case, which is an aspect of how the Caribbean supports differing historical interpretations.

A Woman in Slave Society

A friend of Mary Woolstonecraft and part of a radical literary group, Eliza Fenwick (1767–1840) was an early British feminist. Married in 1788, she separated from her alcoholic husband and tried to earn a living for herself and her two children, including by writing children's books and being a governess. In 1814, Eliza joined her actress daughter, also Eliza, in Barbados. The two opened a school for white girls, and, by 1815, there were forty-two pupils, although Eliza (the elder) found that managing the hired workers, who were slaves, was difficult as she had only limited control over them.

In 1816, crisis hit, with a slave rebellion and a hurricane making it hard for parents to pay fees, while her son, Orlando, died of yellow fever. In 1819, her son-in-law abandoned his wife and their four children. In total, the elder Eliza bought five slaves, one an elderly woman to look after her youngest grandson. White women were frequently slave-owners, and especially in West Indian urban settings, so that in 1817 about half the properties in Bridgetown, Barbados, with fewer than ten slaves were owned by women, many of whom were widows.

In 1822, the Fenwicks moved their school to New Haven, Connecticut, because the business was doing badly on Barbados. As a result, Eliza could not afford to send her grandsons to England for schooling, while she was also concerned about health issues in Barbados and haunted by the possibility of another slave rebellion. The school ran for a while with white West Indies' children boarding, but, when her daughter died in 1828, Eliza could not continue and turned her school house into a boarding house. She died in 1840.

Abolitionism

The abolition of slavery as a cause in Europe had not been helped by the violence associated with the foundation of Haiti; and Abolitionist views first focused solely on ending the slave trade. In Britain, popular action to that end included the boycott of Caribbean sugar and rum in the early 1790s, although it had scant impact according to surviving commercial data. Meanwhile, slave risings or conspiracies in the Caribbean continued to be repressed, for example a conspiracy on Tobago in 1802. The Maroons of

Dominica, already a serious problem in 1785, and more so by the 1810s by when there was fear of the impact on the slaves, were firmly suppressed in 1814, in part as a result of defections and in part due to the burning of their cultivated patches.

The end of both the British slave trade in 1807 and, later, of slavery itself in 1834 (as a result of legislation in Britain in 1833 that had scope across the entire empire), has been ascribed by some commentators to a lack of profitability in the plantation economy of the Caribbean caused by economic developments. These included problems stemming from the impact of the American Revolution, and, crucially, of subsequent British protectionism, on the trade with North America that was very important to the supplies from, and markets of, the latter. This view underplays the multiplicity of factors that contributed to the relevant decisions, and notably the humanitarianism usually stressed in the nineteenth century as the reason.

In addition, as an important accentuation of earlier competition, serious problems were subsequently created for the sugar producers during the French Revolutionary and Napoleonic Wars by overproduction following the British seizure of French, Dutch, Spanish and Danish colonies, although not of Cuba, Puerto Rico or now independent Haiti. Sugar producers from Brazil and the remainder of the West Indies soon replaced the decline in production in the French Caribbean. Low-cost Spanish sugar growers in Cuba were also a factor; while having benefited greatly from the chaos on Saint-Domingue in the 1790s, they took over, in addition, the competitive role to the British colonies formerly provided by Saint-Domingue. This production benefited from the introduction to Cuba in 1796 of the steam engine, from French expertise, energy and capital in the shape of refugees and slaves from Saint-Domingue, and from the investment born of profit. Steam power required more skilled labour, but the skills could be acquired. Cuba's population grew from about 172,000 in 1774 to 272,000 in 1792, the sugar mills increased from 89 to 277, and the average production at each mill tripled. From 1760 to 1789, Cuba exported 325,865 cases of sugar but from 1790 to 1802 the figure was 1,563,046, with a marked increase from 1797. Similarly, French refugees from Saint-Domingue founded over fifty coffee plantations in western Cuba, including those that can be visited: *Antiguo Cafetal Angerona*, with its watchtower, slave quarters and Neoclassical mansion; and *Cafetal Buenavista*, with its slave quarters. The exclusion of British exports from European markets, an exclusion that stemmed from the extent of French conquests, affected the profitability of the British Caribbean.

Yet, there are also significant indications that British slave plantations remained profitable, which in part reflected the ability of plantation owners to innovate. An aspect of this innovation included better care for the slaves, and therefore improved survival rates, so that, by the 1820s, Barbados (but not Jamaica or Trinidad) had reached demographic self-sufficiency in slaves. This situation helped with labour costs and lessened the economic shock otherwise caused by the end of the slave trade and therefore of the provision of new slaves from abroad, unless illegally obtained.

'Monk' Lewis, **Journal of a West India Proprietor** *(1834)*

Known from his successful and very lurid Neogothic novel *The Monk* (1796), Matthew 'Monk' Lewis (1775–1818) spent much of 1815–18 on Jamaica, managing the family estates, only to die on the way back from the yellow fever he had contracted. Enchanted by the beauty of his estates, Lewis liked the people, and his account of plantation life is gripping.

Instead of problems within the slave economy, which was the approach favoured for a while by left-wing commentators, it is more appropriate to look at Abolitionist pressures within Britain. Having abolished the British slave trade in 1807, and that largely due to domestic political pressures, notably from Abolitionism and Evangelicalism, the British put successful pressure on other states to stop the slave trade, which France did in 1815 and the Dutch in 1818. However, British participation in the slave trade continued, both illegal and legal; the latter including the provision of goods, credit, insurance and ships to foreign slave traders. The French had numerous illegal slaving voyages in the late 1810s and 1820s, and, like the Dutch, also sold slaves to Spanish-ruled Puerto Rico, both circumventing treaties banning their import direct from Africa by moving them via their Caribbean ports and reclassifying them.

Although, under British pressure, Spain agreed in 1817 to limit the slave trade, it did little to enforce the treaty. The illicit slave trade was rampant in Havana in the 1820s, and Cuba imported an annual average of 10,700 slaves in 1836–50. The profitable nature of its sugar economy, helped by free-trade moves in Britain, kept the trade successful, as did the commitment to the lifestyle and ethos of slaveholding, and a lack of relevant European immigrant labour: as a Spanish colony with a Catholic monopoly, there was not the openness to immigrants from elsewhere in Europe. The decline of the slave economies of nearby Haiti and Jamaica encouraged an increase of slavery in Cuba, which also led to considerable interest in American pro-slavery circles in annexing Cuba, while, despite the abolition of the slave trade by the United States, American slavers greatly profited from demand in Cuba as well as illegally importing slaves from the Caribbean into the South, many via New Orleans. As a result of the continued flow of new slaves, Cuba in the nineteenth century remained more African than either the British West Indies or the southern United States, to which, in addition, many Europeans migrated. This contrast had important long-term consequences in terms of their societies and cultures; and these consequences continue to this day, although without the strong transatlantic linkage seen in the era of the slave trade.

The wars of independence in Latin America were exploited by many slaves in order to escape or rebel. Simon Bolívar, the most prominent leader of the independence struggle in northern South America, freed his own slaves and, in part in order to please British views, pressed for the abolition of slavery; but he also supported continued control by a white élite and was willing to use violence to that end, notably at the expense of mixed-race opponents. Slavery was abolished in Mexico in 1829 (although with Texas exempted), in Colombia in 1851, and in Venezuela, the part of the Spanish American mainland with the most slaves, in 1854. None of these areas had as many slaves as Brazil, formerly a Portuguese colony.

Yet, in some respects, the Caribbean slave world was also being strengthened even as it was put under pressure. The destruction of the French plantation system in what became Haiti was followed by major expansion in Cuba. Moreover, plantation agriculture, the large-scale importation of slaves, and a switch from cotton and coffee to sugar, all followed the British conquest of underexploited Trinidad from Spain in 1797; and it became more like the late-seventeenth century West Indies than the more mature slave societies of most of the British Caribbean in this period where, by now, a lower percentage of the slaves were African-born and where the work regime was less cruel. The expansion of plantation agriculture in Trinidad reflected the credit and investment readily available as part of the British world, and the profitable opportunities presented by trade within it. Outside the British empire, the same was true of Cuba.

Change was more general, whether or not the slave trade or slavery continued. In Louisiana, indigo, which like tobacco had not done well, was given up in the 1790s, being replaced by sugar, originally introduced by Jesuits in 1751, which now was substituted for production from Saint-Domingue. The first crop of sugar to be granulated in Louisiana was in 1795, and the number of slaves rose from 20,000 then to 100,000 in 1830. The steam-heated vacuum pan, introduced by Edward Howard in 1813, was an aspect of the technological developments associated with sugar. In Louisiana, this was to be followed in 1843 by Norbert Rillieux patenting the multiple-effect evaporator, which lowered the boiling point of the syrup by using enclosed vats. By 1860, about 125,000 slaves worked in the Louisiana sugar plantations, which had increased greatly in scale in the 1790s, 1820s and 1840s in particular. Similarly, cotton production boomed in the American South, production rising to about 5 million bales by 1860, and helping provide commercial and financial opportunities for other parts of America, as well as for the dynamic Lancashire cotton-manufacturing industry in Britain.

From 1823, when the Anti-Slavery Society was established, Abolitionist pressure became again more powerful in Britain, as the Caribbean legislatures had already shown in 1815–16, in response to parliamentary pressure for amelioration in the treatment of slaves and for their registration, that slave-owners had little desire to offer concessions, let alone to end slavery. The programme of amelioration promoted missionary activity and the establishment of some schools for slave children, but there were renewed and reiterated protests from the legislatures about interference, as well as the argument that physical punishment should be maintained. Economic factors were very important to their attitudes, but so also were the racist ideas and fears about difference and what the end of control by enslavement would mean. Aside from its continued profitability, albeit one affected by pressure on the sugar economy, the plantation economy remained an important asset base, while the limited convertibility of plantation assets did not encourage the movement of investment into other

activities: too much money was tied up in mortgages and annui-
ties that were difficult to liquidate in a hurry.

Yet, profitability was affected by the rise in the cost of acquiring and sustaining the workforce, a rise that in part was due to
moves against the slave trade and in part to market forces. Indeed,
as an aspect of costs, by the time of emancipation, the material
consumption levels of the slaves were similar to those of manual
workers in Britain, although this point, which was made by
supporters of slavery there and with reference to factory workers
in New England in the United States, does not extenuate it, as the
primary problem was not invariably ill-treatment (treatment
could, and did, vary) but, rather, the absence of freedom, civic
status and rights to family and self.

In 1830–1, in Jamaica, in response to Abolitionist pressure,
there was talk by the slave-owners of secession from British rule,
which provided opportunities for discussion of southern expansion by the United States. Opposition to reform and abolition was
also seen in Cuba, not least because of *criollo* fears of the black
slave population, fears that very much weakened the reform
movement.

Meanwhile, violence remained a context, not only the violence
involved in strong racism, but also the harsh suppression of slave
rebellions, as with Bussa's rebellion on Barbados in 1816, the
Demerara rising of 1823, and the Baptist War on Jamaica in
1831–2. In the first, named after the slave who led the rebellion,
possibly a response to the belief that emancipation was on the
way but was being obstructed by the Barbadian House of
Assembly, and to Nonconformist preaching, about 3000 to 5000
slaves (smaller numbers used to be given) rebelled across most of
the island in what had been seen as a stable slave society. The
swift repression included the display of the remains of executed
rebels in order to overawe the slave population. In contrast, Bussa
has since 1985 been celebrated by the Emancipation Statue and in
1998 was named one of the ten National Heroes of Barbados.

In part a response to anti- as well as pro-slavery agitation, the Baptist War (a large-scale rising in western Jamaica) led to reprisals by the militia, including the execution of numerous rebels and the burning down of mission buildings, notably the Baptist Chapel at Salter's Hill. Such action was part of the attempt by both sides to weaken their opponents in practical terms and also symbolically. In 1823, planters had burned down the Methodist chapel in Bridgetown, Barbados.

Similarly, there were major risings in Martinique in 1822 and 1831, although they did not involve the whole island, and risings in Louisiana in 1811 and Cuba in 1812; all of which were suppressed. That of 1811, the largest slave revolt to take place in the United States, saw the rebels mostly armed only with agricultural implements. About 250 to 300 men rose in St John the Baptist Parish on the German Coast of the Mississippi River, in doing so taking advantage of the disquiet among creoles about the change in control in 1803 and the impact of the new order, not least on land rights. They aimed to march on New Orleans, free the slaves there, and then take refuge in Haiti, an instance of the role of the latter in encouraging rebellion. However, their failure, with defeat at the hands of the militia and of federal troops, led to the execution at New Orleans and Destrehan of fifty-seven prisoners, their heads placed on pikes along the river. Again drawing on Haiti, white fear in Louisiana played a role in alarm about voodoo, which was based on a body of rituals drawing on West African vodou.

The Cuban disturbances in 1812, named after their leader, José Antonio Aponte, a free black, were aimed against Spanish imperial control as well as slavery, and involved free blacks as well as slaves. Aponte, who belonged to a cooperative society that looked to African social practices, was inspired by the example of Haiti, but also reacting to the spread of Cuba's sugar-slave economy, which, as in Louisiana, had implications for the treatment of free blacks. The opposition in 1812 focused on western Cuba, which was the centre of the sugar economy on the island. It was suppressed, with Aponte's head displayed as a deterrent to fresh agitation.

Abolitionists argued that opposition to slavery by the slaves was undermining the system and that, to avoid bloodshed, it would be much better if it was abolished legally and promptly. In practice, organised opposition by the slaves was limited, in large part due to the coercive context in which slaves were held, the major difficulties of coordinating opposition and the limited opportunities for flight on many islands; but reports of the Jamaican rising helped make slavery appear redundant as the colonists could not keep order. Moreover, from within the empire, the British West Indies colonies were affected by competition from British Guiana (now Guyana) and, far more distant, Mauritius.

In a period when there was scant need to think about the prospect of war, the reformist Whig government pushed through electoral change in 1832 with the Great, later First, Reform Act, followed by passing the Emancipation Act in 1833. Nonconformist Evangelicalism played a major role in the abolition, a charge made by slave-owners opposed to 'the Sectarians', and, indeed, the Baptist Missionary Society founded in 1792 had been followed in 1813 by the Wesleyan Missionary Society. With opposition limited, much of the parliamentary debate revolved around the financial issue of compensation. Rather than the loan originally proposed, £20 million was granted, over £12 million to slave-owners in the West Indies, with the remainder for owners elsewhere including in British Guiana, a decision that arouses outrage today. In the short term, this compensation strengthened the plantation owners' position in the Caribbean by freeing up capital for their use, although at least half of the compensation was paid to beneficiaries in Britain and was capital lost to the region.

The Act came into effect on 1 August 1834, freeing 580,000 slaves in the West Indies: 311,070 of them in Jamaica and 83,150 in Barbados. Initially, as a transition that was seen as necessary for all concerned (although the slaves, of course, were not consulted), other than in Antigua which rejected the idea, all slaves aged over six were to become apprenticed labourers, obliged to work for their former masters for forty-five hours a week: field workers for six years, and others for four, although a clause forbade the punishment of former slaves. This system reflected uncertainty about the practicality of emancipation, an uncertainty also seen in the preferential tariff granted to sugar imported from British colonies, a measure to support the economy against competition from the colonies of other powers that maintained slavery. In the end, this interim labourer system, which was difficult to manage and supervise, and which led to protests from many former slaves, was ended on 1 August 1838, so that the slaves were now free, their movement from slavery often a profound experience at the individual level. Earlier, free black people, some of whom were harsh slave-owners, had been admitted to the full rights of citizens from 1828.

In 1848, slave uprisings on Martinique and St Croix, and the threat of one on Guadeloupe, all helped encourage the end of slavery in the French and Danish colonies. Prior to that, particularly in Martinique, many slaves had fled to British islands. The rising on St Croix, which was suppressed with the help of troops from Puerto Rico, led the governor to abolish slavery, a measure subsequently adopted by the Danish government. The violence in Martinique – a slave demonstration for freedom being fired on by a planter assisted by sailors, leading to the deaths of twenty-five slaves, after which the demonstrators killed thirty-two white settlers – led the governor to grant the demand at once, and fear of the same led the governor of Guadeloupe to follow suit. Again as a reminder of multiple causes and the significance of developments in Europe, the change of opinion in Europe was also very important, particularly the crucial establishment in 1848 of the more liberal Second Republic in France. In 1849, compensation was agreed for the slave-owners by the French government. In 1847, Sweden had abolished slavery on its tiny Caribbean colony of St Barthélemy, which, in the aftermath of a damaging hurricane in 1852 that hit the economy, was sold back to France in 1877. The abolition of slavery on the French colonies in 1848 meant the threat of flight by the slaves on the Dutch side of St Martin. In response, the Dutch freed their slaves on the island; although only in 1863 was slavery formally abolished on all Dutch islands.

Nevertheless, as mid-century neared, slavery was still important in the Caribbean, with Spain and the United States slave societies, and, in the 1840s, the Spanish government became more repressive in Cuba in the face of pressure for abolition. Already in 1838 it had built a new prison in Havana, the *Carcél de Tacón*. In 1841, slaves were 43.5 per cent of the island's population. However, despite the expansion of slavery on Cuba, the general situation as far as slavery was concerned had been transformed from that in 1830.

THE CASTE WAR

Not only international conflict and slavery shaped Caribbean societies, although other elements of their history have often been pushed to the margins. In 1847, the Caste War broke out, an insurrection against Mexican rule in Yucatán, mainly sustained by the Maya-speaking poor and fired by more wide-ranging peasant resentment. The main focus was not independence, but rather disputes over social conditions, notably access to agricultural land and taxation. In this brutal conflict, raiding and the seizure of goods were crucial to rebel logistics, troops destroyed rebel settlements and fields and killed prisoners, and the rebels also killed civilians, including pregnant women. Religion was significant, with the Cult of the Speaking Cross developing from 1850 and providing cohesion for the rebels. Nevertheless, the insurrection had largely been suppressed in 1848. Forced to retreat to the more isolated southeast of Yucatán, a jungle area with few roads, some of the rebels there submitted in 1853, but others continued their resistance for several decades. This looked toward twentieth-century opposition there, which was an aspect of the widespread continuities that have been, and remain, so significant in Caribbean history.

DISEASE

Disease was a potent backdrop to the changes of the period. The smallpox epidemic of 1798, which spread from Veracruz, encouraged the adoption of the English physician Edward Jenner's system of vaccination, which was safer than the traditional variolation method. This helped move the population towards more continuous growth, but it was not really until the early twentieth century that malaria and yellow fever could be managed in hot, wet places. Whereas the Royal Navy succeeded in getting typhus in check, partly thanks to the establishment of the naval hospital at Haslar on the south coast of England, all similar efforts in the West Indies to control malaria and yellow fever failed or were less successful. Yellow fever hit the cities of the region hard, New Orleans for example in 1878; but the last major outbreak in the city was in 1905, and public health education and measures helped wipe the disease out there. Other diseases were also serious, notably cholera, as in Havana and Jamaica in 1850–1, the Bahamas in 1852 and the Leeward Islands and Trinidad in 1854. The spread of cholera was an aspect of the extent of globalisation in the period, but, as in Britain, crowded living conditions and poor sanitation helped drive up the death rate.

THE CARIBBEAN AS A FRONTIER ZONE

The Latin American wars of independence were the particular precipitant of lawlessness in the early nineteenth century, but they were even more disruptive because they also contributed to what was a general crisis of public order, both between and within states. This crisis stemmed from the accentuation of the already serious impact of eighteenth-century great-power conflicts by, in addition, the American and Haitian revolutions and their consequences. Rather than seeing peace as the normal state, it is more appropriate to consider violence and conflict as more commonly the norm, and the end of slavery, itself a key component of violence, did not stop this. The extent to which the end of slavery was the result of slave action is an instructive issue today, and one that is discussed against the background of giving agency to the slaves in ending their servitude, although doing so can risk underplaying the significance of development in distant metropoles.

A Historian of the West Indies

The nephew and heir to a wealthy Jamaican plantation owner, Bryan Edwards (1743–1800) was also a politician in the colonial assembly of Jamaica and, eventually, an MP in Westminster. A defender of slavery, he published histories of the British Caribbean (1793) and of Saint-Domingue (1797). The latter in part was based on a trip Edwards made there in which he saw the consequences of the slave revolt, which he feared would spread to Jamaica. Edwards was an opponent of the abolition of the slave trade and a supporter of the value of the West Indian colonies to Britain. Like Benjamin Franklin and Thomas Jefferson, he also rejected European scientific suggestions that the New World was a harmful environment for plants, animals, peoples and cultures.

8

A New Age of
Capital, 1848–98

I'm Captain Corcoran, K.C.B.
I'll teach you how we rule the sea,
And terrify the simple Gauls;
And how the Saxon and the Celt
Their Europe-shaking blows have dealt
With Maxim gun and Nordenfeldt
(or will, when the occasion calls).
If sailor-like you'd play your cards,
Unbend your sails and lower your yards,
Unstep your masts – you'll never want 'em more
Though we're no longer hearts of oak,
Yet we can steer and we can stoke,
And thanks to coal, and thanks to coke,
We never run a ship ashore!
                    Captain Sir Edward Corcoran, RN, in
                    Gilbert and Sullivan's *Utopia Limited* (1893)

HAITI

The potential of independence was not much more encouraging to some commentators than the inequality and stagnation of the continued reality of imperial influence, and the two were linked in Haiti, where, amidst mass devastation and a marked fall in the population, some of the plantation economy producing for European markets had survived the slave rebellion in 1791, the highly destructive subsequent warfare and independence from

France in 1804. Slavery had gone, formally abolished when Jean-Jacques Dessalines declared independence on 1 January 1804, but the black élite who ran the state used forced labour to protect their plantations from the preference of people instead to live independently as peasant proprietors. Dessalines had insisted that people serve as soldiers or as labourers, and the control over labour continued thereafter. As a result, amidst the development of class and colour divisions, notably prejudice against those with a darker skin, a prejudice also seen elsewhere, for example in Brazil, the pressures of the global economy and the attractions of cash crops selling into international markets triumphed over the potential consequences of independence. In another feature of slavery days, these sales, in turn, were affected by competition from the products of Caribbean colonies. Compensation to France agreed in 1825 in order to gain recognition of independence, which was finally unconditionally granted, hit both living standards and social capital in Haiti.

Political stability proved elusive after the overthrow of Jean-Pierre Boyer, who had unified Haiti in 1820. He remained as president until 1843, when he was overthrown by a rebellion organised by Charles Rivière-Hérard, a general, who, in turn, fell in 1844 in the face of defeat by Dominican rebels and rebellions in Haiti, both by his governmental opponents and by the 'Army of the Sufferers', a peasant force led by a former officer and pledged to black rather than mulatto rule. The next president, Philippe Guerrier, another general, died in office in 1845, being succeeded by Jean-Louis Pierrot, another general who was overthrown in 1846 by Jean-Baptiste Riché, another general, who died, possibly poisoned, in 1847. His successor, Faustin Soulouque, the last of the presidents to have fought in the War of Independence and to have been an ex-slave, was also a general. Once president, he set up a militia, the Zinglins, who terrified mulattoes. A murderous but effective autocrat, Soulouque openly backed vodou, and in 1849 re-established the empire, originally proclaimed by

Dessalines in 1804, becoming Faustin I. A Haitian nobility was also established. On the model of Napoleon, he had an imperial coronation in 1852. Invasions of the Dominican Republic in 1849, 1850 and 1855 failed.

In 1858–9, Fabre Geffrard, a general, overthrew Soulouque, becoming president, surviving coup attempts in 1858, 1861, 1862, 1863 and 1864, and finally fleeing in 1867 in the face of serious division within the country. His successor, Sylvain Salnave, a major who had rebelled in 1864 and 1866, was faced by a peasant rising and disputes with Congress. The latter led Salnave to re-establish the presidency-for-life, but this resulted in a civil war. Fleeing to the Dominican Republic in 1869, he was handed back, court martialled and shot. Nissage Saget, another general, succeeded him, and was able to serve out his term (1870–4) peacefully and in full, although he faced quarrels with liberals trying to introduce parliamentary rule. In 1875, riots and assassinations marred the presidency of Michel Domingue, another general, but his successor, Pierre Théoma Boisrond-Canal, another former general, managed to be president in 1876–9, 1888 and 1902, and to die, peacefully and not in exile, in 1905. Louis Salomon (r. 1879–88), an autocratic moderniser, faced serious rebellions, notably in 1883–4, 1887 and 1888, leading him to resign and flee. In turn, the election of François Légitime, a general, in 1888 led to a battle in which a rival general was killed, but, in 1889, he resigned in the face of opposition from yet another general, Florvil Hyppolite, who suppressed rebellions, improved the economy, and was able to die in office in 1896. His successor, Tirésias Sam (r. 1896–1902), helped oversee a measure of stabilisation.

Frequent changes and the related instability, however, had not helped Haiti's development and also led it very much to have a frontier reputation. From the outset in 1791, Haiti was regularly deployed by imperialists and racists in order to justify their prejudices, as in *A Roving Commission; Or, Through the Black Insurrection at Hayti* (1900) by the British adventure writer and protagonist of empire G. A. Henty: 'the condition of the negroes in Hayti [sic] has fallen to the level of that of the savage African tribes . . . unless some strong white power should occupy the island and enforce law and order', he wrote, the situation would not improve. Henty also claimed that the situation there for the slaves had deteriorated since the 1791 revolution, a highly dubious proposition.

CUBA

After its end in the British and French colonies, slavery continued in the Spanish colonies, as did the illegal slave trade. In 1863, Henry, Viscount Palmerston, the British Prime Minister, a bitter opponent of the slave trade, suggested that 15,000 to 20,000 Africans, and possibly more, were imported into Cuba each year. The British accordingly felt it necessary to press Spain to implement its treaty commitments, but the bribery of officials to ignore restrictions was widespread. Furthermore, although the United States was Cuba's major market for sugar, imports of sugar from Cuba ensured that British consumers were heavily dependent on slave production, which led to well-deserved anger from Abolitionists in Britain.

Slavery remained crucial to the low-cost sugar monoculture of much of the Cuban economy, especially in western Cuba, while, far from being a reactionary survival of an anachronistic past, American and British investment (including in railways), markets and technology, helped Cuban production, not least in response to the end of the preferential measures that had ensured markets for sugar from British colonies. Some British plantation owners emigrated to Cuba where the number of sugar mills had increased to 1531 in 1862 and that of slaves from 197,415 to 323,759. Tobacco was also important, and Havana cigars became widely famed at a time when cigar consumption was rising rapidly. Surviving sugar warehouses from the period, as at Caibarién, testify to the importance of the exports, which underlined the continuing economic value of Cuba to Spain; its psychological place as a source of a continued imperial identity and role was also important, not least to the military. This helped explain the army's determination to retain control. The far smaller scale of the sugar-slave economy on Puerto Rico meant that it could not compete and indeed declined from the late 1840s.

The example of Haiti and anxiety about the increased numbers of slaves accentuated the brutality of life on the Cuban plantations, and this led to violence, suicide and a series of slave risings, in 1825, 1833 and 1843, all mounted by newly arrived slaves, although their scale and organisation were less than suggested by those keen to justify repression.

THE WORLD OF THE FORMER SLAVES

It was not only to be in the United States after 1865 that former slaves found their prospects limited and their conditions harsh. In the West Indies also, many former slaves were pressed into continuing to work in sugar production, as on Martinique. Legal systems were employed in order to limit the mobility and freedom of former slaves, for example by restricting emigration and also what was presented as vagrancy, which, in practice, could simply mean a failure to engage in the world of work on approved terms. Rents were also used to control labour and to reduce labour costs, a policy and process that hit living standards. Resistance, which included strikes as well as workers leaving the plantations, was different in means, tone and response to the situation under slavery, but the advantage of staying included pay and housing. Indeed, the difficult situation for workers in the British colonies after 1838 undercuts any simple attempt to create a contrast between slavery and freedom, although, on the other hand, very different notions of liberty were involved. The conditions of labour for ex-slaves, as earlier for slaves, reflected far more than the legal situation, and for most there was no sweeping change in their lives. Many ex-slaves, moreover, remained dependent, in some form or other, on their ex-masters or on new masters, and could be treated brutally by the government and military, as in Cuba, where black workers suffered disproportionately from government action and military repression. The plight of former slaves, however, did not attract the attention previously devoted to Abolitionism.

Former slaves tended to take up small-scale independent farming, on provision grounds, rather than work on plantations, and this helped lead to demands for fresh labour in the colonies. For example, several thousand free blacks from the British West African colony of Sierra Leone went to the West Indies in the 1840s to satisfy this demand. Nevertheless, despite the availability of cheap indentured labour, notably Indians seeking employment on Trinidad (but also elsewhere, including Jamaica, St Vincent and Grenada), sugar production in the British Caribbean declined. Indentured labour was also employed in Cuba and the French Caribbean, with Indians arriving accordingly in Martinique from 1853. In Cuba (as elsewhere including Martinique), as part of a prevalent racism, indentured Chinese workers were treated harshly and found that, although 'free', they could not buy their way out of their contractual obligations. The arrival of indentured labour had major economic, cultural and political consequences that continue to be felt to the present day in some countries, particularly Trinidad, where Hinduism and Islam are common as a result. The already-pronounced ethnic diversity of the Caribbean was therefore also further enhanced by the ending of slavery; and this addition added new elements to the nearly thirty creole and pidgin languages of the region.

In the face of such diversity, the classification system remained in place for ex-slaves as it did for slaves where slavery continued. For the latter, in Louisiana, slaves were distinguished in inventories as creole (of Louisiana origin), American, in other words from elsewhere in the United States, or African, in short African-born, to distinguish place of origin; and as Negro, Mulatto (mixed white/black) and Grif (mixed Native American/black), to distinguish ancestral background.

The crisis of the British plantation societies was especially marked in Jamaica. Labour availability and discipline were crucial to the ability of estates to hold down costs, but the end of the apprenticeship system in 1838 was followed by large numbers of former slaves leaving the plantations, notably in Jamaica and Trinidad, in order to seek unsettled land for their own where they followed subsistence agriculture. Former slaves thus became independent farmers, a process also seen with former coerced labour in the East Indies, as well as in Africa mostly after the turn of the century. These ex-slaves, to the degree they were able to get land, were important in the expansion of peasant export agriculture in the twentieth century.

This option was not so available in smaller colonies, such as Antigua and Barbados, which lacked free land, and the estate system therefore remained more effective there. In the larger colonies, emancipation led to a fall in estate productivity and profitability as, despite the possibilities offered by the adoption of steam power in the shape of steam milling in place of windmills, sugar production continued to be labour-intensive. Free labour proved more expensive and less reliable (because less intimated) than slaves, greatly increasing the operating costs. Many estates were affected by debt. A lack of liquidity, which was also hit by the crisis affecting plantation underwriters, meant that there was insufficient investment in new technology. In addition, under the Sugar Duties Act of 1846, all duties on imported sugar were equalised in 1851, hitting the British colonies, as did growing competition from imports of often subsidised European sugar beet, notably from Germany. In Jamaica, significant areas went out of cultivation. Individual colonies, moreover, were hit by particular events, a bad hurricane in 1847 precipitating the end of sugar exports from Tobago. There was some substitution, notably by cocoa on Grenada, but none of great scale; and the Royal Commission appointed in 1896 reported that, excluding Jamaica, sugar products were responsible for 75 per cent of the exports of the British Caribbean. The price for unrefined sugar had fallen by nearly 50 per cent from 1881 to 1896.

The development of sugar-beet production is a classic instance of the relationship between Caribbean history and that of distant regions. The cultivation of modern sugar beets dated from Frederick the Great of Prussia's attempt to ensure sugar supplies from beets cultivatable in Germany. Beetroots were the original source and the first factory opened in 1801. Responding to British naval power, Napoleon rapidly followed suit. By 1840, about 5 per cent of the world's sugar came from sugar beets but by 1880, with production concentrated in Germany, but also spreading, notably to Russia, the percentage had risen to over 50 and in 1879 commercial production began in the United States. For British markets, German producers were closer than those in the Caribbean; although the first British sugar-beet factory only appeared in 1912, large-scale British production did not follow until the mid-1920s, and then in the aftermath of wartime shortages of imported sugar. By 2020, British-grown sugar, a highly mechanised process, supplied about half of the national demand.

As the exports of the former British plantation economies declined, so they were less able to attract investment, afford imports from Britain and elsewhere, and develop social capital, which hit living standards. In 1815, the West Indies had been the leading market for British exports, but, by 1840, they had been passed as a market by India, Australia and Canada in that order; and, linked to this, the role of the Caribbean in British shipping needs also diminished. The severance of commercial links with the United States as a result of post-1783 protectionist legislation was a major problem, notably in the 1820s. Similar problems affected other plantation economies and societies such as St Martin, which was divided between France and the Dutch.

Moreover, the Caribbean receded from European attention; in the case of Britain, with the exception of the Morant Bay uprising in October 1865. Edward Eyre, Governor of Jamaica, had proclaimed martial law and, with the use of troops, court martials on often flimsy evidence and the burning down of homes, very harshly, on occasion murderously, suppressed an insurrection, leading to much criticism in Britain, as well as support, for example from Charles Dickens. In practice, both Eyre and the troops broke the law, and the Royal Commission decided that the punishments were excessive and even 'cruel'. Eyre was recalled and criticised in Parliament by the Secretary of State for the Colonies for a lack of sound judgement and impartiality. Similarly, in 1870, a dispute in Martinique became a racial struggle, led to a proclamation of independence, and was firmly suppressed.

Dickens on Eyre's Harshness

His imperial connections in the shape of the careers of his sons contributed to Dickens's strong and disgusting response at the time of reasonable criticism in Britain of Edward Eyre's brutal and illegal handling of the Morant Bay uprising, but other factors also played a role in Dickens's response, including anger at what he saw as a mismatch between the response to hardship abroad and at home, as well as his view that missionaries were humbugs:

> The Jamaica insurrection is another hopeful piece of business. That platform – sympathy with the black – or the native, or the devil – afar off, and that platform indifference to our own countrymen at enormous odds in the midst of bloodshed and

savagery, makes me stark wild. Only the other day, here was a meeting of jawbones of asses at Manchester, to censure the Jamaica Governor for his manner of putting down the insurrection! So we are badgered about New Zealanders and Hottentots, as if they were identical with men in clean shirts at Camberwell ... But for the blacks in Jamaica being over-impatient and before their time, the whites might have been exterminated.

Drawing probably on this episode, Dickens later referred harshly to popular accounts of imperial cruelty when he mocked the foolish reports about Neville Landless, the alleged murderer of Edwin Drood in the novel named after the latter:

Before coming to England he had caused to be whipped to death sundry 'Natives' – nomadic persons, encamping now in Asia, now in Africa, now in the West Indies, and now at the North Pole – vaguely supposed in Cloisterham to be always black, always of great virtue ... and always reading tracts of the obscurest meaning, in broken English, but always accurately understanding them in the purest mother tongue.

The economic problems that affected the British Caribbean appeared to some at mid-century to demonstrate the continued value of coerced labour, not of course their own. So also did the British acceptance of indentured Indians into the region, which was not a remedy open to the Spaniards or Americans. Indeed, emancipation appeared an uneconomic risk. The case of the British Caribbean thus apparently fortified the lesson learned from Haiti, in that, if the latter apparently demonstrated the serious, destructive and bloody risks posed by Abolitionism and independence, the former indicated the problems that would follow from Abolitionism and continued imperial control. The British Abolitionist Stephen Cave, who, in 1849, published *A Few Words on the Encouragement given to Slavery and the Slave Trade by recent Measures and chiefly by the Sugar Bill of 1846*, noted that 'the miserable failure of emancipation in Haiti' was 'the favourite theme of all advocates of slavery'.

MID-CENTURY NEW ORLEANS

The most booming city in the Caribbean world was New Orleans, which benefited greatly from the development of its Mississippi River hinterland, a development speeded by the potential of steamships, by the opportunities offered by rail, not least in linkages to steamship river ports, by population growth in the hinterland, and by the opportunities of an expanding world economy with a strong demand for cotton. There was extensive immigration to the city, which had a foreign-born population of about 40 per cent, many Germans and Irish. The population rose from about 116,000 in 1850 to nearly 170,000 in 1860, by which time America was producing about 80 per cent of the cotton traded in the world. Later in the century, there was to be a significant Italian immigration, with many finding work in the docks, but also leading to ethnic tension, as in 1890 when the murder of the Superintendent of Police, David Hennessy, was attributed to the Mafia and led to riots in which Italians were killed. At the same time, this was a tension born of the opportunities presented by economic growth.

Tourism

With economic development, and more particularly steamships and railways, facilities for travellers increased, notably with purpose-built hotels, not only in New Orleans but also in other cities, such as the aptly named *Hotel Inglaterra* in Havana (1856), the oldest in Cuba. Relief from the European and North American winter also encouraged tourism, a process greatly facilitated by the establishment of steamship routes and tourist hotels, including the Royal Victorian Hotel in the Bahamas (1861), Crane Beach in Barbados (1887), and the Titchfield Hotel in Port Antonio, Jamaica, in about 1891, rebuilt in 1905. The Dutch went to Curaçao, the French to Martinique, and the Americans to the Bahamas.

AMERICAN EXPANSIONISM

Meanwhile, the period saw growing great-power competition linked in particular to American expansionism and to more specific episodes such as the French and Spanish attempts to recover influence in the 1860s. The acquisition of Cuba, which would bring more slaveholding states into the Union, was a goal of many Americans, including President Franklin Pierce (r. 1853–7). In 1851, Joseph Crawford, the activist British Consul in Havana, reported that Southern cooperation would lead to revolution against the unpopular Spanish government, which, indeed, was the goal of some influential Cubans and Southerners. Alliance with the slaveholding South would provide safety for the slaveholders who dominated Cuban society, and, in 1844, had helped repress a slave rebellion that had broken out in western Cuba the previous year. The Ostend Manifesto, a claim, in 1854, by the American envoys in Britain, France and Spain that America could seize Cuba if Spain refused to sell it, increased tension. Nearby America was Cuba's foremost trading partner, taking most of Cuba's sugar, and being the major source of its imports. Indeed, Cuba represented an important market for America.

Spain, however, rejected American interest in purchase in 1848 and 1854, and America lacked the necessary military strength to conquer Cuba against Spanish forces which, in 1850 and 1851, had seen off filibustering expeditions (i.e. unauthorised warfare against a foreign state) by Narcisco López, a Caracas-born former Spanish general, who was executed. A supporter of slavery, he had held out the idea that Cuba would follow Texas into the Union and thus help the South, and New Orleans was his base from 1850. The flag López designed later became the flag of Cuba, but he received scant support on the island on either occasion. Britain, meanwhile, deployed warships in Cuban waters as a deterrent to American attack. The forward projection potential offered by American plans to develop a naval base in the Dominican Republic had also proved fruitless.

Encouraged by the California gold rush, American interest in the development of a rail and/or canal route across Central America greatly increased in the 1850s, at the time when there was no rail route across the United States; but this interest proved unavailing. Already high, tension in the region rose from 1848 when the Nicaraguans who had occupied Greytown (previously San Juan del Norte) on the Mosquito Coast, a centre of British influence (the kings were crowned in British Honduras, now Belize), were expelled with the help of British warships from Jamaica. The Americans were concerned, as the river on which Greytown sat was likely to be part of the route for a canal across the isthmus. In 1853, moreover, President James Buchanan (r. 1857–61) pressed Britain on the Bay Islands to the north of Honduras, a British settlement that had been established as a colony from the previous year, which he presented as a valuable naval and commercial station near the isthmus commanding the

Caribbean. Naval bases were regarded by him (and others) as the currency of competition and both America and Honduras rejected British claims to the Bay Islands.

This was part of the definition of power and clarification of authority after the Latin American wars of independence; an often uneasy clarification that also registered serious Anglo-American competition, and one that posed problems for local allies. Indeed, in 1854, in pursuit of the interests of the Accessory Transit Company, a Cornelius Vanderbilt company which transported passengers and goods across Nicaragua, an American warship and marines destroyed Greytown. In response, the British reinforced the West Indies fleet, but did not use force and pressed only for compensation. The lack of key British political, military or economic interests in Central America, not least at a time when Britain was engaged in the Crimean War (1854–6) with Russia, which definitely took precedence, affected British policy, and led to an acceptance of the American position that the Mosquito Coast should be placed under Nicaraguan sovereignty.

WILLIAM WALKER AND THE PURSUIT OF CENTRAL AMERICA

The 1850s were also the years of renewed American filibustering, including John Quitman's preparations to seize Cuba in 1853–4, preparations abandoned because President Franklin Pierce withdrew his initial support, Henry Kinney's unsuccessful pursuit of control of the Mosquito Coast in 1855, and those of the indefatigable William Walker. Having failed in his invasion of Mexico in 1853, the idea of a Central American state to fulfil his view of manifest destiny for himself, as well as to create a modernised and pro-American Nicaragua, entranced Walker, who, in 1855, sought to exploit the civil war there. Victorious, he declared himself president in 1856 and annulled the Emancipation Act of 1824 banning slavery. In 1856, however, Walker's Nicaraguan forces were defeated when they invaded Costa Rica, while Walker fell out with his previous sponsor and, in effect, filibuster, Cornelius Vanderbilt, and his Accessory Transit Company, who, in 1857, paid for Costa Rica to invade and overthrow Walker. Another invasion attempt by Walker on Nicaragua failed later that year, and, in 1860, after he seized Trujillo in Honduras, he won no backing, was turned over to the Hondurans by a British warship to which he had fled, and was shot. The British were consistently opposed to filibustering. Moreover, as another aspect of the attempted suppression of illegality, privateering was largely ended by the Declaration of Paris of 1856; although the United States did not sign it.

Walker's reputation today reflects the still contentious nature of links with the United States. In Latin America, there is a tendency to regard him as an expansionist American filibuster, and not as a liberal moderniser. His shooting prefigured that, in very different circumstances, of Archduke Maximilian of Austria, the French-backed claimant to imperial authority in Mexico, whose execution in 1867, depicted in a famous series of paintings by Édouard Manet, brought to an end a different episode of fili-bustering, this one state-sponsored but again benefiting from a civil war.

POWER POLITICS IN THE 1860S AND 1870S

The nature of opportunity in the Caribbean was changing, for local states as well as filibusters. Thus, in 1851, Britain and France used a joint naval blockade of Port-au-Prince to force Emperor Faustin I of Haiti to a truce with Santo Domingo; although in 1855 he renewed the war. Imperial ambitions were not only in flux in Hispaniola. Britain became less active in the Caribbean, although France was to be far more so in the 1860s.

British claims on the Mosquito Coast became more modest in the 1850s. Suzerainty had been claimed there until 1850, but the British protectorate came to an end with the recognition of

Nicaraguan sovereignty in 1860, although the interests of the Moskitos were protected and there was no full incorporation of the area into Nicaragua until 1894, and that after a confused conflict that also involved Honduras and British Marines.

Meanwhile, the northward extension of the protectorate in Honduras was recognised as coming under Honduran sovereignty in 1859, as were the Bay Islands, Lord John Russell, the Foreign Secretary, expressing his concern that year about the health of island bases in the tropics. These British withdrawals, which reflected a lack of political and public commitment to a longstanding part of Britain's informal empire, and certainly no wish to extend British influence or possession, did not open the way for American occupation: there was no annexation of the Bay Islands which were actually transferred to Honduras in 1861. There were other American interests. In 1861, Mexico rejected President Abraham Lincoln's approach to purchase Cozumel as a settlement for freed American slaves. The following year, an American entrepreneur, Bernard Kock, leased the Île-à-Vache from Haiti in order to establish cotton production produced by freed slaves. However, the short-changed labourers became rebellious and in 1863 the contract was broken. Furthermore, on a longstanding pattern, British accommodation of American interests did not extend to governmental support for the American purchase of Cuba, while in 1865 the destruction of the British Consulate in Cap Haïtien, Haiti, by rebels led to firm action by a British naval squadron.

In 1861, while America was divided by civil war, political instability in Mexico and its default on international debts led to Britain, France and Spain occupying Mexico's leading port, Veracruz, in order to take over customs revenue to help repay the loan. In 1862, as the French took the intervention further, intervening in the conflict between Mexican liberals and conservatives, Britain and Spain withdrew. Spain, however, under its interventionist prime minister, General Leopoldo O'Donnell, was willing to resume control of Santo Domingo in 1861 in order to help the President resist domestic opposition and because O'Donnell felt that Spain should still have a major role in Latin America. In 1863, the French seized Mexico City and arranged the offer of the crown of Mexico to Archduke Maximilian of Austria, who was crowned Emperor of Mexico in 1864. Concerned about the build-up of French strength and French links to the Confederacy, President Abraham Lincoln (r. 1861–5) and the Union backed Maximilian's republican opponents in the Mexican Civil War. They were the liberals while Maximilian was backed by the conservatives and by clerical interests.

THE AMERICAN CIVIL WAR

Meanwhile, combined operations played a significant role for the Union in the American Civil War (1861–5), and particularly so in the Caribbean, notably with the seizure of New Orleans on 1 May 1862. This strangled the Confederacy's export of cotton and affected its shipbuilding capacity, as well as delivering the largest city in the Confederacy. In doing so, David Farragut overcame the Confederate warships (the massive *Louisiana* could not move for want of her engines, while the *Manassas* only mounted one 32-pounder) and bypassed, at night, Fort Jackson and Fort St Philip, two substantial forts with numerous guns, but only after the river was freed of obstacles. Later Confederate attempts to regain New Orleans failed. Farragut and General Benjamin Butler pressed on to capture Baton Rouge on 12 May 1862. The occupation of the city was an unhappy one. While some in New Orleans did not want to hear about the Civil War, many of the citizens disliked the Yankees and expressed this by public displays of Confederate support and by actions such as pouring chamber pots over Union officials and troops including, allegedly, Farragut. An attack on the Union flag above the mint led to a hanging. The merchants adapted, however, to the occupation, notably because they were able to continue their trade to the Caribbean and were happy to ship sugar to New York. Associated with the Union, free blacks found themselves in a difficult situation due to local hostility, but, in 1863, thousands of slaves were freed in Louisiana.

The war continued. In July 1863, the Union forces captured Port Hudson after a costly siege, while, in 1864, Farragut followed up by successfully fighting his way into Mobile Bay on 5 August, despite mines which claimed one Union ironclad and could have claimed more had they worked better. The Confederate ironclad CSS *Tennessee* was overwhelmed in this battle. In April 1865, Farragut provided support to Union forces that captured Confederate positions around that bay.

THE AFTERMATH OF CIVIL WAR

Victory in 1865 left the Union with a massive and well-honed military, on land and sea; and American non-recognition of Maximilian's government became more significant as, after the Civil War, American forces were moved south to the Mexican frontier. Both America and France had exploited Mexico: America, in 1846–8, by launching a war of aggression and seizing much territory, and France by trying to turn the country into a satellite state. However, the French capture of Mexican ports highlighted the contrast between input, in the shape of force projection, and outcome, in the shape of much more difficult control over much of the interior. French naval strength enabled coastal success, as with the capture of the port of Guaymas in 1865 and the reinforcement that year of Matamoros, which thwarted an attack on that port; but could not deliver more.

American politicians, meanwhile, and with some reason, saw Napoleon III, Maximilian, Mexican conservatives and Southern exiles as key elements in a far-ranging geopolitical and ideological combination directed against liberal progress in Mexico, and, therefore, against American interests. With the encouragement of Maximilian, some ex-Confederates developed plans for creating settlements in Mexico, for example the New Virginia Colony.

American pressure, notably the threat of war, played a role in Napoleon III's decision in 1866 to withdraw his troops from Mexico, a decision that took effect the following March, but, as so often in history, a focus on just one factor is misleading. There was in particular the need to confront a Prussia newly strong as a result of the complete defeat of Austria in 1866. In the aftermath of this withdrawal, Maximilian fought on, was besieged at Santiago de Querétaro, was rapidly defeated and, once captured, court martialled and shot on 19 June 1867.

There was also conflict in Central America, conflict that was an instructive counterpoint to the relative stability of the British, French, Danish and Dutch West Indian colonies, although not of Cuba. Foreign intervention was the norm in Central America, as conservatives and liberals not only fought each other within states, but also both looked for support from foreign colleagues. Thus, Guatemala and Nicaragua supported their clients in Honduras in 1863. These conflicts were affected by continuing American interest in routes from the Caribbean to the Pacific, which played a major role in the Treaty of Comayagua with Honduras in 1864. Hostilities in the region continued, as in 1871 when the liberals overthrew the regime in Guatemala. Moreover, in Mexico, Porfirio Díaz, unwilling to accept defeat in the presidential election of 1875, rebelled and seized power, beginning a long dictatorship.

Like France, Spain was in no position to pursue its New World ambitions, with acute instability in Spain and American pressure leading to a pulling back. As a result, moreover, of local opposition, which in 1863 led to an insurrection, Spain in 1865 abandoned its attempt to control the Dominican Republic, which had indeed turned out to be a fruitless commitment that encountered popular fears that Spain would reintroduce slavery as well as the serious inroads of yellow fever on its troops. O'Donnell was also under considerable political pressure in Spain. However, his interventionism, which included naval hostilities with Peru and Chile, was a reminder of the imponderables of Caribbean history. Had the

Confederacy succeeded, then the role of France and Spain in the Caribbean might well have been far more significant and lasting.

The success of the Dominican War of Restoration (1863–5) was followed by pronounced instability in the Dominican Republic, with frequent insurrections, grave financial problems and partisan politics. A dictatorship under Ulises Heureaux followed from 1882 until his assassination in 1899.

US President Ulysses S. Grant (r. 1869–77) had favoured the annexation of the Dominican Republic if its people backed the proposition; only, after a plebiscite in 1870 voted in favour, to be thwarted by Congressional opposition in the United States which led to the failure by a narrow majority to ratify the treaty. Also in 1870, the Senate decided not to proceed with the purchase of the Danish Virgin Islands, which Denmark had agreed to sell in 1868, although the threat from German submarines were to change American attitudes in 1917. Grant also faced liberal pressure to support the Cuban insurrection against Spanish rule, pressure that looked toward the situation in 1898 when America intervened, but he was unwilling to provide such support.

The Swan Islands

Named after Captain Swan, who was recruited to piracy by compulsion, these became a source of guano for fertiliser in the 1840s, and this led to a claim to them by America in 1856 under the Guano Act. Ninety-five miles off Honduras, and the most northerly part of the Bay Islands archipelago, the Swan Islands were used for a variety of American purposes, including as a hurricane weather station from 1838, but the rival Honduran claim was accepted in 1971 and became effective in 1972. In contrast, Navassa Island near Haiti remains under the United States.

LOUISIANA AFTER THE CIVIL WAR

The huge debt left by the Civil War helped restrain American expansionism, as did the very rapid post-war demobilisation, and the problems of trying to contain white violence in the Southern states. Notably, in New Orleans the army intervened to prevent a pogrom of black people in 1866, the Knights of the White Camelia were active from the late 1860s, and the White League, which claimed to fight 'armed negro militia and metropolitans', sought to seize control of Louisiana in the 1870s. In 1873, in the Colfax massacre, about 150 black people were killed. In 1874, in 'the Battle of Liberty Place', the White League, in an attempt to wrest control of Louisiana from Vermont-born William Pitt Kellogg, the Republican governor from 1873 to 1877, occupied several key city-centre sites, only for the revolt to be quashed by federal troops. In an ultimately futile attempt to impose a Reconstruction that enabled civil rights for black people, federal troops remained in Florida and Louisiana until 1877. However, there was not sufficient federal or local support for Reconstruction to overcome the challenge of white supremacism. Black people lost their hope of land and many became sharecroppers or worked on estates where they had formerly been slaves. In 1896, the *Plessy v. Ferguson* Supreme Court judgment affirmed segregation legislation. Politics in New Orleans by then was very much a competition between two factions of white Democrats; the Ring, which was based on immigrants and organised labour and led by the corrupt machine boss John Fitzpatrick; versus reforming businessmen.

In 1868, the Fourteenth Amendment to the Constitution had guaranteed citizenship and equality for anyone born in the United States, while the Reconstruction Constitution of Louisiana had decreed black male suffrage and equal rights for all to public education and accommodation. An African American, Oscar Dunn, had become Lieutenant-Governor of Louisiana, an outcome that appeared fantastical by 1896. Indeed, in 1898, white

Democrats took firm control of the legislature and introduced a new constitution that segregated public schools and imposed poll taxes and literacy tests as qualifications for voting. In the aftermath, as in 1868–80, many black people left Louisiana, where limited opportunities were accompanied by a marked recalibration of control and oppression. After Kellogg, no Republican was elected governor of Louisiana until 1980, by which time the Republican Party had changed totally.

Rebellion in Cuba

War led to the end of slavery in the United States in 1865. It was also crucial in Cuba. As with the original Latin American wars of liberation, there was a close link between political division in Spain and the outset and course of rebellion in Cuba, because the first insurgency, in 1868, was connected to a successful army rebellion in Spain. Launching the 'Ten Years War' of 1868 to 1878, the insurgency stemmed from the failure of the reform movement launched by *criollo* planters in 1865, the refusal of Spain to extend more political participation to Cuba, and the degree to which rebels seeking independence were ready to free their slaves.

Although much of the *criollo* support for the earlier Latin American wars of liberation was due to a rejection of reformism imposed on them from Spain, whether Bourbon or from Joseph Bonaparte, liberalism was the cause, or at least a major contributory cause, of many of the revolutions or would-be revolutions in the nineteenth-century Western world, notably separatist liberal ones as in Poland, Hungary, northern Italy, Ireland and Cuba. The late 1860s, moreover, appeared to be a time when liberalism was in the ascendant, with the liberals victorious in the Mexican Civil War and the conservative Southerners defeated in its American counterpart. This was the background to the declaration of Cuban independence on 10 October 1868, a declaration that promised 'a constitutional government created in an enlightened manner'. The background was a breakdown in relations. The 1865 demands for representation in the Spanish Parliament, judicial equity with Spaniards, tariff reform and full enforcement of the slave trade ban had been rejected, taxation was increased and opposition silenced, while the economy deteriorated in 1866–7. Conspiracy against Spanish rule was followed by rebellion in eastern Cuba.

In Cuba, the rebels concentrated on taking advantage of the difficult, often mountainous terrain, thick overgrowth and numerous rivers, through ambushes and by harrying Spanish forces with rifle fire, especially if, as at Palo Seco in 1873, the Spaniards formed infantry squares and thus offered concentrated targets. The Spaniards were also hit hard by yellow fever.

In turn, the Spaniards benefited greatly from ethnic, geographical and social divisions among the Cubans and from the willingness of many Cubans, in part as a result, to support Spain, and notably so in the west. In particular, from 1870, the Spaniards were helped by ethnic tensions, as Cuban whites increasingly rejected what they now saw as a black-run revolution focused on opposition to slavery, while conservative loyalists, fearing a repetition of Haiti, provided powerful support for Spain. These longstanding attitudes and divisions became more significant in the nineteenth century, underlining the mistake of seeing states as units. On the pattern of longstanding practices in Caribbean warfare, as well as civil wars in Spain, Spanish forces employed harsh measures, which included, in the case of Cuba, wholesale executions, the killing of rebel families, and the forced relocation of the rural population so as to create free-fire zones and to prevent the rebels from gaining access to civilian aid, an issue that remained important in later insurrections.

In turn, the rebels waged economic warfare, destroying sugar mills and plantations. Insurgent activity rose to a height in 1872–3; but the rebel leadership was hit by military and political divisions, deaths of leaders in 1873-4, and by the failure of an invasion of western Cuba in 1875. Once civil war in Spain ended in 1876, 25,000 troops were sent to Cuba, and a combination of military action and conciliatory promises, notably more political representation for the *criollos* and freedom for the rebel slaves, led to a settlement there in 1878, the Pact of Zanjón, that restored Spanish control. The *Guerra Chiquita*, or Small War, of 1879-80 registered the failure of those who rejected the settlement.

The devastating insurgency, in which about 200,000 people were killed, saw the partial abolition of slavery in rebel areas, which encouraged the move for gradual abolition in the island as a whole. Slavery was liberalised and abolished in stages in 1878, when the slaves who had fought in the war were freed; 1880; and, finally, 1886; having already taken place in Puerto Rico in 1873. The Dutch, meanwhile, had abolished slavery in 1863 without such a struggle. The Spanish government, however, was unwilling to accept a reformist agenda including universal suffrage. This was a parallel to the situation in the United States in the failure to sustain Reconstruction.

Affected by the socio-economic dislocation of the period, the Cuban insurgency resumed in 1895. Revolutionaries had continued to be active, notably in the Cuban exile community in the United States, and this was the basis for an insurrection, launched on 24 February, that focused in the east. The Cuban Revolutionary Party under the rapidly killed José Martí played a key role in what became a large-scale conflict that highlighted the problems of both guerrilla and counterinsurgency warfare. With limited weaponry, and faced by a very large Spanish army, the insurgents hit the economy, destroying the sugar and tobacco crops, in an attempt to create mass unemployment and to force refugees to become a burden on the Spaniards. The insurgents were initially successful in evading attempts to engage them in battle, in part because the Spanish forces attempted to cover the entire country. Raids and ambushes played a major role, and control over supplies was important to both the regulars and the insurgents. Preventing opponents' access to supplies was the goal of many operations. Thus, in December 1895, the insurgents ambushed a Spanish column at Mal Tiempo, capturing 200 rifles and replenishing supplies of ammunition. The use of machetes in this attack underlined the extent to which insurgency warfare still involved hand-to-hand conflict. In this close-combat ambush, the Spaniards were not able to bring their impressive Mauser rifles effectively to bear.

In turn, the Spaniards sought to fix their opponents so that they could use their firepower, as at Manacal earlier that month, when Spanish artillery helped drive the insurgents from a defensive position. Valeriano Weyler, who became governor general in January 1896, had extensive experience of the range of counter-insurgency operations, including in Cuba in 1868–72. Weyler combined terror tactics and defensive lines with effective field offensives. He also had a social strategy based on the enforced movement of people to the towns, where, surrounded by barbed wire in what the Spaniards called concentration camps, they were hard hit by disease and food shortages. Due in particular to yellow fever, 150,000 to 170,000 Cubans died in the camps, a major part of the maybe 10 per cent of the population who died in the war. Meanwhile, the insurgents were driven from western Cuba in 1896. Faced with heavy costs, as well as by a simultaneous independence struggle in the Philippines, the Spaniards tried to be more accommodating, replacing Weyler in October 1897, offering, under a new liberal ministry that took office following the assassination by an anarchist of Prime Minister Antonio Cánovas del Castillo in August 1897, a new colonial constitution, and establishing a new government in Havana; but without success. Cuba remained divided, while successful American intervention in 1898, which led to the end of Spanish rule, prevents us from knowing how long Weyler's policies would have achieved results, which is a key counterfactual in Cuban history.

AMERICA TO THE FORE

The build-up of American naval power from the 1880s and, even more, 1890s, with the 'New American Navy', owed much to East Coast industrial interests, especially Pennsylvania shipyards and steelworks, linked to politicians and commentators keen not only to present America as a great power, but also as able to take a central role in global power politics. 'Manifest Destiny' was being repurposed and with new resources. Economic strength was readily present in New Orleans, where the World's Industrial and Cotton Centennial Exposition in 1884 was in part a demonstration of regional economic hegemony. The capacity of the port, which replaced Veracruz and Havana as the focus of maritime links, was increased when open wharves were replaced by covered ones from the late 1890s, while jetties were developed at the South Pass of the Mississippi. Harbour facilities were widely improved around the Caribbean, even in poor Haiti, in response to the need to cater to steamships and the prospects of increased trade, for example banana exports from Costa Rica.

From the late 1880s, the American navy developed a concept of offensive sea control by a battleship fleet, and pressed successfully for the launching and maintenance of an offensive battle fleet in peacetime. Presidents Benjamin Harrison (1889–93) and Theodore Roosevelt (1901–9) were strong supporters of the naval build-up.

The rise of American assertiveness and economic and naval power led in 1898 to war with Spain, a power which appeared to be redundant and a feeble obstacle to Americans' conviction of their country's 'Manifest Destiny' for greatness and to their insistence that Cuba be granted independence. The explosion in Havana of the battleship USS *Maine* on 15 February 1898 with 260 deaths was blamed without evidence by jingoistic American newspapers, notably those of William Randolph Hearst, especially the *New York Morning Journal*, on Spanish sabotage, while

Spanish cruelty in Cuba was also a theme, albeit greatly exaggerated by the press. Despite the tale being oft-repeated, Hearst did not cable, 'You furnish the pictures and I'll furnish the war.' In the background, racist attitudes to Hispanics played a role, and many of the attitudes seen in the Mexican–American War were reiterated. Victory was regarded as foreordained, and the American public was given much information on relative resources, as in the 'Strategic Map of our war with Spain'.

The navy played a key role in the Spanish–American War, gaining and using maritime superiority in order to isolate Spanish forces. On 3 July 1898 complete victory was obtained over the Spanish fleet off Santiago, with four modern cruisers and two destroyers sunk after they left the protected anchorage, in an easy but poorly commanded American victory over warships in poor condition and badly led. This victory gave vital leeway in Cuba to the inadequately trained American army and also encouraged the surrender of Santiago. The operational advantage of naval strength was further demonstrated on 21 July when a squadron captured Bahia de Nipe on Cuba's north coast, destroying the warship guarding the port and providing a new sphere of operations for the army. Naval power was also crucial in the capture of Puerto Rico, enabling successive bombardment (May), blockade and invasion (July). On 2 July, the *Graphic* commented: 'The mobility conferred upon the Americans by their sea-base made it impossible for the Spaniards to resist the landing.'

The American army was less effective, but benefited greatly from the Spanish failure to dispute its landing in Cuba. The Spaniards were confident that they knew how to operate in Cuba and that the Americans, who lacked comparable experience, could be defeated. Indeed, the climate and terrain created problems for the Americans, many of whom died of typhoid. However, the Spanish force in Cuba was in a vulnerable state. It had been intensely politicised for decades, and this affected both the quality and the quantity of command: there were far too many officers.

The determination to restrict expenditure ensured that the army lacked training. Despite a manpower advantage, the effectiveness of rifles and artillery using smokeless powder, and some tactical proficiency, the Spaniards in Cuba were poor at the operational level, retiring into a weak defensive perimeter around Santiago and not attacking American communications. In a key development, Santiago surrendered on 17 July.

Although support for the war was distinctly muted in the former Confederacy, victory more generally brought a strong sense that the Caribbean was America's backyard. In contrast, Cuban nationalists were concerned, not least because the Americans restricted their role, although not to the same degree that Filipino nationalists faced as the Philippines were transferred from Spanish to American control. Before he died in 1895, José Martí had been very worried about American intentions toward Cuba.

Whereas Puerto Rico was annexed, American officials took power in Cuba for a while, and sought to create a client state, as the Italians unsuccessfully had tried in Abyssinia (Ethiopia) and the French were to do successfully in Morocco. The constitution imposed in 1901 included, in the shape of the Platt Amendment, a right to American intervention in order to protect the independence of the country, a provision capable of a very wide interpretation to the benefit of the United States. The Americans also, in 1903, gained a perpetual lease for the southern portion of Guantanamo Bay for use as a naval base (established in 1898), with the local population moved out.

Moreover, American political and military dominance in the aftermath of war, and the loss of links with Spain, led to economic dominance as American capital rushed in, searching for a new investment opportunity in an undervalued and now illiquid economy, and one that appeared to have more investment opportunities than the American South. Land and assets were bought, notably much of the sugar industry, creating a new edge to existing social divisions. More generally, such divisions were accentuated across the Caribbean by economic changes. The rural world found itself squeezed to provide food and goods for markets both regional and further afield. Like imperial rule, liberation for Cuba was a matter of élite control and international markets, but without real economic or political participation, or social justice; a situation that helped produce discontent that led to social disorder, notably in 1912, as it had earlier done with the Mexican Revolution that began in 1910. Albeit with very different circumstances and contexts, there was a parallel in Cuba with Haiti after independence, but Cuba avoided the more serious level of disorder seen in Haiti.

CONCLUSIONS

In Cuba, the opposition to imperial control from Spain matched in some respects the hostility to federal pretensions in the United States. Southern white people were more united behind that cause than Cuban white people, while black people played a smaller direct role in the American crisis than that in Cuba. Political contingencies, moreover, were crucial, not least the absence of foreign intervention in the American Civil War and its key role in Cuba in 1898, a role that transformed the situation at several levels, including the resource dimension and the naval side. The Cuban insurgency was to be played up by Fidel Castro as a suitable prelude that anchored his achievement and provided a validation in terms of linking the independence struggle to his conflicts with the United States. As a result, streets, libraries, squares and statues commemorated Martí, the last two for example in Cienfuegos, while the Order of José Martí is one of Cuba's major honours. Earlier, the symbolic link with Spain was broken with independence in gestures such as the movement of Columbus's (alleged) funeral monument from the cathedral in Havana to that in Seville, although it is also claimed that his tomb is at the 'Lighthouse to Columbus', a mausoleum-museum in the Dominican Republic inaugurated in 1992. Parallels between the American South and the Caribbean were also to be seen in the plight of black people in both areas after slavery, a plight that was primarily economic but that also had significant political dimensions.

The Caribbean had changed. In Cuba, as very differently in Catalonia, there was an inability on the part of successive Spanish governments to search for an effective compromise and, instead, a determination to preserve central control. However, whereas Catalan separatism or, at least, autonomy lacked effective foreign support after the War of the Spanish Succession (1702–13), America's newfound great-power activism transformed the situation for Cuba in 1898. Although there were mixed feelings because American acquisitions might threaten Britain's Caribbean islands, the British government was not particularly concerned about the Spanish–American War which, indeed, generated a wave of Anglo-Saxonism in Britain. Moreover, the outcome of the war expedited British recognition of American predominance in the western hemisphere, as seen with the Hay–Pauncefote treaties of 1900–1. British policy was certainly heading in that direction at any rate, from the Venezuela crisis of 1895 onwards at least, but the demonstration of American military and naval power, and of a willingness to use it, all in 1898, encouraged this development. America might deploy power rather than gain territory, but this power was increasingly in evidence.

Developments in the East Indies were very different, for there was no rising regional state to challenge European power as the United States did in the Caribbean. Indeed, there was to be no such state until Japan, an Asian state that had Westernised, notably with its weaponry, came to the fore in 1941–2. The Dutch had faced serious problems in conflict in Sumatra and Java in the 1820s, and in part depended on local allies. In mid-century they made gains – in Borneo, Sulawesi, Bali, Sumatra and New Guinea

– but the process was slow, in part because of the problems of campaigning – logistics, disease and native opposition – and in part because of only limited will and resources. Nevertheless, Dutch expansion continued. Limits, as earlier in the Caribbean, owed much to the presence of other powers. Thus, New Guinea was divided by the Dutch with Britain and Germany. However, in the East Indies, the struggle for power was essentially between the Dutch and native powers, and there was no equivalent to the range of powers present in the Caribbean. Amidst that range, it was very much America that had come to the fore, and with a dominance expressed not in the territory directly controlled but in an ability and willingness to deploy clear strength.

9

The Age of American Power, 1898–1945

Everybody looked on in wonder; then a little black boy broke the spell by saying, 'Oh, by and by the Negro will have better ships than that.' Once upon a time that crowd would have laughed that boy to scorn. Who knows? Perhaps that boy in the future may be the Nelson of the Negro Race.

In its issue of 23 August 1924, *Negro World*, the pan-Africanist New York publication of the anti-imperial Jamaican activist Marcus Garvey, gave a response to the visit to Kingston, Jamaica, of a powerful British naval squadron during the 1924 Empire Cruise. A more insightful comment might have been to note the rising power of America. At the same time, power politics were overshadowed by natural disasters, notably the eruption of Mont Pelée in Martinique, which killed about 40,000 people in 1902, and the damaging earthquake that hit Kingston in 1907.

AMERICAN POWER PROJECTION

Unlike Puerto Rico, Cuba was not annexed after American victory in 1898, but there was no doubt of the shift in power. Naval strength measured that very clearly in the Caribbean, and bases were a key currency of geopolitics, as air bases were later to be. Under an agreement in 1903, the Americans retained control of the naval anchorage at Guantanamo as a sovereign base and the power to control sea lanes that came with such a base. In contrast, in 1905, Britain withdrew its garrison from Barbados, while the naval dockyard at Port Royal was closed. The Royal Navy's North America and West Indies station was abolished in 1907, but restored in 1915.

The social dimension to American dominance could be very bleak. In 1912, the Americans sent Marines into Cuba as a whole in order to protect their extensive property interests in the face of a large-scale, mostly black, peasant uprising motivated by the strains of economic change, social pressure and political discrimination. The uprising focused on the plunder and destruction of property, but was brutally suppressed by the Cuban army, which forcibly removed peasants from the countryside and summarily killed large numbers of black men, possibly up to 35,000. Possible for Puerto Rico, annexation no longer appeared an option for Cuba, but, as in Mexico and Nicaragua, the disruptive consequences of American activity remained acute.

American power was dramatised in the new geopolitics of the Panama Canal, which provided a link for warships and merchantmen between the eastern and western seaboards of the United States, transforming what had been a barrier between them. The project, originally and unsuccessfully begun with French capital, had ended in 1914 as a triumph for American engineering and power, for, in 1903, Panama became an independent state carved out from Colombia under American protection, and, under the Hay–Bunau-Varilla Treaty, the United States gained control over what became the Canal Zone. This provided a parallel to British control over the Suez Canal, but one that was to be less problematic politically. To a degree, Panama was an instance of what some Americans had sought as a result of detaching Cuba from Spain.

Taken over by the Americans in 1904, the construction of the Panama Canal owed much to the combination of Caribbean labour, notably from Barbados and Jamaica, and the American army, which played a major role in its planning and organisation, as well as in providing a measure of protection from disease, in part using expertise gained from operating in Cuba. In 1901, building on the 1881 thesis of the Cuban doctor Carlos Finlay, Major Walter Reed, an American army doctor, confirmed that yellow fever was a mosquito-borne, viral disease; rather than being spread by other means such as contaminated water or bedding, a discovery that led to the draining of swamps in order to hit mosquito habitats. The engineering of the canal was formidable, and was seen in that light. Thus, Lake Gatun, a drowned valley near the midpoint, became what was then the world's largest artificial lake.

The Panama Canal, over which America retained control until 1999, was a key indicator of American dominance of the Caribbean, while the opening increased the strategic significance of the Caribbean in American naval plans, which, in turn, accentuated the need to defend the Canal Zone and the routes that focused on it. The British were worried about the impact of the Panama Canal, the Royal Navy being particularly anxious because, thanks to the canal, the American fleet could pass from the Atlantic to the Pacific, and vice versa, thereby greatly increasing American seapower. The Americans controlled the canal and the Canal Zone until the Torrijos–Carter treaties of 1977, named after the two presidents, superseded the 1903 treaty by guaranteeing that Panama would gain full control of the canal from the end of 1999. At the same time, America retained the permanent right to ensure that all ships were able to use the canal thereafter, so that there should be no equivalent to the Egyptian closures of the Suez Canal. The 1977 treaties were ratified that year by referendum in Panama, but faced criticism before being passed by the American Senate.

Prior to the opening of the canal, the threat of American intervention in 1902–3 had encouraged Britain, Germany and Italy to end their blockade of Venezuela in pursuit of unpaid debts, a situation very different to the French, Spanish and British pressure on Mexico in 1861–2 when the Americans had been able to do nothing. Separately, Germany had considered Margarita Island off Venezuela as a base but, in 1900, decided it was unsuitable. In contrast, the Charleston Navy Yard, established in 1902, supported American power projection into the Caribbean, where its navy took to holding regular manoeuvres. The Spanish–American War was followed by increased investment in the navy, which became the world's third largest after Britain and Germany, and it was a navy that was used. Warships carried a Marine expeditionary force to ensure a peaceful (albeit coerced) election in the Panama Canal Zone in 1908, represented the United States at the inauguration of a new Cuban president in 1909, and landed Marines there in 1912. In 1913, a policy of keeping three or four battleships in Mexican waters was followed as a means of supporting American interests in Mexico. The navy enabled the landing of Marines at Veracruz in 1914, and also the occupations of Haiti in 1915 and of the Dominican Republic in 1916.

Such interventions were in large part a response to instability, as with the Mexican Civil War that began in 1910, and the pronounced instability in Haiti in the early 1910s culminating, in 1915, with the mob lynching of the President in response to the execution of his opponents including a former president. The policy of interventionism reflected imperialist assumptions, but not a drive for territorial expansion. At the same time, American power and influence, political, economic and cultural, lessened that of other powers, for example those of France and Germany in Haiti, as well as overshadowing the regional strength and role of the Royal Navy.

American interventionism was a matter in part of a progressivist ideology linked to improving Caribbean societies, not least by ensuring political stability, economic improvement and financial security. Control over local customs revenues and police forces were part of the equation.

FIRST WORLD WAR

American interventionism in the Caribbean became more pointed as a result of concern about German policy in the First World War (1914–18), which was a reason for the intervention in Haiti. American neutrality, under strain from German submarine warfare on international trade, was made more so by worries about German interest in the Caribbean, where Germany in 1902–3 and 1908 had deployed warships in order to pressurise Venezuela. During the First World War, there were fears of Germany encouraging Mexican opposition to the United States, which was one of the reasons for American entry into the war. In 1917, when America first broke off diplomatic relations with Germany (3 February) and then declared war (6 April), it pressed other neutral countries to follow suit, and many did so, Cuba and Panama declaring war on 7 August, and Guatemala, Nicaragua, Costa Rica, Honduras and Haiti following suit in 1918. Venezuela under its pro-German president, however, remained neutral, as did Colombia and Mexico.

The British and French colonies had been involved in the war from the outset in 1914, and were hit by the serious human, social and economic strains of the conflict. Thus, as a result of the conscription imposed in 1913, Guadeloupe and Martinique produced nearly 13,000 troops, and suffered many casualties. Members of the British West Indies Regiment experienced racial discrimination, which led to a mutiny in December 1918 at Taranto in Italy. This was to contribute to black nationalism in the Caribbean. Moreover, wartime strains, which contributed to strikes in the British Caribbean in 1917–18, encouraged an increase in nationalism, as in Jamaica, where the experience of wartime racism was significant, and also in British Honduras (Belize) and Trinidad.

As there were no colonies or allies of the Central Powers in the Caribbean, the war saw no related conflict on land there; nor any territorial change, bar the American purchase of the

Danish Virgin Islands in 1917. This was a measure in part motivated by the war against German submarines, although that was not the sole factor, as America had earlier sought to acquire the islands, most recently in 1902, when Denmark's Parliament refused the sale.

Jazz

The combination of syncopation, improvisation, ragtime and the blues was to be crucial to jazz, which developed in New Orleans and drew on local music making, for example by the talented cornetist Buddy Bolden, as well as on the national popularity of ragtime by 1910. Jelly Roll Morton, who was presented as the 'inventor of jazz', released the 'Jelly Roll Blues' in 1915. New Orleans in that period was a hardworking city focused on the docks, but one also devoted to pleasure. From 1898 to 1917, there was a legal red-light district in the city called Storyville.

AMERICAN INTERWAR POWER

The interventions to protect American interests in Haiti and the Dominican Republic, from 1915 and 1916 respectively, led both to a measure of accommodation by sections of local society, notably élites and emerging middle-class groups, and to continuing nationalist resistance. Popular guerrilla movements in the 1920s proved able to limit the degree of control enjoyed by occupying American forces who found that rebel ambushes restricted their freedom of manoeuvre. American bombing was no substitute, especially in the face of guerrilla dominance of rural areas at night. However, the Americans were not defeated in pitched battles, and, in 1922, the guerrillas in the Dominican Republic conditionally surrendered, American forces leaving two years later. Instead, created by the American occupiers as a way to help maintain both order and their interests, the *Guardia Nacional* became a key force.

American influence remained central. *The Times* on 9 December 1929 described Major-General John Russell, the American high commissioner in Haiti from 1922 to 1930, as the 'real ruler', and not Louis Borno, president from 1922 to 1930. Russell, indeed, selected Borno's replacement, Louis Roy. Moreover, the commander of the army (formerly National Guard) in the Dominican Republic, Rafael Trujillo, who became dictator there in 1930, a verdict endorsed in an election in which he received, depending on accounts, 99 per cent of the votes or more votes than there were voters, was aligned with the United States. He used force and terror to entrench his vast fortune, corruptly acquired, and, in 1937, in order to strengthen his position, had the Haitians living in the country killed in the Parsley Massacre, which was an instance of a long-standing rivalry between the two halves of the island, one that underlined the extent to which black–white differences were not the sole basis for tension. Between 12,000 and 35,000 people were murdered.

The Americans dominated the region militarily, not least due to their naval power and to the operational effectiveness of the Marine Corps. Thus, in December 1929, 350 marines were sent on the cruiser *Galveston* from Guantanamo Bay to support American operations, while in April 1931, the Sandinista siege of an American-hold position near the Caribbean coast of Nicaragua led to the dispatch of Marines from the Panama Canal Zone on the *Asheville*, and the light cruiser *Memphis* was sent from Guantanamo Bay. The American withdrawal from Nicaragua in 1932, bringing to an end a commitment that had been expanded in 1926, and also from Haiti in 1934, owed much to a sense of the intractability of the local situation and an unwillingness to devote more resources; but the ability to leave the situation to supposedly friendly national governments and militaries was important, while America's strength and regional presence provided an opportunity to intervene anew if required.

In line both with longstanding themes and with the greater conservatism of the 1920s, American attitudes to Caribbean society were apt to be inflected by a habitual racism, both toward blacks and Hispanics. 'Anglos' were presented as heroes. This was so even in films and novels that sought to be more sympathetic as with the Cecil B. DeMille, Paramount Pictures production of *The Buccaneer* (1938), which was based on Jean Lafitte.

THE BRITISH CARIBBEAN

With their empire seriously overstretched, economically, financially and politically, after the First World War, the British made no comparable effort to project their influence into Central America nor the independent Caribbean islands, but, instead, sought to retain control of their colonies without having to devote many resources to that end. Strikes in 1919 helped underline the apparent volatility of the situation. In the most populous colony, Jamaica, administrators and officers had for a long time been concerned as to how best to maintain control with a very small force, and the military strength available was seen as the crucial support of a moral authority on which rule rested. The extent to which this authority was accepted by the colonised in the nineteenth century should not be exaggerated; but there is little doubt that it was under far more challenge by the interwar years, in part because the war had encouraged a sense of separate, alongside imperial, consciousness. Colonial governors, however, with their support for equality, notably in the administration of the law, tended to represent an imperial consciousness different to that of settler élites who tended to advocate white superiority, and in all respects. The pattern of sentencing in homicide trials reflected this tension. Alongside difficulties in this relationship, the longstanding jockeying between executive and legislature, came pressure for an extended franchise.

Hégésippe Légitimus (1868–1944)

Légitimus was a Caribbean socialist whose career testified to changes in the French Caribbean. Only the second black deputy elected to the French National Assembly (the first was in 1793), he was one of the founders of the Socialist Party of Guadeloupe, serving in the National Assembly in 1898–1902 and 1906–14 and as Mayor of Pointe-à-Pitre from 1904. The decline in sugar prices after the American Civil War hit living standards in the West Indies. Opposed to the white settler class and to the dominance of Guadeloupe's business and politics by mulatto interests, Légitimus pressed forward black concerns, and is commemorated on the island with street names, plaques and a bust.

SOCIO-ECONOMIC TRENDS

The global Depression of the 1930s reduced investment for colonial development, limiting the resources available to provide jobs at all levels, while the rapid decline in markets for colonial goods such as sugar hit local economic systems, cutting off credit and investment. As a result, social tensions became more potent, including disturbances on Trinidad sugar estates in 1934, a general strike of agricultural workers on St Kitts in 1935, labour disturbances in Jamaica that year, and related issues in British Honduras and Barbados. The scale of protests increased from

1937, when there were riots in Barbados and Trinidad, and there were numerous deaths. Similarly, there were major strikes in Cuba in 1930, 1933 and 1935, and disturbances on Martinique. On Jamaica, where unemployment was high, tensions to a degree were linked to activism by trade unions and the League of Coloured Peoples and, in 1938, helped cause a major crisis including rioting. Trade union politics became more significant, and there was pressure for political change. The Moyne Commission that reported in 1939 on the situation in the British colonies criticised the land-tenure system and recommended the federation of the colonies, social welfare and development payments from Britain; but did not back universal suffrage. The outbreak of the Second World War, however, diverted attention and lessened tensions.

Rastafarianism

A religious and social movement that began in Jamaica in the 1930s, offering identity and meaning to the poor and a criticism of a colonial culture derived from Britain and conventional Christianity. The name came from Ras Tafari, the pre-coronation name of Haile Selassie, ruler of Ethiopia (1930–74), and there were important links to what was, until its conquest by Italy in 1935–6, the only non-colonised country in Africa, including iconography, colours and Old Testament references to religious orthodoxy. Pan-Africanism, drug culture and, eventually, reggae music became part of the mix and led to serious cultural tensions in Jamaica in the 1950s, although these became less significant from the 1970s. Moreover, from the 1980s, Rastas became less numerous in Jamaica, in part due to the rise of Pentecostalism.

Economic trends interacted with differing experiences in particular areas. These led to movement in search of work, as earlier from the British Caribbean islands and Martinique to build the Panama Canal. Large numbers of pretty desperate Barbadians and Jamaicans sought work on the canal, and, as with other workers from the islands, had higher death rates than the whites because they were left to set up shanty dwellings in the jungle and received poorer quality food. The British islands also produced workers for the Cuban sugar industry, its important Central American banana counterpart, the rapidly expanding Venezuelan oilfields round Lake Maracaibo, and the oil refineries of Curaçao and Aruba. Money brought or sent back from Panama and elsewhere was a major factor in the history of the eastern Caribbean as it enabled many to qualify for the vote for the first time, and thus helped to further political modernisation.

In addition, between 1900 and 1930, about 200,000 Haitians moved to Cuba where there was more work and better pay, while Haiti was hit by greater political disruption, including the social strain stemming from the rise in food prices linked to the deployment of American Marines from 1915 to 1934. In Cuba, such contract labour was a substitute for slaves and indentured labour, and was particularly important for the sugar and coffee plantations, but immigration fell foul of local hostility, notably against blacks. Banned in Cuba in 1931, this immigration led to large-scale deportations, notably to Haiti and Jamaica. West Indian immigration into Venezuela and Central America was also banned.

Tourism

The interwar period saw a marked rise in tourism, albeit one that was affected by the Depression. Alongside the improvement in steamship services came the development of air services, first private flight and then scheduled services. A cult of the sun helped, with tans seen as an aspect of vitality. By 1938, there were over 100,000 visitors a year to the West Indies. Cuba built an airport for Havana in 1929–30. The first aircraft to land in Barbados did so in 1939, and the passenger service there began the same year.

CUBA

American power had played an insistent role in the 1900s and 1910s, and, in 1919, the prohibition of alcohol in the United States was followed by a boom in American tourism to Cuba, with Havana attracting most visitors. American investment financed hotels and other developments, again especially in Havana. In 1924, however, Gerardo Machado, a general of the War of Independence, was elected president on the slogan 'Water, roads and schools', and, in part, on the platform of limiting American intervention. He initially benefited from the economic growth of the 1920s, notably with sugar exports to the United States, for example to supply Hershey chocolate bars and Coca-Cola. The wealth of the period can be seen in buildings such as the large *Iglesia del Sagrado Corazón* in Havana, built between 1914 and 1923, the National Capitol, the seat of the Parliament, opened in Havana in 1929, and the *Antiguo Ayuntamiento*, the government buildings in Cienfuegos built in 1929.

At the same time, most wages were low and education, health and housing for the bulk of the population were limited. In addition, there was widespread corruption. In spite of a promise not to stand for re-election, Machado did so in 1928, and became increasingly authoritarian, with his government responsible for the murder of opponents, notably students. The Depression slashed the already precarious value of the sugar crop and accentuated the crisis, and, in response, the Americans in 1933 sought to stabilise the situation by finding an acceptable replacement to Machado. Confronted by a general strike, and, crucially, by a developing loss of military support, he fled in 1933, dying in Miami six years later.

A provisional government, under Carlos Manuel de Céspedes y Quesada, only held power briefly, but was overthrown that year by the Sergeants' Revolt, a coup led by Fulgencio Batista, that led to the presidency of Ramón Grau, while Batista became head of the army, which was increasingly the centre of power, whoever was president. 'Fierce riots in Cuba' were in the British morning paper of the fictional Mrs Bertram in Alan Melville's novel *Weekend at Thrackley* (1934), although she domesticated the item as 'Some sort of a to-do in Cuba.'

Grau introduced reforms, notably the nationalisation of the American-owned Cuban Electric Company, and a rise in the minimum wage, and in 1934 abrogation of the Platt Amendment defining American dominance, as in a 1901 amendment to the Cuban constitution. American pressure, however, led Batista to overthrow the reformist Grau in 1934, replacing him with Carlos Mendieta. In a pattern reminiscent of many Latin American politicians in the early twentieth century, Batista talked about progressive policies, indeed of a miniature Cuban version of a New Deal, and, even more, of Getúlio Vargas's *Estado Novo* (New State) in Brazil; but, in practice, attainment was limited and corruption serious. It had received an important boost when Prohibition meant that Havana became a major site not only for alcohol production but also for its smuggling into the United States.

Cuba in *The Ghost Breakers*

Based on a 1909 play that was turned into 1914 and 1922 films, the 1940 horror-comedy version of *The Ghost Breakers*, with Bob Hope and Paulette Goddard, presents a heroine who inherits a plantation with its abandoned mansion on a small island off the Cuban coast. A dubious Cuban solicitor is shot dead in New York, while a ghost and a zombie are part of the action in Cuba, and Morro Castle is shown in the background when the protagonists enter Havana by sea.

SECOND WORLD WAR

Again, with no Axis colonies in the Caribbean, the Second World War in some respects was a reprise of the First World War, with no fighting on land, but the situation was made different by the German conquest of France in 1940, which gave the German navy the opportunity to pursue its *Weltpolitik* from Atlantic bases. Moreover, the attitude of the authorities in the French colonies became of note. Initially, they backed the collaborationist Vichy regime.

Fu Manchu in the Caribbean

Villainy of a different source was seen in *The Island of Fu Manchu* (1941), a Sax Rohmer novel in which the villain operates a submarine base from the crater of a dormant volcano in Haiti. First serialised in *Liberty Magazine* from November 1940 to February 1941, the target for Fu Manchu is the American navy, and he is tracked down by his long-time British opponent, Sir Denis Nayland Smith, to Haiti

---

where voodoo mysticism (there is a chapter on 'The Zombies') backs Fu Manchu's diabolical technology. The Panama Canal plays an important role in the action, as does the villain's search for treasure in Haiti. The plot is a jumble, with Fascism playing a role, but also rivalry within the evil Si-Fan organisation.

Again, America was neutral at first. Yet its alignment was clearly indicated in September 1940 when it provided surplus destroyers to Britain in return for ninety-nine-year leases on bases including in Antigua, the Bahamas, Jamaica, St Lucia and Trinidad, bases that were to be the source of an important extension of American influence on Caribbean life. Moreover, concern about the German naval build-up, as well as about Japan, encouraged America to do the same; and its naval build-up was far more significant for the Caribbean.

The German declaration of war on America on 11 December 1941 was followed by a German submarine campaign in the Caribbean where most of the independent powers had automatically followed the United States: Cuba, the Dominican Republic, Guatemala, Nicaragua and Haiti declaring war on Germany that day, Honduras the next, and Panama and Mexico in 1942; although Colombia did not follow until 1943, and Venezuela not until 1945. These moves represented the failure of significant German attempts to weaken the United States in its backyard, although these had focused on South America, and not the Caribbean. Once they joined the war, none of the Caribbean states played a significant, let alone crucial, role; but they offered bases for the United States, as well as room to operate against submarines.

Aimed principally at oil movements from Venezuela, but also hitting Allied shipping more generally, German submarine attacks inflicted much damage. The struggle proved difficult in

1942, with nearly 300 ships sunk, as well as the shelling of the refinery on the Dutch island of Aruba, which was a key processor of Venezuelan oil. Moreover, the movement of bauxite, a crucial material in the production of aluminium, which was important to aircraft frames, was challenged. The sinking of shipping affected the availability of food on the British islands, the price of which rose.

The attacks led to the deployment of American forces, notably aircraft which threatened submarine movements on the surface. New air bases were established by, and for, the Americans in Cuba, the Dominican Republic, Haiti and Panama. Cozumel acquired an airport during the war. Air bases also served against submarine operations in the Atlantic and to protect the Panama Canal, the prime requirement for the Caribbean Defense Command created by the Americans in May 1941. The naval and air bases provided by the British were also developed and used. In response to the growing difficulties of operating in the Caribbean, the Germans moved their submarines to focus on the mid-Atlantic.

Alongside the building of the bases, which provided employment but caused labour disputes and could reflect racial tensions, as with the Panamanian reluctance to accept black Jamaicans, the British and Americans sought to control the region. The fall of the Netherlands to German invasion in 1940 was followed by British forces moving in to protect the Dutch West Indies from German takeover. These troops were freed for other duties when replaced in February 1942 by the Americans. The latter also served to block the Venezuelan wish to send troops and thus give force to their territorial interest: in 1929, Venezuelan rebels had seized Fort Amsterdam on Curaçao.

Vichy-controlled Martinique and Guadeloupe were block-aded by the British, preventing the movement of French warships there; a blockade taken over by the Americans after they entered the war. However, because the French high commissioner, Admiral Georges Robert, did not make any threatening moves, there was no invasion or bombardment, unlike with the successful British invasion of Madagascar in 1942. In mid-1943, Vichy control was ended without invasion and due to local pressure.

The Americans and British allied with local dictatorships, notably those of Cuba's Fulgencio Batista, the Dominican Republic's Rafael Trujillo and the Haitian oligarchy, and helped them by purchasing their goods, thus securing export markets despite wartime disruption. The Americans bought Cuba's entire sugar crop. The dictatorships not only allied with America and Britain but also proved willing to accept Jewish refugees from Europe.

In a different, democratic context, and against a background of violent discontent in the 1930s, Puerto Rico's links with America were strengthened, which looked toward the granting of US Commonwealth status. The *Partido Popular Democrático* of Luis Marín, encouraged by Governor Rexford Tugwell, offered a model not seen elsewhere on the islands, where change occurred as a result of the war, but not really democratisation.

The link between the victorious allies and the dictatorships ensured that there was an essential stability in the Caribbean, one that during the Cold War was to be translated into American links with the clearly anti-Communist dictatorships. This looked toward a continuity that lasted until the decade beginning with the overthrow of Batista in 1959. In contrast, there was far less continuity in South or South-West Asia or in Eastern Europe.

This period saw an engagement of the Caribbean colonies in the wider war. Thus, about 16,000 West Indians volunteered for service, many in the Caribbean Regiment, which was sent overseas in 1944, seeing service in the Middle East and Italy, while others joined units in Britain. Some of these men faced racism that helped sharpen their political awareness. There were many other effects of the war, ranging from the dispatch of refugees from Gibraltar and Malta to Jamaica, to the location of American units in the British Caribbean, which contributed to the redirection of attention there onto the United States. Shipbuilding expanded considerably in New Orleans, including the building of Higgins boats (amphibious landing vessels) and PT boats (patrol torpedo boats).

COMPARISON

The contrast between the Caribbean and the power politics of the East Indies was particularly clear at the outset of the period. The Dutch in the 1900s greatly extended and enforced their control in the latter. In 1906, when they intervened in South Bali, the two ruling *raja* families fought their final battle (*puputan*) at Den Pasar and Pamĕcutan, being slaughtered as they advanced in the face of Dutch firepower. In 1908, when the Dutch attacked the Dewa Agung of Klungkung, he staged his own *puputan*. In Sulawesi, in 1905–6, Dutch power proved effective against both developed states, in the case of the Bugis and Makasarese, and against the head-hunting Toraja. Resistance to Dutch rule in Borneo and Sumatra was defeated in the 1900s. As a result, the East Indies were more under European control by 1910 than they had ever been, with the Dutch enjoying a dominance greater even than that of Spain in the sixteenth century; although the Dutch position owed much to good relations with Britain for which Spain had no counterpart, either in the sixteenth century or in the early twentieth.

The East Indies essentially under one power was an area subject to Western commercial penetration and to related economic development, notably of oil in Borneo and Sumatra. There was no immediate equivalent in the Caribbean, but growing American economic dominance provided a parallel. This dominance was not challenged during the Second World War in which, instead, the American political and military role in the region increased, in large part, and certainly so in 1941–2, as a response to anxiety about German plans. In contrast, the rapid and total conquest of the Dutch East Indies (as well as of the British positions and the Portuguese in East Timor) by Japan caused a completely different situation during the war and was to have post-war consequences greater than those in the Caribbean in either world war, and only really comparable in the very different circumstances of Haiti and Cuba after the respective earlier overthrows of French and Spanish rule in 1791–1804 and 1898.

10

The Cold War, 1945–90

*The Caribbean Comes to Washington: The
Truman Assassination Attempt*

Pro-independence activists in Puerto Rico were largely peaceful, but there were violent episodes from 1935, with assassinations on the one hand and police massacres on the other. In 1950, there was nationalist violence in Puerto Rico including in the capital, San Juan, as well as an assault in Washington on Blair House where President Harry S. Truman lived during the renovation of the White House. The two would-be assassins attacked the police officers protecting the house. In two brief exchanges of fire, a police officer was killed, as was one of the assailants. The other was sentenced to death, but Truman commuted this to a life sentence.

Truman backed a referendum in Puerto Rico in 1952 in which 81.9 per cent of the return supported continuing as a US Free Associated State as enacted in 1950. The independence movement saw this as a continuation of colonialism, not least as there was no option in the referendum in favour of independence. In 1954, five Congressmen were wounded in Washington when nationalists fired from the visitors' gallery in the House of Representatives.

American dominance was the key theme in the Cold War, but both dominance and the Cold War were divided into two very different phases in the Caribbean as a result of the Cuban Revolution that led to Fidel Castro gaining power in 1959. That was not an inevitable development, but it came to condition a lot of the discussion of the region in the outside world.

The Second World War entrenched American dominance, not only as the key victorious power, but also because the other colonial empires were much weakened by the war; while both the war and America's continuing and highly obvious economic and financial strength encouraged the focus of regional links on the United States. Although far more was involved, American dominance was in part expressed by the retention of bases in British colonies, as well as by continuing alliances with corrupt dictators, as with Cuba, the Dominican Republic, Nicaragua and Venezuela, where Marcos Pérez Jiménez, an army officer, became a member of the junta that seized power in 1948 and was president from 1952 to 1958. The Americans showed in Guatemala in 1954 that they were not prepared to allow independent governments, or indeed states, to move in a leftwards direction; although the intervention there that led to the overthrow of the reformist government of Jacobo Árbenz was a matter of the US Central Intelligence Agency (CIA) and local allies, rather than the American military. Moreover, the strong dependence of Britain, France and the Netherlands on the United States for their security did not encourage them to challenge American views, while, with their focus on Asia and/or the Muslim world, these imperial powers had only limited interest in their Caribbean colonies.

A Planter's Punch

A Planter's Punch is what Emilio Largo offers James Bond when they first meet in Ian Fleming's novel *Thunderball* (1961). A cocktail made of dark rum, grenadine syrup, sugar syrup, orange, pineapple and lemon juices, and Angostura bitters, it is usually served on the rocks. It allegedly was developed at the Planters Hotel in Charleston, but in fact originated on Jamaica, a rum island. As with other cocktails, the quantity of the ingredients is really a matter of individual choice.

THE CUBAN REVOLUTION

Cuba worked out very differently to Guatemala. Corrupt governments, under Ramón Grau (1944–8) and Carlos Prío Socarrás (1948–52), were followed in 1952 by Fulgencio Batista as a result of a coup that pre-empted the election of a presidential successor. Running third in the contest, he came to power with military backing, and the Americans rapidly recognised his success. Proving far less interested in reform than he had been when in power in 1940–4, Batista ran a spoils system, notably focused on Havana, which some saw as a Latin Las Vegas, although it was not a new city like the latter. Alongside American tourism, corruption thrived, with Mafia interests marshalled by Meyer Lansky, a major gangster known as the 'Mob's Accountant', correctly alleged to have become very significant. In 1946, the Havana Conference held at the *Hotel Nacional* consolidated the Mafia's interest in Cuba. Batista took a cut from the casinos and helped support their construction, profiting also from that. Gambling, racing and prostitution were to the fore, and each very much served the tourists.

Separately, the wealth, cars and attractive bungalows of the urban middle class, notably in west Havana, was a major contrast to the acute poverty of much of the rural population and of some of that of Havana. At the same time, Cuba before the revolution was one of the most developed countries in Latin America, a point Fidel Castro was to ignore. Indeed, Cuba was richer than much of southern Europe, which also had a lot of acute poverty. An imposing legacy of the period is the large statue of Christ overlooking Havana, commissioned by Batista's wife, Marta, and finished in 1958.

Castro, a young lawyer and an unsuccessful Congressional candidate in 1952, had launched a rebellion on 26 July 1953, but the attack on the Moncada barracks in Santiago failed, and many of those involved were tortured (a frequent practice of the secret police) or summarily executed. Lucky to evade capture for a while, Castro and his younger brother, Raúl, were tried and imprisoned instead, and, in 1955, after being released under a general amnesty, exiled. From Mexico he founded the *Movimiento 26 de Julio* and, in late 1956, invaded Cuba by means of a leaky yacht, beginning a guerrilla campaign in the Sierra Maestra mountains.

Although they sent ten Sherman tanks in 1957 (the British adding fifteen Comet tanks in 1958), the Americans failed to support the Batista regime against the insurrection. The regime was unsuccessful in its use of aircraft in the Sierra Maestra, where the insurgents presented a far more disparate target than the Marines who had unsuccessfully rebelled in the city of Cienfuegos in 1957, or than the activist urban movements of opposition to Batista, notably the *Directorio Revolucionario* under José Antonio Echevarría, which failed to assassinate him in 1957. Batista's military response crowded out alternatives to armed struggle. Castro's was not the only form of armed resistance to Batista, although he pushed aside, at the time and in memorialisation, other instances, not least those committed to liberal democracy.

Fighting in Cuba

'What you need against guerrillas are guerrillas ... It is rough country and there is no use sending tanks and heavy artillery up there.' Allen Dulles, the influential director of the Central Intelligence Agency, explained American options to the Senate Foreign Relations Committee in 1959 after Castro took over. The tanks supplied to Batista had not prevented the defeat of his demoralised troops in the battle of Santa Clara the previous December.

Castro benefited from the extent to which his insurrection was not yet seen by the American government as Communist. After victory by Castro's ally Che Guevara in the Battle of Santa Clara (28–9 December 1958), notably over a government armoured train, Batista fled before the advancing rebels with his extensive loot on 1 January 1959, and Castro entered Havana on 8 January. Having taken refuge in the Dominican Republic, Batista moved on to Portugal, dying in Spain in 1973, possibly thus pre-empting an assassination attempt by Castro's agents.

Although a stop-gap government, with Manuel Urrutia as president, held power for several months in 1959, harsh repression of those opposed to Castro followed his triumph, whether or not they had been loyal to Batista. Castro was unwilling to restore democracy and rapidly turned against capitalism, as well as purging Havana of what was deemed anti-social, such as prostitution and casinos. Revolutionaries, such as Huber Matos in 1959, who complained about the Communist direction of the regime were arrested and imprisoned, and in Matos's case tortured. Castro's regime soon faced American opposition as it pushed through a socio-economic revolution, notably the nationalisation of assets, including land and the oil refineries, and also moved towards the Soviet Union, which was looking for allies in the Third World. In February 1960, there was the first Cuban–Soviet trade agreement, and, that October, Cuba nationalised all American businesses.

As a variant of the usual debate over the causes of the Cold War, it is sometimes claimed that Castro would not have moved in this direction had America proved less hostile; but the evidence, instead, suggests that authoritarian Communism reflected Castro's tendencies and views, and that he was a tactician in pursuit of a strategy to that end, rather than someone choosing between strategies. Conversely, although Castro later claimed to have been a Communist from the outset, we should be careful not to repeat the regime's own narrative. In 1960, he was certainly a nationalist and a power-hungry *caudillo* with authoritarian leanings. However much ideologically driven, the opening to the Soviet Union was definitely also a power strategy.

Our Man in Havana (1958)

Written by Graham Greene, who had visited Havana several times in the early 1950s, this black comedy of an espionage story is based on Greene's wartime work for MI6 and in particular on duplicitous German agents in Portugal. Among the characters, a local strongman, Captain Segura, draws on the Batista regime. The Castro regime permitted the filming of the story in Havana in 1959, to which Greene returned. In his short story, 'For Your Eyes Only' (1960), Ian Fleming offered a harsher view of the corrupt cruelty of the Batista regime, which is linked in the story to an ex-Gestapo officer.

In 1960, American-backed sabotage operations allegedly began, notably the destruction, with many casualties, of an arms shipment being unloaded from the freighter *La Coubre* in Havana harbour on 4 March. The incident was exploited by Castro like the explosion on the USS *Maine* in 1898 had been by the Americans. Some among the large number of anti-Castro exiles who had fled to Florida used aircraft to send supplies to opponents of Castro based in the Cuban mountains. However, in April 1961, President John F. Kennedy's failure to provide the necessary air support to a force of 1300 CIA-trained exiles was blamed for the total defeat of their invasion at the Bay of Pigs. Subsequently, there has also been a stress on the bureaucratic momentum that left the CIA unwilling to accept that the plan was based on misleading assumptions about the prospects of success, including that a popular uprising might occur. The newly elected Kennedy certainly allowed political concerns to overwhelm military considerations; but emphasising American choices, which is the standard American approach, underestimates the strength of resolve and numbers on Castro's side. Indeed, Dean Acheson, the Secretary of State, observed '25,000 Cubans are better than 1,500'. Castro also had more and better tanks, and had successfully infiltrated his opponents; while commanding his forces well, he was underestimated by the Americans.

The air dimension itself indicated the role of a number of factors. On 15 April, American aircraft, disguised with Cuban markings and piloted by Cuban exiles, bombed Cuban airfields, but this attempt to destroy the Cuban air force failed as the aircraft had already been moved and camouflaged. When the exiles landed on 17 April, they met damaging air attacks, while, the next day, bombers sent to open the way for the landing of the necessary supplies for the stranded invasion force were mostly shot down. The supplies never arrived, and the force surrendered.

Subsequently, the Cuban regime faced guerrilla opposition in the Escambray Mountains for a number of years, opposition, supported by the numerous exiles in Florida, that has largely been forgotten, although there is a relevant (propagandist) museum in Cienfuegos, which displays models of engagements. No one else was visiting when I went. The opposition was essentially overcome by the mid-1960s. The frontier between Castro's revolution and its opponents now lay outside Cuba, and was firmly policed by the regime. One aspect of this frontier was the hijackings of Cuban aircraft from 1958 and of American aircraft from 1961. The latter provided Castro with propaganda coups as well as the money gained from returning the aircraft. Such hijackings increased greatly in the late 1960s, but decreased from 1972, in part due to the introduction of metal detectors in American airports in 1973.

THE CUBAN CRISIS, 1962

Underestimating the strength of anti-American nationalism in Cuba itself, the Americans feared that the country would serve as the base for successful Soviet and Cuban subversion across Latin America, which was more accurate as an account of the intentions of Castro's lieutenant Che Guevara, and of attempts, notably in the Dominican Republic, Congo and Venezuela, than of the realities on the ground, as Che's total failure in Bolivia in 1967 was to reveal. The debacle of the Bay of Pigs was followed on 30 November 1961 by the authorisation by Kennedy of the CIA's Operation Mongoose, which involved covert American operations, including sabotage, in order to try to provoke revolt and thus the overthrow of Castro. Propaganda and assassination attempts were part of the equation and the operation was sustained until the end of 1962, although American plots to kill Castro continued thereafter. In 1961, USS *Oxford*, the first of America's spy ships equipped with radio interception devices, was used to intercept telephone communications from Cuba.

Meanwhile, the Soviets, who treated the Cuban Revolution

with great enthusiasm as a reprise of their own in 1917, decided to help counter American pressure. As so often with the role of external factors in Caribbean history, this was not simply due to events in Cuba, but reflected, instead, the serious deterioration in relations between the United States and the Soviet Union over the U-2 incident, developments in Berlin, and the failure of arms control negotiations. This deterioration helped lead to Soviet commitments to Cuba, both military and economic, commitments that, in turn, assisted Castro in defeating opponents within the revolution and driving his policies forward.

Believing, in part due to American naval exercises, inaccurate reports that an invasion of Cuba was imminent, maybe in order to help the Kennedy government in the November 1962 midterm elections, Nikita Khrushchev, the Soviet leader, decided to send nuclear missiles, plans entailing secretly dispatching 230,000 tons of materiel and sending 42,000 military personnel. Thanks, however, to effective American aerial surveillance, secrecy was lost and, on 4 September, the Americans warned the Soviets against deploying any significant offensive capability in Cuba. Khrushchev, nevertheless, persisted, keen to protect Cuba and to bring Washington within range.

On 14 October, a U-2 spy plane obtained proof that medium-range nuclear missile sites were under construction in Cuba, a breach of Khrushchev's assurance. Agreed on the need for a response to get the missiles, which were a clear threat, removed, American decision makers were divided on whether to launch a pre-emptive military strike. Concerned about the implications of such action, Kennedy determined on a blockade to stop the shipment of missiles, and both sides made military preparations, including for an American invasion of Cuba, which was to be preceded by a massive air assault. America was able to call on a range of Caribbean bases, including Guantanamo Bay (Cuba), San Juan (Puerto Rico), and Pensacola and Key West in Florida. The Soviets initially planned to deploy eight surface ships, four conventional submarines and seven missile-armed submarines to Cuba, but this plan was cancelled, and only the four conventional submarines (each with one torpedo equipped with a nuclear warhead with a capability similar to that of the bomb dropped on Hiroshima) were deployed. They were forced to the surface by the Americans. On 25 October, the blockade took effect and the Soviet ships carrying the missiles stopped. Having decided not to escalate the crisis, Khrushchev agreed to dismantle the missile sites in return for an assurance that there would be no invasion and the American missiles in Turkey would be withdrawn. The bellicose Castro was furious that he backed down, and this step was also criticised by China's Mao Zedong.

Confrontation, nevertheless, continued, with Cuba seen by the Americans as a Soviet base. From 1962, the Soviets operated 'research and survey' spy vessels in the Caribbean, sailing from a centre near Havana built in 1962–6 that had a state-of-the-art communication system. The first big visit of Soviet surface naval units was in 1969, when one cruiser, two destroyers, a nuclear submarine, two attack submarines, a submarine tender and a tanker began what became a pattern of visits that, in 1970, included a submarine depot ship.

Meanwhile, alongside moves against racism, and campaigns in favour of healthcare and literacy, Cuba became very much an oppressive, one-party state, and with a large number of political prisoners held in brutal conditions, while many were executed. This turn to autocracy was in response to a range of factors, including the Cold War, ideology, a determination to hold onto power and the difficulties of turning a movement into a government. There were tensions, however, with the Soviet Union until 1968, when Castro, threatened with severance from Soviet financial assistance, supported the Soviet invasion of Czechoslovakia. The regime's inefficient planned economy, combined with the American economic blockade, led to an economic crisis, as well as the beginning of rationing. For the people, rice and beans were the diet.

In response, in an attempt to mobilise support from a widely discontented population, the revolution was presented in an active programme of political mobilisation highlighted by Castro's lengthy speeches as an ongoing struggle for national sovereignty and anti-American nationhood. At the same time, large parts of the opposition and old élites had fled to the United States. There was support for Castro, notably from intellectuals (until the late 1960s) and sections of the rural population, the working class and black people, but this was a dictatorship with all the problems that entailed.

Ernest Hemingway and Cuba;
Leicester Hemingway and Jamaica

The difficulties in the relationship between Cuba and America were in part captured by Ernest Hemingway who had a house outside Havana from 1940 to 1960, during which time he wrote several novels there. Happy to praise the overthrow of Batista, his house and books were expropriated in 1961 after the Bay of Pigs invasion. Hemingway was a key aspect of the celebrity culture that had joined Cuba and America, one that ranged widely from literati to film stars, such as Errol Flynn and Lana Turner. Under Castro, the celebrities, instead, were left-wing Latin American cultural figures.

Seeking to employ the American 1856 Guano Islands Act, Ernest's younger brother, Leicester, founded New Atlantis on an anchored bamboo raft off Jamaica in 1964 as a source of funds (selling stamps) for his interest in marine research; but his claim was not recognised and, in 1966, a storm damaged the raft, which was then looted by fishermen.

In practice, from the 1970s, Cuba became an informal Soviet colony instead of being an American one. Indeed, when I visited a senior East German academic in East Berlin in December 1980, he showed me with pride a Cuban orange he had been given; while historian Simon Dixon's memory of a research trip to Leningrad in 1985–6 is of surviving on expensive Cuban grapefruit. The Cubans fought at great cost to advance Soviet Cold War goals in Africa, notably in Angola from 1975, when 36,000 troops were sent, to 1991, but also elsewhere, including in Ethiopia. This involved often brutal warfare including, in Angola, counter-insurgency operations, and led to casualties as well as discontent within Cuba itself, alongside giving the regime a role. Castro was enthusiastic about the commitment of Cuban troops who, speaking a similar language and often black people, could be popular in Angola, or at least presented as popular, and the Cubans helped pull the Soviets into the conflict there. General Arnaldo Ochoa, who fought in Angola and Ethiopia, became a popular hero, too popular for Castro who had him executed in 1989, charged with drug smuggling, which was an activity in which Castro himself was involved.

More positively, many Cuban doctors and teachers were sent to Africa. To Nelson Mandela, Cuban success over UNITA and South African forces in Angola and Namibia in 1988 'inspired the fighting masses of South Africa', but 'the great debt that is owed the people of Cuba' was one on which the latter, of course, were not consulted at all. Meanwhile, in Cuba, the secret police maintained the megalomaniacal Castro in power, with the Committees for the Defence of the Revolution a form of surveillance of the people, by the people, for the dictatorship.

What Castro Had for Breakfast

Quail eggs made for nice breakfasts for the 'Leader of the Revolution', while malnourished fellow-Cubans searche-drubbish bins or queued for the few things available. Castro was also a great fan of ice cream, able to eat ten scoops at a sitting. Demanding particular foods in short supply, such as elvers (baby eels), Castro was also prone to lecture kitchen staff on how best to cook, for example red snapper.

DOMINICAN REPUBLIC, 1965

As a consequence of Castro's success in Cuba, American policymakers became more anxious about the Caribbean, as well as Central and South America. In response not so much to the British imperial recessional as to concerns about Latin America, which were greatly magnified by fears about Cuba, America adapted its policies, not least offering sponsorship and support with the Alliance for Progress (1961) and the establishment of the Agency for International Development (1961) and, more questionably, the National Endowment for Democracy (1983). The first left the former British colonies to Britain, although Haiti was grouped with the Latin American recipients of aid.

Both the Cuban Revolution and the American response helped accentuate political tensions in the Caribbean. Easily surviving an effort by Castro to overthrow him, the brutal and corrupt Trujillo was assassinated in 1961 in a local conspiracy in which the CIA had been active. His son, Ramfis, sought to maintain power in the Dominican Republic after the poorly handled coup, but his unpopularity, combined with American pressure, led to his depar-ture. Political instability was not ended by the election in 1962 of

Juan Bosch and the left-wing *Partido Revolucionario Dominicano*, and in 1963, in the aftermath of a failed attempt by Bosch to overthrow François 'Papa Doc' Duvalier, the hostile dictator of Haiti, the military seized power, establishing a government known as the Triumvirate (1963–5). In turn, in 1965, 43,000 American troops and 1748 from the Inter-American Peace Force were sent into the Dominican Republic, in Operation Power Pack, in order to stop civil violence in part linked to interservice rivalry and the alleged but greatly overstated threat of a Communist takeover. In very different circumstances to the contemporary Vietnam commitment, the Americans succeeded.

The result was the establishment of an anti-Communist government, under Joaquín Balaguer, a figure from the previous corrupt Trujillo dictatorship, that was the beneficiary of fraudulent elections. Democracy was postponed until the 1990s. It was also delayed in Haiti, where Duvalier, a longstanding tyrant, was succeeded in 1971 by his son Jean-Claude, 'Baby Doc', who was also murderously brutal and totally corrupt. Large-scale rioting in 1985 led in 1986 to the dictator's departure, a measure encouraged by the US government of Ronald Reagan.

Britain, in turn, intervened in Anguilla in 1969, although this was a small-scale matter. Objecting to being governed as part of St Kitts and to being forced into a federation with St Kitts and Nevis, the St Kitts police were evicted in 1967, a referendum voted heavily for secession, and, in 1969, independence was declared. An interim British administration was rejected, but, on 18 March, twenty-two London policemen (to the amusement of the British press) and 300 parachutists, landing by helicopter, peacefully restored order. Anguilla was allowed to secede from St Kitts and to become a separate British dependency, and it continues to be a British overseas territory. In 1964, a crisis in the Panama Canal Zone, in which American troops fired on rioting Panamanians, led to a short-term breach in diplomatic relations, but the crisis was settled without further violence.

The Contrast of the Caribbean

'Prince's Club, in the foot-hills above Kingston, was indeed a paradise. Pleasant enough members, wonderful servants, unlimited food and cheap drink, and all in the wonderful setting of the tropics,' Ian Fleming wrote in *Octopussy* (1966), 'it was paradise all right, while, in their homeland [Britain], people munched their spam, fiddled in the black market, cursed the government and suffered the worst winter weather for thirty years.'

NICARAGUA

There was no crisis comparable to that in the Dominican Republic for over a decade but, in Nicaragua, the left-wing Cuban-backed Sandinista guerrilla movement gained power from the Somoza dictatorship in 1979. Seeking to ensure human rights and democratic government, President Jimmy Carter had wanted Anastasio Somoza to yield power to a moderate government able to hold fair elections, but Somoza refused. The end of American aid was followed by the Americans beginning negotiations with the Sandinistas, and then by Somoza's fall.

In a parallel with developments in Iran after the fall of the Shah in 1978-9, the Sandinistas, however, were not to fulfil Carter's hopes, and their alignment with Cuba led his successor, Ronald Reagan, to impose pressure that included the mining of its harbours and the secret arming, from 1981, of the Contras, a counterrevolutionary movement based in neighbouring Honduras. Although the Contras helped to destabilise Nicaragua, inflicting considerable damage, they could not overthrow the Sandinistas.

GRENADA, 1983

In contrast to indirect pressure on Nicaragua, the Americans successfully used their military in October 1983 in overwhelming strength in Operation Urgent Fury against Grenada, a former British colony and member of the Commonwealth, a step taken without consulting the British, much to the anger of Queen Elizabeth II, the head of state. However, the American intervention was facilitated by the active cooperation of several Caribbean governments, who formally appealed for help and sent police and troops to take part, notably Jamaica and Barbados, but also Antigua, Barbuda, Dominica, St Lucia, St Vincent, and St Kitts and Nevis. The Americans benefited from being given the use of the Grantley Adams airport in Barbados, and from intelligence gathered in advance of the intervention by members of the Barbados Defence Force.

American action was motivated by concern about Grenada's leftward move since a 1979 coup, and the possibility that it would lead to a Cuban and Soviet military presence, and there was a tendency to see Grenada as another Cuba. The island acquired strategic significance as a result of the development of the airport at Point Salines by the Cubans as an airlift base, with a 9000-foot (2750-metre) runway, able to support their interests in Africa and Central America. Without a joint-force theatre commander or the necessary preparation, the American operation saw inadequate inter-service coordination, which led, despite the rapid seizure of both Grenadian airports, to delay, as each service fought its own war, and to most American losses being due to 'friendly fire'. Originally built by the French, the bastioned Fort Frederick was bombed by the Americans. Despite the flaws in execution, the Cuban and Grenadian forces defending the island were totally defeated and the government was changed, with democratic elections following in 1984.

THE END OF THE COLD WAR

Initially, Mikhail Gorbachev, who came to power in the Soviet Union in 1985, was willing to defend Soviet interests in the Caribbean, and that year, in response to an American trade embargo of Nicaragua, he both increased economic assistance to Nicaragua and promised Cuba help if it backed Nicaragua against an American military attack. Subsequent Soviet disengagement from foreign commitments, however, led to a very different situation, and, in 1989, American diplomatic pressure led to free elections in Nicaragua that resulted in the replacement of the Sandinista government. That year, in a major show of force, the Americans were also able to invade Panama and to overthrow the drug-dealing Manuel Noriega regime without fear of external intervention. Instead, Guillermo Endara, the opposition candidate whom Noriega had fraudulently defeated, was installed by the Americans. The execution that year in Cuba of General Ochoa, intended to be head of the Western Army, and the imprisonment of José Abrantes, the Interior Minister, may have been linked to trying to deny America an opportunity to invade.

In 1990, greatly weakened by the end of over $4 billion-a-year's worth of Soviet economic assistance, including oil, Cuba, the principal means of Soviet action in the region, and, after the change in Nicaragua, the only country ready to defy the United States, declared a 'Special Period in Time of Peace' in order to deal with a national economic emergency. Measures included the encouragement of foreign investment, which was a marked rejection of Castro's priorities, and the introduction in 1994 of convertible pesos which could be exchanged for dollars at a rate of one to one, providing a way to secure dollars, limit inflation and ease tourism. In turn, in order to make it easier to receive remittances from Cuban exiles, in 2019 a ban on dollar transactions was ended and citizens were allowed to open accounts that could receive them. Currency manipulation by the state was matched by

the day-to-day corruption and black-market activity by the population that were central to survival in a dysfunctional socialist economy. On my first trip to Havana, I found rooms in museums
closed unless a gift was given to the custodians.

Decolonisation

Meanwhile, across much of the Caribbean in the decades from
1945, there had been other developments that owed nothing to
violence. This was especially true of decolonisation, which was
more peaceful than the situation in much of the world. The
French colonies, however, were incorporated into France as overseas regions in 1946, gaining representation in the National
Assembly and the same legal rights as French citizens. This was
part of a tradition in which France tries to make her overseas territories departments of the mother country, whereas Britain prefers
self-government and independence.

Under an agreement of 2010, the Dutch islands are part of the
kingdom of the Netherlands, but are separate countries, although
with their population enjoying full Dutch citizenship. In the
British and Dutch West Indies, there was not to be the military
rule seen in many former colonies in Africa and Asia. In part, this
reflected the smaller role of the military in the West Indies, but
the more well-grounded nature of the Caribbean societies, and
notably the presence of a large middle class, played a role. There
was also a commitment to the idea of improvement through
education, respectability and social uplift, one that drew on the
powerful matriarchal quality of households and on Christian
commitment. Through education, the islands managed to develop
a sizeable middle class that helped in the transition from colonialism to independence. The churches played a big part in this
through their establishment of a chain of colleges and schools
that helped to educate a segment of society. Castro told the British
ambassador in the early 1980s that, although he loathed Britain,

he loathed it a little less than other imperialist nations because, unlike them, Britain had left its colonies in a fit state to govern themselves.

In accordance with the Moyne Report of 1939, the British sought from 1945 to establish an inter-island federation, on the pattern of similar attempts in Africa and South-East Asia, not least protecting the smaller islands, but, in the face of disparate interests, the West Indies Federation (1958-62) failed. This was principally due to tensions over the degree to which a federation meant a powerful federal government, as Trinidad, the site of its headquarters, sought, or not, as the other major player, Jamaica, argued. In addition, there were economic and financial issues, as well as differences of personality. In 1961, with opinion there hardening against federation, the Jamaican government held a referendum that decided on secession from the Federation, and that led Trinidad to decide to do likewise.

Prior to that had come the move toward democracy, with universal adult franchise in Trinidad and Tobago from 1945 and Barbados from 1951, and local government made democratic, as well as a move toward full internal self-government, which was seen in Jamaica in 1959, and in both Barbados and Trinidad and Tobago in 1961. There were also changes in relationships between the islands, with the Turks and Caicos Islands and the Cayman Islands no longer dependencies of Jamaica from 1959. As a result, they were able to maintain their links with Britain when Jamaica became independent.

The failure of the West Indies Federation was followed by independence for Jamaica (1962), Trinidad and Tobago (1962) and Barbados (1966); and separate militaries accordingly. Under the Associated Statehood Act of 1967, Antigua, Dominica, Grenada, St Kitts–Nevis–Anguilla, St Lucia and St Vincent gained full self-government, while Britain remained responsible for external affairs and defence. Cohesion was limited and the states moved to full independence: Grenada in 1974, Dominica

1978, St Lucia 1979, St Vincent 1979, Antigua and Barbuda 1981, and St Kitts and Nevis 1983. After independence, the former colonies were linked in the Organisation of Eastern Caribbean States, which was established in 1981 and has more members and associate members than there were British colonies, including Guadeloupe and Martinique. Meanwhile, the Bahamas had gained independence in 1973 and British Honduras, as Belize, in 1981. However, in the face of territorial claims from Guatemala, the British provided an army and air force garrison for Belize.

SOCIO-ECONOMIC CHANGE

The agricultural economies of the Caribbean were affected by protectionism and preferential tariffs elsewhere, the European Union proving a particular issue, not least with banana imports. Moreover, employment was hit by precarious profit margins and mechanisation. There were also more specific issues. Thus, in the 1970s and 1980s *monilia* (blights) hit the production of cacao, notably in Costa Rica. In turn, the land was planted with bananas and, later, pineapple, although the latter posed environmental problems. These were both specific to particular plants, for example water requirements, but, more generally, a consequence of monoculture. Meanwhile, with European sugar-beet production providing effective competition, most Caribbean sugar plantations ceased to produce sugar and concentrated on rum and/or tourism.

The attempt to lessen dependence on plantation goods, and the need to support a larger population and greater social capital, encouraged economic diversification. Tourism, financial services and shipping have been crucial sectors for such diversification, but success has varied. New Orleans remains a key centre for shipping, while the Dominican Republic has developed impressive facilities, but other territories lack comparable harbours, in part due to geography and in part to a shortage of investment.

There were also transport improvements related to better road and air links, and both car and lorry (truck) use increased. A major development was the bridge over Lake Maracaibo in Venezuela. Opened in 1962 as the longest prestressed concrete bridge in the world, this ended dependence on ferries and also the sense of isolation from the rest of Venezuela, a sense that had led periodically to speculation that the region of Zulia would become an independent state. Oil wealth gave Venezuela opportunities for infrastructure lacking to most states, but they were to be squandered by the governments of Hugo Chávez (1999–2013) and Nicolás Maduro (from 2013).

As elsewhere in the Third World, there was large-scale urbanisation in parts of the Caribbean, and the grid-like colonial city centres were often swamped by development. The results varied. In some cases, the wealthy moved out to newbuild suburbs with running water, and there was also institutional movement. In these cases, there was also a crumbling of buildings and infrastructure in increasingly poor centres, as in Havana. In other cases, there was a rebuilding of central areas. Even more was planned. Thus, in Havana in the 1950s, José Luis Sert produced a set of plans to destroy much of Old Havana and replace it with tall concrete and glass buildings, although his schemes were never implemented.

With less wealth, in Caribbean cities there was far less urban development than in Pacific cities, and thus the urban fabric remained relatively unchanged with few urban high rises. Indeed, Atlantic-facing Miami is, as a financial centre, the Hong Kong of the Caribbean. There was generally no attempt to ensure housing quality or, indeed, to maintain what had been built. Urbanisation, moreover, saw only limited infrastructure provision and generally inadequate standards.

There were major problems in running economies dependent

on imports and in maintaining expectations of living standards and social welfare, not least in the face of rising populations, global economic competition and mechanisation, particularly in agriculture and food processing. Ambitious political and governmental policies did not help. As a result, there was generally a reliance on foreign sources or support. These varied, with Britain, France, the Netherlands and the United States providing support for current or earlier possessions; while the Soviet Union did so for Cuba.

International bodies also provided part of the help for Caribbean islands, notably, although not for Cuba, the International Monetary Fund (IMF), but its assistance came with requirements, and these led to political issues. Thus, in 1980, an IMF agreement that required wage freezes and cuts to welfare led to protests in Jamaica, and the agreement was then abandoned by the government. Between 1981 and 2013, Jamaica defaulted on its bonds four times and restructured foreign loans eight times.

Emigration was part of the equation. It had been an important part of Caribbean life since the end of slavery, but the movement of people thereafter had been largely within the Caribbean region. After the Second World War, in contrast, there was large-scale movement to the imperial metropoles, including, for Puerto Ricans, New York, although it also attracted large numbers of immigrants from the Dominican Republic and Jamaica.

Meanwhile, and again creating new networks for Caribbean families, the West Indian diaspora in Britain grew significantly from the arrival from Jamaica of the *Empire Windrush* in London in 1948, largely as a response to labour shortages, notably in foundry work, nursing and on the buses, shortages that led to an active sponsorship of immigration that accorded with Commonwealth idealism, although the immigrants often met with a racist response, particularly with the Notting Hill

Riots in London in 1958. Some of those who arrived in the 1950s and early 1960s planned to save money in order to buy land in the West Indies and return; but most only gained low-paid jobs and never earned enough. French financial support for its former colonies is in part designed to limit emigration to France.

TOURISM

Millions of Tourists in the West Indies

1959	1.3
1965	3.9
2007	17.0
2013	25.0

Much of the benefit of tourism was to foreign companies and spent on imported foreign products; while, alongside tourism providing employment, much of this was low-wage, and the rise in land prices had consequences for local housebuilding. Pressure on the environment is also serious, including water usage and sewerage.

James Bond in the Caribbean: The Novels

An enthusiast for the Caribbean, living part of the year on Jamaica at his house Goldeneye, Ian Fleming introduced his readers to it in his second novel, *Live and Let Die* (1954). Bond travels to Jamaica and is briefed about the Isle of Surprise, an offshore island recently purchased by Mr Big: 'Since 1950 Jamaica has become an important strategic target, thanks to the development by Reynolds Metal and the Kaiser Corporation of huge bauxite deposits found on the island ... the activities on Surprise might easily be the erection of a base for one-man submarines in the event of war.' Indeed, Reynolds had started to export bauxite from Ocho Rios in 1952 and Kaiser from Port Kaiser in 1953, while Alcan built an alumina-processing plant near its mines, and, from 1952, exported alumina from Port Esquivel. Duvalier, Trujillo and Castro were different examples of real Caribbean Mr Bigs.

Bond returned to the Caribbean in *Dr No* (1958), with the uncovering of a major conspiracy behind the guano-digging activities of Dr Julius No on the island of Crab Key, a fictional dependency of Jamaica that Fleming based on Inagua in the Bahamas, which he had visited in 1956. The Soviet-backed Dr No had been overriding the instructions sent to test rockets launched 300 miles away from the American missile-testing base on Turks Island, a British colony. The novel presented British control as precarious, with the Colonial Secretary drawing attention to an increase in self-determination, while Fleming writes of one bastion of colonial rule: 'Such stubborn retreats will not long survive in modern Jamaica. One day Queen's Club will have its windows smashed and perhaps be burned to the ground.' There were indeed disturbances in Jamaica in 1946, 1959 and 1960, but at the end of the book there is an impressive display of imperial power with a British warship and troops sent to Crab Key.

In *Thunderball* (1961), the Anglo-American rocket base at North-West Cay on Grand Bahamas is SPECTRE's target; while in *The Man with the Golden Gun* (1965), the Mafia and the KGB are linked in Jamaica, with sabotage planned against Reynolds Metal, Kaiser Bauxite and Alumina in Jamaica, as well as against the Jamaican and Trinidadian sugar-cane crop in order to improve the sales position for Cuban sugar. Unlike at the close of *Dr No*, the officials are no longer British, and praise has now to be distributed at the behest of the independent government of Jamaica, which downplays Bond's role.

James Bond in the Caribbean: The Films

The feature-length films, which began with *Dr No* (1962), were subsequently to take the engagement with the Caribbean further, notably by providing a visual impression of opulence, particularly in *Thunderball* (1965), which depicted a world of luxury hotels, sumptuous villas, yachts, parties, open-air clubs and diving among coral. There were, however, other themes, notably the Cold War, as in the opening scene of *Goldfinger* (1964), which brought in Cuba and drugs; the latter also a theme in *Live and Let Die* (1973), much of which was set in the fictional San Monique, and in *Licence to Kill* (1989), which was set in 'Isthmus', in other words Panama. Cuba returns in the opening scene of *Octopussy* (1983) and in *Die Another Day* (2002). Providing, in its depiction, the idea of a frontier of civilisation and an opportunity for the malign conspiracy, voodoo played a major role in the film *Live and Let Die* (but not the earlier novel), which was given an additional setting in New Orleans.

In his first 1965 script version for the film *Casino Royale*, Joseph Heller began with a dynamic opening sequence, with a white dinner-jacketed Bond in the Caribbean stealing microfilm, triumphing at roulette, blowing up a submarine and winning the girl. In a later version of this frequently rescripted film, the villain is consumed at the end as lava escapes from a reactivated volcano.

Conclusions

Race continued to play a role in Caribbean life, but it was a changing one, in large part due to independence for former colonies, which, despite continuity in important respects, proved a transformative experience, and led to a very different social ethos and public history. Moreover, desegregation was important in the United States, although it was resisted. Thus, despite the 1954 Supreme Court *Brown v. Board of Education* ruling, Louisiana only desegregated its public schools in 1960.

In addition to the changing political context of the Caribbean, there were the many general demographic social trends of the period, notably major population growth, urbanisation, the decline of deference, the rise of individualism, and the greater significance of women and the young. In the Caribbean, the working out of these themes was in part a question of the development of what came to be seen as a distinctive culture, a distinctiveness which owed much in particular to the role of music in both the culture and the era. At the same time, while finding the culture attractive, tourists did not always grasp the character of life, the nature of social issues and the extent of problems.

Returning to the theme of comparison with the East Indies, the disruptive character of the Second World War helped encourage a violent post-war nationalistic opposition to the reimposition of Dutch colonial rule. When combined with Dutch exhaustion after the war and American hostility to the Dutch attempt, this opposition led to independence for what became Indonesia in 1949. There was to be no equivalent in the Caribbean, nor to the expansionism Indonesia subsequently achieved in western New Guinea and East Timor, and unsuccessfully pursued in north Borneo and Brunei. Nor, other than in Central America, was there to be an equivalent to Indonesia becoming a military dictatorship. As so often, the contrasts remind us of the extent to which the distinctive character of a region's development can best be understood in a comparative light.

11

The Caribbean Today, 1990–

A Rum Collins

In the Bond film *Thunderball* (1965), Emilia Largo offers Bond a Rum Collins, a cocktail consisting of light rum, lime juice, sparkling water and sugar. Ice, of course, is essential. It is a variant on the gin-based Tom Collins.

As the guns largely stilled in Central America at the end of the 1980s and the start of the 1990s, an emphasis on conflict as a central theme for much of Caribbean history became less appropriate. Indeed, the prime form of killing thereafter was that of a degree of criminality that challenged social norms and peace, and led accordingly to the deployment of troops alongside the police, as in Jamaica in 1999 and subsequently, leading in 2005 to an unsuccessful call for a merger with the police. Gangs linked to drug production and transport are a particular problem in the Caribbean, and notably so in Colombia and Mexico and everywhere in between. For both, relations with the United States are closely linked with drugs and related public order. Thus, the United States finances Colombia's fight against drug cartels. In Mexico, about 250,000 people were killed in 2009–18. The links between drug networks and society could reach to the top of the latter: in 2018, Tony Hernández, brother of the President of Honduras, a country with major problems in this sphere, was arrested in the United States on drug-trafficking charges.

A key aspect of the Caribbean's significance became that of a transit zone for drug flows to Europe and to the United States. Fast boats, light aircraft and, eventually, submarines criss-crossed the Caribbean to this end, and major states deployed warships in response, not least because the local navies were far too weak to do so and required assistance, including air support and intelligence surveillance, to that end. Drug trafficking was a new version of older established patterns of smuggling and piracy. Thus, part of the population of Providence Island was recruited by drug cartels for their navigational skills, and many as a result were imprisoned abroad.

There was also anxiety about the possibility of 'narco-states', with governments, or at least sections within them, providing cover for drug networks and obtaining money accordingly. The cause of the American invasion of Panama in 1989, this situation remained pertinent and helped explain American interest in the Caribbean and, in particular, in Colombia, as well as American concern about Venezuela. However, this concern owed more to the instability and anti-Americanism associated with the pro-Cuban, left-wing Chávez government, and its equally pro-Cuban, left-wing, successor government under Nicolás Maduro. The Venezuelan and Cuban governments have repeatedly provided classic instances of the presidentialism that could so readily compromise democracy and the rule of law.

REWRITING HISTORY: CUBA

Esta es la Historia (*This is History*, 1980) by Gilberto de la Nuez (1913–92) offers the history of Cuba all in one painting. Everything, including the landing of Christopher Columbus, the opening of the Spanish era, the blowing up of the USS *Maine* in 1898 and Castro's revolution, is simultaneous in the painting, forcing interest in what would otherwise be distant, and violence is a key theme.

Tourists visiting Cuba as it opened up found a public history that bestows virtue on the Castro regime, although with a backstory to the late nineteenth-century insurgencies against Spain. In contrast, there is hostility toward what is not favoured, for example in the inscription added to the memorial to the victims of the explosion on the USS *Maine*, an inscription that linked American imperialism in 1898 to the Bay of Pigs in 1961. Memorialisation, more generally, dwells on Castro's overthrow of the autocratic Batista regime in 1959, and not, of course, on the serious hardships suffered by much of the population under Castro's rule. The theme is of teleology in action thanks to heroism.

Housed in Batista's presidential palace, the *Museo de la Revolución* provides great detail on the Cuban revolution and exhibits on the 'Construction of Socialism'. Alongside the museum is the *Granma* – the boat that took Castro from Mexico to Cuba in 1956 to begin the revolution, military vehicles from the Bay of Pigs invasion, and a monument to those who died in the revolutionary struggle. The museum of the Ministry of the Interior depicts exhibits relating to the numerous assassination attempts made on Castro, as well as details of other CIA and Cuban-exile operations. A Cuban Sea Fury aircraft is on display outside the Museum of the Revolution. Seventeen had been purchased by Batista from Britain in 1958, and four of them saw service in opposing the Bay of Pigs operation. Santa Clara has a number of memorials to Che Guevara, while, in Cienfuegos, there is the monument to the Martyrs of 5 September 1957.

The Castro narrative, propagated through memorialisation and education, is the sole public history most Cubans now alive have encountered. Thus, the years after 1898 are denigrated as a 'pseudo-republic'. However, this account is challenged by family narratives and, linked to this, by the presence of an outer world that offers a very different perspective, notably in the United States where many Cubans have relatives who keep a close eye on the island.

REWRITING HISTORY: VENEZUELA

For Hugo Chávez, the populist president (r. 1999–2013), Simon Bolívar (1783–1830), the revolutionary who fought successfully for Latin American independence from Spain, and then faced domestic opposition, served as a powerful talisman and point of reference. In 1992, when he mounted an unsuccessful coup, Chávez stated that Bolívar was his inspiration. Later, seeking to position himself in history, Chávez, as president, claimed to be leading a 'Bolívarian revolution' against the 'empire', the latter no longer Spain, but now the United States. Ignoring the extent to which Bolívar was an Anglophile conservative, Chávez drew on him for his anti-US Bolívarian Alliance for the Americas. Chávez also claimed that immediately before he gained power, Venezuela had been weakened by a neo-liberalism he blamed on the United States.

In 2000, Chávez gave Castro a replica of Bolívar's sword, which, as part of the creation of a revolutionary heritage, was in turn given to the *Museo José Martí* in Havana, the museum of Cuba's liberation hero, José Martí. Killed in battle with Spanish forces in 1895, Martí was referred to by Castro in seeking to polish his nationalist credentials during his quest to overthrow Batista. The joint Chinese–Venezuelan communications satellite launched in 2008 was called the Simón Bolívar satellite by the Venezuelans, with Chávez proclaiming it a 'step towards sovereignty', but the satellite failed in 2020.

CRUISES

Despite its relative distance from non-American major centres of wealth, the Caribbean became one of the two major destinations for cruise passengers, the other being the Mediterranean. In 2019, out of an estimated 30 million cruise passengers, a third went to the Caribbean, which, in part, was a reflection of the ability of wide-body jet aircraft to deliver large numbers to the region at a cost that struck outsiders as cheap. Being to the warm south of the United States, the third most populous country in the world, was important, as was an accessibility by aircraft from Europe. The scale of activity was seen in December 2019 when two Carnival ships collided at Cozumel in Mexico, a major cruise harbour for Yucatán.

Entrepreneurial activity and receptiveness by Caribbean states was significant. In the first, the key element was the ability of cruise companies to order ships of an hitherto unprecedented size, with Carnival and Royal Caribbean being the major names. These ships could also be used because of the development of appropriate terminals, notably at Fort Lauderdale in Florida. Moreover, the companies sought with considerable success to make cruising attractive for the mass market and all ages.

In addition, Caribbean countries built facilities for the liners, as in the Dominican Republic and Yucatán. Whereas anchorages and quays had previously been for ships of a more modest size, facilities were developed in order to attract the big liners. Significantly, the island that was most reluctant to do so was Cuba, where, as in Santiago, good anchorages were not matched by appropriate docking facilities, and the ad hoc landing arrangements could be unintentionally amusing. This situation eventually led, in the late 2010s, to the expansion of the cruise port at Havana. In 2018, it had two berths, which in 2017 had welcomed 328,000 passengers, and there were plans for four more by 2024. In May 2016, Carnival's *Fathom Adonia* became the first American-based cruise ship to call on Cuba in over fifty years.

However, in June 2019, the Trump administration announced that it was cutting off all cruise travel from the United States to Cuba, as well as ending the popular people-to-people category of travel that allowed Americans to visit Cuba despite the embargo. As a result, whereas Cuba received 4.7 million international visitors in 2018, it had to revise down subsequent estimates.

European-based cruise companies could not make up for the American market, and no cruise ships visited Havana between 5 June and 30 October in 2019.

Resorts elsewhere were developed to satisfy cruise passengers. Thus, in 1986, Labadee, a beach in Haiti controlled by Royal Caribbean but surrounded by barbed wire, became a destination that by 2018 had over 700,000 passenger visits, with the government earning $12 for each. Customs, immigration controls and the use of Haitian currency were all not necessary. In 2015, Amber Cove in the Dominican Republic was similarly opened by Carnival. The Caribbean offered to passengers varied greatly. In Haiti, there was a mock village with a vodou show in order to provide a safe shore excursion. As in Haiti, concerns about passenger safety were seen on Jamaica.

Many tourists did not come to the region's islands but, instead, to its coasts, arriving by car or aircraft. Thus, in 2011, 8.75 million people visited New Orleans, putting $5.47 billion into the local economy. Florida and Yucatán were also particular beneficiaries of such tourism.

THE LESSER ISLANDS

Most tourism is, as has long been the case, to the eastern Caribbean; albeit with the southern (the former Dutch Antilles) and the northern/central, in the shape of the Dominican Republic and now Cuba, increasingly fashionable. The 'opening up' of Cuba in recent years has greatly encouraged the latter. That, however, leaves the western Caribbean as the island region that attracts fewest tourists. This area is best reached by boat, although it is possible to fly to Roatán in Honduras's Bay Islands. Roatán is distinctly different to mainland Honduras as, thanks to British rule and influence in the nineteenth century, including the deportation of St Vincent 'Black Caribs' in 1797, and migration from the Caymans from the 1830s, the population is overwhelmingly black, English-speaking and Protestant; although the mainland officials are the opposite. This is an instructive cultural frontier, one that is part of the Garifuna diaspora from St Vincent. There are islands to the east of Nicaragua that belong to it or to Colombia. To the north of eastern Panama, there are the over 400 San Blas Islands: the *Archipélago de las Mulatas*, home to the indigenous Kuna Indians, who have had a measure of autonomy since the 1920s, but are threatened by rising sea levels.

ISLANDS IN CRISIS: HAITI AND PUERTO RICO

The very different political circumstances of the Caribbean make cooperation between the islands difficult, but there can be marked similarities. The inroads of devastating earthquakes and hurricanes are one such, as with the earthquake on Haiti in 2010 and Hurricane Maria on Puerto Rico in 2017: the latter killed 2975, while Puerto Rico was hit by an earthquake in January 2020. Both islands suffer from financial crisis, with Haiti subject to the IMF, while heavily indebted Puerto Rico was declared bankrupt in 2017 as, with limited economic growth, it could not make its annual creditor payments.

At the same time, there is a major contrast due to the political context. Although Puerto Rico is an unincorporated territorial possession and not a state, Puerto Ricans have been citizens of the United States since 1917, which enables them to go freely to the mainland. In the 1950s, the Puerto Rican population of New York rose from 187,000 to 613,000. Moving to the mainland provides Puerto Ricans with an opportunity and safety net (including remittances from family members) that is lacking in Haiti where, in 2019, over half the population lived below the national poverty line of $2.41 a day. Yet, although Puerto Rico has the highest GDP per capita in Latin America, its poverty rate is higher than the poorest American state and there is serious unemployment.

In Haiti, the shortage of food and clean water is acute, while widespread corruption and gang violence are serious problems. The first democratically elected president, Jean-Bertrand Aristide, took office in 1991, only to be overthrown that year in a military coup. American pressure in 1994 led to the removal of the coup regime, and Aristide was president again in 1994–6 and from 2001, only to be removed in the coup in 2004. Large-scale violence followed, but a measure of stabilisation ensued under René Préval, president from 2006 to 2011, only for corruption and disorder to revive under Michel Martelly, president from 2011 to 2016. The political system is anarchic, with a multitude of political parties, no parliamentary majority, no budget passed since that for 2017–18, high inflation, and the president since 2016, Jovenel Moïse, ruling by decree, and with the legislative election due in October 2019 not held. Rising fuel prices caused unrest in 2019 and street protests linked to inflation have helped to accentuate the crisis of governance. Demonstrations have led to over 200 fatalities, with the security forces using live ammunition.

Cuba

The crisis of the collapse of Soviet support led to the economy shrinking by 35 per cent, to widespread power cuts and shortages, and resulted in Castro seeking international investment. Amidst crises in living standards, as well as public services such as transport, small-scale private enterprise was legalised, and in 1993 the dollar was declared legal tender. Although the American trade embargo was tightened, there was no overthrow of the Fidel regime, which went on being controlling in its mix of coercion and paternalism, and, indeed, it proved more durable than most Communist regimes. Alongside a propaganda war with America, economic shortages continued into the 2000s, but, again, the regime maintained power.

In 2008, Raúl Castro, who had been minister of the Revolutionary Armed Forces since 1959, formally took over the presidency from his sickly brother, who died in 2016. There was a measure of economic liberalisation under Raúl, but not of political freedom, and the economic changes did not constitute the reforms necessary to help provide a context for obtaining the foreign exchange of which Cuba is so short. The same continues to be the case under Miguel Díaz-Canel, who succeeded Raúl Castro as President of the Council of State in 2018, becoming President of Cuba in 2019, and, indeed, to an extent the post-Castro years as yet do not really appear to be a viable context for discussion of difference. None of the elections are contested. Born in 1931, Raúl Castro remains First Secretary of the Communist Party of Cuba, a post in which he succeeded his brother in 2011.

Surveillance, arrests, public shamings, job dismissals, travel restrictions and beatings are all part of governance, as are the intrusive Committees for the Defence of the Revolution established in 1960 and rationing, and its counterpart, the black market. In 2018, Decree 349 meant that permission from the Ministry of Culture was required before artistic works could be shown in public, and banned 'anything that violates ... the normal development of our society in cultural matters'. Protests against the new law led to violent arrests. Thus, repression continued alongside a loosening of economic restrictions. It was symptomatic of the situation that the artist Tania Bruguera was repeatedly arrested in 2014–15 after, as part of a performance art piece, she invited people to speak freely into a microphone in Cuba's *Plaza de la Revolución*.

The Chinese model showed that authoritarianism was less marginal on the world scale than it might have appeared in the 1990s, but it is unclear that the Castro legacy has much to offer the young, and the strain on living standards is readily apparent. So also with the social capital on which Cuba prides itself, notably the health service, as opposed to the social capital that evades it, such as a good sewage system and adequate roads. Exacerbated by drought, a shortage of investment has contributed to the poor infrastructure that leads to problems with the water supply, as on my first visit to Havana. Fuel shortages in 2019 led to a governmental cut in bus services and affected both industry and agriculture. The comparison as far as Cubans is concerned is with Cubans in the United States where many live in Florida, and not with the situation on other Caribbean islands. *Stampede* (2014), a photograph by Jorge Otero Escobar (b. 1982) that shows him acting out his anxiety, referred, as Cuba opened its border to the United States, to the challenge from its global culture.

Cuban Control

The use of doctors represents a classic instance of Cuban authoritarianism. A producer of large numbers of doctors, who could be trained at far lower cost and paid far less than elsewhere in the Americas, Cuba sent doctors abroad in order to gain goodwill, in fulfilment of its mission, and, increasingly, in order to wield influence and gain money. By 2015, there were 50,000 doctors and nurses abroad, many in left-wing states. In 2019, Cuba's medical services produced 46 per cent of its exports, and 6 per cent of GDP. Venezuela took 20,000 doctors and nurses and provided cheap oil in return. However, most of the doctors' salaries continue to be taken by the government, which also holds their passports in order to prevent them freely emigrating. Cuba's doctors abroad are in effect trafficked; and this is a new form of indentured labour in which they choose salaries and living standards that are higher than in Cuba. From 2006 to 2017, the United States offered these doctors permanent residency and over 7000 accepted, which was a major comment on Cuban society and government.

Geopolitics

Russia's position in the Caribbean was compromised by its own economic difficulties and by the weaknesses of its regional partners: Cuba and Venezuela. Both suffered from serious economic problems and mismanagement, and Venezuela was hit hard in the 2010s and early 2020s by the major fall in the price of oil. Its economic collapse led to large numbers of refugees, many of whom went to Colombia or Trinidad. The *Admiral Kuznetsov*, the only Soviet aircraft carrier, when deployed to the Caribbean, faced serious operational difficulties, notably with its engines and its deck landings.

In contrast, China proved more adept both at extending economic aid, for example to Antigua, Costa Rica, Dominica, Grenada and Jamaica, notably in infrastructure projects, and in creating a degree of resulting dependency. For Antigua, the key investment has been in power generation, and in Dominica a new airport and roads. Over $3 billion has been invested by China in Jamaica, leading to the building of the North–South Highway in 2013–16. The latter, however, has left Jamaica with a $730 million debt to China, while the Chinese developer collects a $32 toll for the 66-kilometre (41-mile) journey. Moreover, the children's hospital built for free in 2019–20 was constructed with a largely Chinese workforce, especially at the senior level. In 2016, a Chinese state-owned company bought the Alpert bauxite mine and refinery, which had closed in 2009, but it was closed again in 2019. That year, Jamaica was the tenth Caribbean country to sign on to China's Belt and Road Initiative, but it announced it would stop borrowing from China.

The impressive queues of ships daily waiting to go through the Panama Canal are fully laden when transiting from the Pacific northwards and westwards to the Caribbean, and carry East Asian goods to the United States and Europe. Geopolitics, indeed, is crucial to discussion of canal links from the Caribbean to the

Pacific. Plans for a canal across Nicaragua were renewed in the 2010s and, in 2013, Nicaragua accordingly signed a memorandum of understanding with the Hong Kong Nicaragua Canal Development Group. This established the basis for the construction and management of a canal for fifty years, and, in 2014, a 278-kilometre (173-mile) route was approved. However, the financing proved inadequate, and the project has not begun, although expropriatory land acquisitions have been pushed through by the Nicaraguan government.

China, moreover, shifted its investment focus to politically (and geologically) more stable Panama. There, the Panama Canal expansion project began operations with New Panama vessels in 2016. This ship classification was based on the new locks' dimensions. From 2018, the Canal Authority permitted ships with twenty rows of containers and a 51.25-metre beam and 15.2-metre draught. The entrances to the American East Coast ports of New York, New Jersey, Norfolk, Baltimore and Miami, as well as to Mobile, Halifax and Liverpool, were widened accordingly, thus underlining the wider significance of the Caribbean.

Despite Chinese moves, the Americans clearly remained the dominant players in the Caribbean and in benign ways such as hurricane predictions, as well as less welcome ones, such as drug imports. In 2020, economic and political pressure on Venezuela revealed a continued American presence. Regional tensions were shown in April when a Venezuelan naval patrol boat, the *Naiguatá*, sunk after ramming the *Resolute*, a cruise liner, off Tortuga, apparently unaware that in order to sail in Antarctic waters it had a reinforced hull.

CONTINUITIES

Very different economic opportunities seem almost integral to Caribbean life, and there is an ethnic dimension that is readily noticeable in some areas, for example Louisiana. At the same time, there is much else at stake, with two examples of note. In the Dominican Republic, prior to the coronavirus crisis, labour shortages were tackled in part by hiring workers from poverty-stricken Haiti, who were encouraged by being told of the money they would be able to remit back home. The reality, on the sugar plantations, is a form of slavery with armed guards policing the workers who lose their freedom, are poorly paid, and are forced to purchase food at overpriced company stores. On Cuba, as an aspect of a controlled society where, more positively, there is less economic inequality than in most of the region, the state workers, such as doctors and teachers, who are lauded in the government's ideology, are poorly paid, and then only in the official currency, doctors earning the equivalent of $50 a month in 2018; whereas those linked to the tourist industry benefit from hard-currency tips and therefore are better off. As a result, doctors and teachers took on additional jobs as taxi-drivers. Race, indeed, proves a less harsh master than the pressures of economic control and/or the role of the state.

Recent Crises

The global coronavirus crisis that began in 2020 followed on from the global financial crisis that began in 2008. The latter hit prosperity elsewhere, and thus reduced demand for Caribbean products, notably tourism, but also the sale of raw materials, such as bauxite from Jamaica. As a result of these issues, debt rose greatly, as in Puerto Rico, and/or was transferred via subsidies, as in the French islands. Jamaica signed an IMF agreement in 2010 but failed to reach the fiscal targets and the IMF terminated the deal, which helped to accentuate the flight of capital, a problem across much of the Caribbean. In 2013, when Jamaica's public debt stood at 147 per cent of GDP, one of the worst in the world, a new agreement was reached with the IMF, which included expenditure cuts and a three-year wage freeze for public-sector workers that was designed to limit inflation. By the time the programme finished in 2019, debt had fallen below 100 per cent of GDP and unemployment had fallen from over 15 per cent to under 10 per cent, with tourism helped greatly by the recovery of the global economy. At the same time, there were many problems for Jamaica before the coronavirus crisis that began in 2020. Growth was low, as was average income, which in 2019 was just under $5000, while a weak dollar hit companies dependent on imported goods or oil, infrastructure and investment remained inadequate, and corruption and crime were major problems. In 2018, tourism and remittances from Jamaicans abroad provided about 16 per cent of GDP, and this created significant issues when the new crisis began in 2020, while, more generally, the situation then was similar to that following the 1929 Depression.

Not only Cuba, Venezuela, Haiti, Puerto Rico and Jamaica had major difficulties prior to the crisis. There was a more general dependence in the Caribbean on international economic, and often political, links, whether in the form of tourism, shipping, finance, exports, oil prices or subsidies, and this dependence, itself a cause of precariousness as well as profit, was seen in societies that had considerable poverty as well as pressures on their social fabric. So also with Mexico, Guatemala and Honduras, which suffered from serious lawlessness, corruption, low growth, population flight and unstable politics; as in Honduras, notably from 2017, with the election of that year seen as problematic. In contrast, Costa Rica, Panama and the Dominican Republic had growth, thanks in large part to sound macroeconomic policies and to becoming effective service exporters able to benefit from the global economy.

The state of the economy was crucial not only to providing the necessary domestic demand to sustain activity, investment and productivity, but also to ensuring a significant middle class hopefully able to encourage consensual politics. In many countries, however, both elements were missing, and, against a background of criminality, politics was in tension between populists, who did not understand economics, and élites only mindful of their interests. Moreover, economic growth potential and rates were affected by the lack of natural resources in most islands, while the populations of all except the very largest are too small to support 'offshore' manufacturing plants, and the larger island countries, notably Cuba and Haiti, are not able to provide economic opportunities to the smaller. More generally, the lack of economic benefits of scale and linkage between the islands, widely seen during the colonial period due to protectionism, has continued into the post-colonial period. There is also the problem that while some locations work well as offshore financial centres and tax havens, the numbers employed in such activities are not large.

The 2020–1 coronavirus pandemic hit this already very difficult situation hard, as a fall in economic growth meant that income per person dropped, while the number of poor people increased. Depression came to the fore, and currencies fell in value, the Mexican peso dropping to its lowest ever level against the dollar. As in the Depression of the 1930s, external factors were very important, notably the American recession which hit the Caribbean economies hard, but so also with the accentuation of previous problems. The Venezuelan economy shrank more than 65 per cent in 2013–20, with the UN World Food Programme in April 2020 reporting that 9.3 million people were 'in need of urgent assistance', and 20 per cent of children under five were either 'acutely malnourished' or with stunted growth. Over 4.5 million people had left the country, but the COVID-19 pandemic hit the remittances crucial to families left at home.

On the islands, tourism had directly accounted for 15.5 per cent of GDP and 14 per cent of employment, but it stopped completely in 2020. So also with cruises. Indeed, in 2020, Carnival issued a bond with a dividend payment of 11 per cent, which, given near-zero interest rates, reflected a major crisis in confidence. Shipping more generally was affected, and Panama refused to allow any ship with confirmed coronavirus cases on board to pass through the Panama Canal. On a longer timescale, however, climate warming may be more damaging than COVID-19.

The problems of life in Caribbean society, notably widespread poverty, help explain why for many of its people it is a place to escape from. Once one gets beyond the beaches, the countryside can be spectacular in its natural beauty, but it is often forlorn and wretched in its lived space and for its people. This situation has not greatly changed in the last two centuries, and is very different from the world of the holidaymakers, as it was earlier from that of the estate owners.

Death in Paradise

Filmed on Guadeloupe and first shown in 2011, this commercially very successful but somewhat simplistic Anglo-French production, an artful mixture of comedy and whodunnit, has a London detective transferred to Saint Marie, a fictional British Caribbean island where much of the population speaks French. The island is a cross between Marie-Galante and Dominica. Voodoo is found on the island which also has sugar plantations.

12

Contingencies and Conclusions

....

A Dark 'n' Stormy

A Caribbean evening in Barbados, very dark but not at all stormy, was when I first had one of these excellent drinks; well, not actually one. Pleasant in itself, I drink it for medicinal purposes to help ease a throat sore from too much lecturing. Dark rum (dark) and ginger beer (stormy) over ice, usually with the addition of lime juice, the drink was developed after the First World War, apparently in Bermuda. The Hour Glass, the best pub in Exeter, makes the most satisfying in the city with Angostura bitters added.

The range of 'what ifs?' in Caribbean history is enormous. Many obvious ones relate to military and related political possibilities, such as British victory at the battle of New Orleans in 1815; which, in practice, however, would only have been a delaying factor in American expansion. At the same time, there are other military and political counterfactuals that hinge less on an individual event, such as a specific battle, but rather on an important possibility, for example the Spaniards in the early sixteenth century deciding not to project power from the islands to the mainland.

A Different New World

In 1762, Arthur Dobbs, the activist governor of North Carolina, offered the British government a prospectus for a New World based on the British model:

> publish manifestos in the Spanish tongue on landing ... declaring the Spanish colonies free states to be governed by laws framed by themselves after the model of British liberty under the protection of Britain as a perpetual ally with a free trade most favourable to Britain ... to retain, as cautionary pledges of the future friendship and fidelity of those colonies, Vera Cruz, Havana, Portobello and the isthmus of Darien, Cartagena, Hispaniola and the other Spanish islands. Spanish Florida to be entirely ceded to Britain ... to send missionaries to civilise and Christianise the natives where the Spaniards have no settlements and to form them into regular polities under the direction of governors truly Christian and educated for that purpose in Britain at the expense of the public.

Dobbs was not alone. On 2 February 1762, the *London Evening Post*, one of the more influential newspapers, proposed the conquest of the isthmus of Darien, while 'Ibericus', writing in the *London Chronicle* of 7 January 1762, pressed for the conquest of Florida and Louisiana in order to complete the British empire in North America: 'it will fix our colony's security beyond the reach of rival states in future times to endanger'. In the *London Evening Post* of 25 May 1762, 'Anglicus' made the same point about Louisiana. Such comments looked back to late-sixteenth-century hopes and forward to American ambitions in the Caribbean in the nineteenth century.

There are also contrasts between political systems/societies/cultures that can be re-evaluated, asking, for example, whether non-European societies could have developed differently and more successfully. There are also contingencies and counterfactuals in environmental terms, most significantly with diseases, which was very much the case with the coronavirus pandemic that started in 2020.

Much of the history of the Caribbean has been subordinated to non-regional powers from the sixteenth century on, and so also for the peoples who are now there. The theme of a difficult and lasting legacy from slavery is understandably present. The CARICOM (Caribbean Community) action plan in 2014 called for funding from the former slave-trading nations for education and health in the West Indies to eradicate illiteracy and chronic health conditions. Sir Hilary Beckles, a prominent Barbados historian who chaired the CARICOM Reparations Commission, established in 2013, that produced the 2014 report, argued:

This is about the persistent harm and suffering experienced today by the descendants of slavery and genocide that is the primary cause of development failure in the Caribbean. The African descended population in the Caribbean has the highest incidence in the world of the chronic diseases hypertension and type 2 diabetes, a direct result of the diet, physical and emotional brutality and overall stress associated with slavery, genocide and apartheid ... The British in particular left the black and indigenous communities in a general state of illiteracy and 70 per cent of blacks in British colonies were functionally illiterate in the 1960s when nation states began to appear.

Indeed, there is a physiological link between descendants of survivors of the Middle Crossing and slavery, and hypertension and diabetes. So also with the situation of black people in the American Deep South. Thus, in 2020–1, the black people of Louisiana were particularly hard hit by coronavirus, in large part due to poverty, less access to healthcare and a higher rate of underlying health problems, notably diabetes, hypertension and heart disease, which black people there tend also to acquire at younger ages.

Subordination, nevertheless, did not mean that Caribbean peoples lacked an ability to influence the process, which is part of the history that is frequently underplayed. This influence had a number of dimensions. Thus New Orleans, while Caribbean in its culture and in many ways very different to the South of the United States, was both greatly affected by the South and of major significance to it as its maritime entrepôt. Yet, that significance was wielded by white interests.

Linked to the point about subordination, and to those of mutual influence and influences, comes the concept of Caribbean history as a matter of frontiers, and notably those of identities and behaviour, as opposed to formal control. This approach helps bring in the role of culture, whether religion or food, music or sport. It is their role in identities, indeed, that helps make the history of the Caribbean so dynamic.

Cricket

Caribbean sport very much reflects past and/or present international links. Baseball plays an important role in Cuba, Puerto Rico, the Dominican Republic and, to a far lesser extent, Mexico, unlike the football otherwise dominant in Latin America. The former British colonies show much more interest in cricket. Initially, the local players were predominantly white people and the playing of cricket was an aspect of the degree to which the empire was a Greater Britain. This was eased by the more intensive imperial circulation that followed the development of steamship and telegraph links, and was subsequently to be taken forward by air services and radio.

Benefiting from the winter weather, English touring teams were a key part of the new practice, Robert Lucas bringing one out in 1894–5 and Arthur Priestley another in 1896–7. Local teams were deployed or established in order to play them. The competition encouraged the formation of representative teams to play for particular groupings including the West Indies as a whole, as well as the Leeward Islands and the Windward Islands. The West Indies Cricket Board joined the Imperial Cricket Conference in 1926 and the West Indies played their first Test match in 1928. Learie Constantine (1901–71), the most prominent player of the period, was a Trinidad all-rounder, who pursued his career in English club cricket as well as the West Indies Test team and, after the Second World War, became a barrister and politician as well as serving as Trinidad's high commissioner in London from 1961 to 1964.

After the break of the war, Test cricket resumed in 1948, with West Indies' bowlers taking many wickets that year, defeating England in 1950, and becoming increasingly a black-dominated side. Barbados-born Gary Sobers was a key player, with a high batting average, and served as captain for the West Indies from 1965 to 1972. Repeated victories in the 1970s and 1980s included 5–0 victories in Tests over England in 1984 and 1985–6 that were known as 'blackwashes', with West Indies' bowlers devastating the England team. England did not fight back with vigour until 1989–90 and 1991, and by 1995 the two sides were regularly even. In 2000, England regained the trophy which it won anew in 2003–4. The relative decline of West Indies cricket in the 1990s and 2000s was variously explained, including with reference to a lack of financial support and a sometime reluctance to part with distinguished players in favour of younger talent. However, there was a degree of recovery in the 2010s, at ICC T20 World Cup Championships in 2012 and 2016. Cricket remains important to Caribbean sport and there are grounds across the islands.

Reggae

Beginning in Jamaica in the late 1960s, this music style became very much linked to the island. Drawing on Rastafarian ideas, reggae built on a range of musical genres, including mento (a Jamaican dance music), calypso, jazz and African folk music, and was characterised by a heavy bass sound, Jamaican lyrics and offbeat rhythms. A key influence was Bob Marley (1945–81), a Jamaican singer-songwriter who was a Rastafarian icon and bestselling international star.

Including the United States in the Caribbean serves to underline the extent to which the growth rates in the region have varied greatly. Other comparative indices are also challenging, notably the contrast between those in East Asia (bar North Korea) and, on the other hand, the Caribbean with the exception of the United States. A political determination to ignore macroeconomic factors is clearly the key issue in Cuba and Venezuela, both of which were relatively far stronger economically in the pre-Castro and pre-Chávez past, but that does not suffice as an explanation for the region as a whole. A number of reasons have been advanced, not least the argument that relative failure is a consequence of American economic and, more particularly, financial hegemony, an explanation that can also be extended to analyse America's Caribbean littoral and Caribbean islands. Thus, from 1976 to 2006, Puerto Rico benefited greatly from tax breaks, notably no federal tax, provided to encourage industry, which led to pharmaceutical companies in particular locating there.

That explanation, however, has its limitations, not least if the last three centuries are considered, as the experience of gaining independence from European colonial empires was more widespread across the world, and the question is how best to explain differences between particular countries in the region and also more widely: St Lucia is obviously not Singapore. Relative political stability might be a key variant in the Caribbean, as, with the major exception of the Civil War, the United States was far more stable than the other large states, and especially so in the period from 1865. Reconstruction ended without significant violence and, thereafter in America, there was no comparison with the civil wars seen most notably in Mexico.

Yet, in much of the Caribbean there has been no such stability over the last two centuries, and this has serious political and economic consequences. Thus, in Nicaragua, the second poorest Caribbean country after Haiti, anti-government protests in 2018 were crushed with great brutality and over 300 deaths, as well as the dismissal of critics. Many fled in the aftermath. Tension continued thereafter, with violence from government supporters in what in many respects was a continuation of longstanding political divisions and conflict.

More generally, irrespective of rule by particular powers, or, more recently, regional collaborative mechanisms, variation is a central theme of the Caribbean, past, present and, one can be confident, future. So also is chance in the ever-present danger of hurricanes, a danger that underlines the multifaceted frontier character of the Caribbean. Hurricane Maria in 2017 caused damage estimated at $91.61 billion, notably in Dominica and Puerto Rico, while in 2019, Jamaica sent troops to the Bahamas to help deal with the devastating consequences of Hurricane Dorian. Global warming is making storm systems more intense and therefore more destructive, and flood risks have risen. Such is a reminder of the hazards of an apparent paradise.

Selected Further Reading

....

Abulafia, David, *The Discovery of Mankind: Atlantic Encounters in the Age of Columbus* (New Haven, CT, 2009).

Andrews, Kenneth, *The Spanish Caribbean: Trade and Plunder, 1530–1630* (New Haven, CT, 1978).

Ayala, César, *American Sugar Kingdom: The Plantation Economy of the Spanish Caribbean, 1898–1934* (Chapel Hill, NC, 2003).

Barber, Sarah, *The Disputatious Caribbean: The West Indies in the Seventeenth Century* (New York, 2014)

Beckles, Hilary, *A History of Barbados* (Cambridge, 2006).

Bethell, Leslie, *Cuba: A Short History* (Cambridge, 1993).

Bjarkman, Peter, *Fidel Castro and Baseball* (Lanham, MD, 2019).

Block, Kristen, *Ordinary Life in the Caribbean: Religion, Colonial Competition, and the Politics of Profit* (Athens, GA, 2012).

Blouet, Olwyn, *The Contemporary Caribbean* (London, 2007).

Brenner, Philip and Peter Eisner, *Cuba Libre: A 500-Year Quest for Independence* (Lanham, MD, 2017).

Brown, Jonathan, *Cuba's Revolutionary World* (Cambridge, MA, 2017).

Bulmer-Thomas, Victor, *The Economic History of the Caribbean Since the Napoleonic Wars* (Cambridge, 2012).

Burnard, Trevor, *Jamaica in the Age of Revolution* (Philadelphia, PA, 2020).

—, *Mastery, Tyranny and Desire: Thomas Thistlewood and His Slaves in the Anglo-Jamaican World* (Chapel Hill, NC, 2004).

—, *Planters, Merchants, and Slaves: Plantation Societies in British America, 1650–1820* (Chicago, IL, 2015).

Burnard, Trevor and John Garrigus, *The Plantation Machine: Atlantic Capitalism in French Saint-Domingue and British Jamaica* (Philadelphia, PA, 2016).

Cañazares-Esguerra, Jorge (ed.), *Entangled Empires: The Anglo-Iberian Atlantic, 1500–1830* (Philadelphia, PA, 2018).

Carballo, David, *Collision of Worlds: A Deep History of the Fall of Aztec Mexico and the Forging of New Spain* (Oxford, 2020).

Childs, Matt, *The 1812 Aponte Rebellion in Cuba and the Struggle against Atlantic Slavery* (Chapel Hill, NC, 2006).

Daut, Marlene, *Tropics of Haiti: Race and the Literary History of the Haitian Revolution in the Atlantic World* (Liverpool, 2015).

Dubois, Laurent, *Haiti: The Aftershocks of History* (New York, 2013).

Duffy, Michael, *Soldiers, Sugar and Seapower: The British Expeditions to the West Indies and the War Against Revolutionary France* (Oxford, 1987).

Dupuy, Alex, *Rethinking the Haitian Revolution* (Lanham, MD, 2019).

Fick, Carolyn, *The Making of Haiti: The Saint Domingue Revolution from Below* (Knoxville, TN, 1990).

Foote, Nicola (ed.), *The Caribbean History Reader* (London, 2013).

Geggus, David, *The Impact of the Haitian Revolution in the Atlantic World* (Columbia, SC, 2001).

Gibson, Carrie, *Empire's Crossroads: A History of the Caribbean from Columbus to the Present Day* (London, 2014).

Gilroy, Paul, *The Black Atlantic: Modernity and Double Consciousness* (Cambridge, MA, 1993).

Gobat, Michel, *Empire by Invitation: William Walker and Manifest Destiny in Central America* (Cambridge, MA, 2018).

Goslinga, C. Corneliis, *The Dutch in the Caribbean and in the Guianas 1680–1791* (Assen-Maastricht, 1985).

Hanna, Mark, *Pirate Nests and the Rise of the British Empire, 1570–1740* (Chapel Hill, NC, 2015).

Heuman, Gad, *The Caribbean* (London, 2013).

Higman, B. W., *A Concise History of the Caribbean* (Cambridge, 2011).

Hughes, Ben, *Apocalypse 1692: Empire, Slavery, and the Great Port Royal Earthquake* (London, 2017).

James, C. L. R., *Beyond a Boundary* (London, 1963).

Knight, Franklin, *The Caribbean: The Genesis of a Fragmented Nationalism* (New York, 1990).

Krise, Thomas, *Caribbeana: An Anthology of English Literature of the West Indies 1657–1777* (Chicago, 1999).

McNeill, John, *Mosquito Empires: Ecology and War in the Greater Caribbean, 1620–1914* (Cambridge, 2010).

Mawby, Spencer, *Ordering Independence: The End of Empire in the Anglophone Caribbean, 1947–1969* (Basingstoke, 2012).

Palmié, Stephan and Francisco Scarano, *The Caribbean: A History of the Region and Its Peoples* (Chicago, IL, 2011).

Pares, Richard, *War and Trade in the West Indies 1739–1763* (Oxford, 1936).

Restall, Matthew, *The Maya World: Yucatec Culture and Society, 1550–1850* (Stanford, CA, 1997).

Restall, Matthew and Amari Solari, *The Maya* (Oxford, 2000).

Rupert, Linda, *Creolisation and Contraband: Curaçao in the Early Modern Atlantic World* (Athens, GA, 2012).

Schwartz, Stuart, *Sea of Storms: A History of Hurricanes in the Greater Caribbean from Columbus to Katrina* (Princeton, NJ, 2015).

Taylor, Michael, *The Interest: How the British Establishment Resisted the Abolition of Slavery* (London, 2020).

Turner, Sasha, *Contested Bodies: Pregnancy, Childrearing, and Slavery in Jamaica* (Philadelphia, PA, 2017).

Vidal, Cécile (ed.), *Louisiana: Crossroads of the Atlantic World* (Philadelphia, PA, 2014).

Walvin, James, *Freedom. The Overthrow of the Slave Empires* (London, 2019).

Willoughby, Urmi, *Yellow Fever, Race, and Ecology in Nineteenth-Century New Orleans* (Baton Rouge, LA, 2017).

Index

Abercromby, Major-General Sir Ralph, 154–5
Abolitionism, 7, 139–40, 154, 175–85, 192, 194, 199
Abrantes, José, 257
Accessory Transit Company, 202–3
Acheson, Dean, 247
Adams, John, 161
Admiral Kuznetsov, 277
agriculture, early, 29–30, 34–6
Aguada Fénix astronomical site, 31
alcohol prohibition, 232–3
Alvarado, Pedro and Jorge de, 45
American Civil War, 172, 204–10, 217, 229, 289
American Declaration of Independence, 142
American navy, 214–15, 221–3
American Revolution, 143, 155–6, 176
Anglo-Dutch wars, 80, 93
Angola, Cuban intervention in, 252
Anguilla, British intervention in, 254
Anne, Queen, 109
Apalachees, 42
Apalachicola, river, 168
Aponte, José Antonio, 182–3
Arawaks, 28–9, 42, 46, 70
Árbenz, Jacobo, 242
Aristide, Jean-Bertrand, 274
'Army of the Sufferers', 190
Aruba, 231, 236
Asiento, 109, 114
Atkinson, Richard, 132
'Atlantic history' (the term), 58
Aury, Louis-Michel, 168
Austen, Jane, 145, 156
Autes, 42
Aztecs, 32–3, 42–3, 61

Balaguer, Joaquín, 254

banana exports, 214, 260
Baptist Missionary Society, 183
Baptist War, 181–2
Barbados, Bussa's rebellion, 181
Barbados Slave Act, 78–9
Barbuda, 78, 107, 256, 260
Barings Bank, 167
Batista, Fulgencio, 233, 237, 243–6, 269
Battle of Liberty Place, 209
Bay Islands, 201–2, 204, 272
Bay of Bengal, 17, 154
Bay of Pigs, 247–8, 251, 269
Beckles, Sir Hilary, 285
Bellin, Jacques-Nicolas, 106
Benbow, Vice-Admiral John, 108
Bernard, Simon, 169
bigamy trials, 80
Blane, Gilbert, 21
Blauvelt, Abraham, 70
Blondel, François, 69
Blue Mountains, 17, 75
Boiling Lake, 17
Boisrond-Canal, Pierre Théoma, 191
Bolden, Buddy, 226
Bolívar, Simon, 162, 179, 270
Bonaire, 69, 72
Bonaparte, Joseph, 162, 210
Bonny, Anne, 111
Borno, Louis, 227
Bosch, Juan, 254
Botany Bay, 154
Bowlby, Peter, 165
Boyer, Jean-Pierre, 190
Brazil, *Estado Novo*, 233
Brigand Wars, 151
British settlers, 101–4
Brontë, Charlotte, *Jane Eyre*, 3–4
Brooke, Sir James, 11
Browne, Thomas, 156

Bruguera, Tania, 275
buccaneers, *see* pirates and privateers
Buchanan, James, 201
Buenos Aires, battle of, 169
Burr, Aaron, 160–1, 164
Butler, General Benjamin, 205

cacao, 25, 30–1, 50, 76–7, 97, 140,
    260
California gold rush, 201
cannibalism, 37, 86
Cánovas del Castillo, Antonio, 213
Caracas Company, 140
Caribbean Defense Command, 236
Caribbean plate, 15–16
Caribbean Regiment, 237
Caribs, 28–9, 36, 41–2, 46, 57, 59,
    64–5, 71, 121–2, 151
    deportation of 'Black Caribs', 272–3
CARICOM, 285
Carlyle, Thomas, 57
Carmarthen, Francis, Marquis of, 142
Carter, Jimmy, 255
Caste War, 185–6
Castillo de Jagua, 90
Castillo do la Real Fuerza, 54
Castro, Fidel, 130, 217, 242, 244–53,
    257–8, 268–70, 274–5
Castro, Raúl, 244, 274–5
Catalan separatism, 218
cattle herding, 78
Cave, Stephen, 199
Cayman Trough, 18
Central Intelligence Agency (CIA),
    242, 245, 247–8, 253, 269
Céspedes y Quesada, Carlos Manuel,
    233
Charles I, King, 80
Charles III, King of Spain, 129
Chávez, Hugo, 261, 268, 270
Chibchan-language family, 29
China
    Belt and Road Initiative, 277–8
    Manchu China, 43
    Ming China, 38, 92
    Mongol China, 43
Chixculub crater, 15
cholera, 174, 186
Christian proselytism, 44–9, 80, 85

Christie, Agatha, A Caribbean
    Mystery, 12–13
Cimarron natives, 54
Claibrone, William, 160
Clarence, William, Duke of, 134, 141
climate, Caribbean, 17–20, 92
climate change, 26, 28, 282
Clinton, General Sir Henry, 133
Club Massiac, 139
Cochrane, Admiral Thomas, 163–4
cocoa, 104, 196
Code Noir, 79, 106, 131, 150
Codrington, Christopher, 83
coffee, 72, 81, 130, 139, 179, 231
Coleridge, Henry Nelson, ix
Colfax massacre (1873), 209
Columbus, Bartholomew, 47
Columbus, Christopher, 39–41,
    217–18, 268
Columbus, Ferdinand, 31
concentration camps, 213
Constantine, Learie, 287
contract labour, 231
coronavirus pandemic, 8, 279–82,
    286
Corsica, French purchase of, 129
Cortés, Hernán, 42–5
cotton, 18, 24, 30, 68, 76, 96, 100,
    160, 167, 179–80, 204–5
Courland, Jacob, Duke of, 71
Crab Island, 84
Craven, William, 7th Lord, 156
Crawford, Joseph, 200
creole languages, 140–1
cricket, 287–8
Crimea, Russian seizure of, 135
Crimean War, 202
Cromwell, Oliver, 66–7, 88
cruise ships, 270–2, 278, 281
CSS *Tennessee*, 206
Cuba
    American interventions, 214–18,
        221–4, 232–3, 247–8, 257
    Aponte rising, 182–3
    British conquest of, 125–6
    Cuban missile crisis, 248–50
    Cuban Revolution, 242–53, 257–8
    doctors, 276
    end of slavery, 192–3, 200–1

history, 268–9
indentured workers, 194
post-Castro era, 274–6, 279, 289
rebellion, 210–13
sugar production, 192–3, 201,
    211–12, 231–3, 237
tourism, 271–2
cuisine, Caribbean, 63
Cuitláhuac, 43
Cult of the Speaking Cross, 185
Cumberland, George, 3rd Earl of, 55
Cumby, Captain William, 156
Curaçao, 19, 69–70, 72, 77, 81, 108,
    140, 152, 155–6, 200, 231, 236

Dalrymple, Major-General William,
    121–2
Danish Virgin Islands, 208, 226
Danish West India and Guinea
    Company, 95–6, 114
Darien scheme, 284
Dark 'n' Stormy, 283
de Gerard, Henrik, 90
de Graaf, Laurens, 90
Death in Paradise, 282
Declaration of Paris (1856), 203
decolonisation, independence and
    democracy, 258–60
Demerara rising, 181
Depp, Johnny, 109–10
Dessalines, Jean-Jacques, 149, 190–1
Díaz, Porfirio, 207
Díaz-Canel, Miguel, 275
Dickens, Charles, 57, 197–8
disease, 21–5, 46, 48, 66, 68, 92, 101,
    186, 222–3
    see also cholera; influenza; scurvy;
    smallpox; venereal diseases;
    yellow fever
Dixon, Simon, 252
Dobbs, Arthur, 284
Domingue, Michel, 191
Dominican Republic, American
    interventions in, 224, 226, 253–4
Dominican War of Restoration, 208
Douglas, Captain Sir Charles, 135
D'Oyley, Lieutenant-General Edward,
    75
Drake, Francis, 53–6, 117

drug trafficking, 267–8
Dulles, Allen, 245
Dundas, Henry, 159
Dunham, Rear-Admiral Sir Philip
    Charles, 157
Dunn, Oscar, 209
Dutch Crisis (1787), 123, 138
Dutch East India Company, 118
Dutch West India Company, 70–1
Dutty, Boukman, 150
Duvalier, 'Papa Doc' and 'Baby Doc',
    254
dyewoods, 96

earthquakes, 1, 5, 16, 25, 83, 221, 273
East Indies, 10–11, 26, 37–8, 58–60,
    91–2, 118–19, 154, 218–19, 238–9,
    266
Echevarría, José Antonio, 244
Edwards, Bryan, 187
Elizabeth I, Queen, 51, 54
Elizabeth II, Queen, 256
Elphinstone, Captain John, 20
Emancipation Act (1824), 202
Emancipation Act (1833), 5, 183
Empire Cruise (1924), 221
Empire Windrush, 262
encomienda, 49
Endara, Guillermo, 257
English Civil War, 66
English East India Company, 111
Enríquez, Don Martín, 52
Escobar, Jorge Otero, 276
Estrées, Jean, Comte d', 81
Ethiopia (Abyssinia), 216, 252
Eyre, Edward, 57, 197–8

Farragut, David, 172, 205–6
Fatiman, Cécile, 150
Fédon, Julien, 151
Fenwick, Eliza, 174–5
Ferdinand VII, King of Spain, 162
filibusters, 143, 168, 201–3
Finlay, Carlos, 223
First World War, 225–6
Fitzpatrick, John, 209
Fleming, Ian, 27, 243, 246, 255
    James Bond in the Caribbean,
    263–5

Fletcher, Benjamin, 111
Florida
    ceded to British, 126–7
    limits of Spanish control, 93, 121
    post-Civil War, 209–10
    return to Spanish control, 133,
        135–6, 138
    Spanish conquest of, 6, 42, 45, 60,
        85
Flynn, Errol, 54–5, 251
Fowle, Rev. Thomas, 156
Franciscans, 6, 8, 86
Franco-Dutch War, 81
Franklin, Benjamin, 187
Frederick the Great, King of Prussia,
    196
Freeman, Captain William, 73–4
French Guinea Company, 109
French Revolution, 138, 142, 146, 171
French Revolutionary and Napoleonic
    Wars, 142, 147–58
French settlers, 104–6
French West India Company, 71
Fronde civil war, 71

Gaines, Brigadier-General Edmund,
    169
Galveston Island, 168
Garvey, Marcus, 221
Gauld, George, 128
Geffrard, Fabre, 191
geology, 15–18, 27, 58
George III, King, 127, 152
German Coast, 26, 182
Ghost Breakers, The, 234
Gibraltar, 108, 136, 162, 238
Gilbert and Sullivan, 189
ginger, 76
Goddard, Paulette, 234
Goffe, John, 103
gold and silver, 31, 47–8, 53, 57
Golding, William, 2
Gorbachev, Mikhail, 257
Gordon, Colonel, 22
Grammont, Michel de, 90
Gran Chichimeca, warriors of, 60
Granada, fall of, 40
Grand Turk, 17, 19
Grant, Ulysses S., 208

Grasse, François, Comte de, 135
Grau, Ramón, 233, 243
Great Depression, 229, 232, 281
Greene, Graham, *Our Man in Havana*,
    246
Grenada
    American invasion, 256
    Fédon's rebellion, 151, 155
Grenville, William, Lord, 147
'Grif' (the term), 101
Grijalva, Juan de, 42
Guadeloupe
    re-establishment of slavery, 148–9
    surrenders to British, 157–8
    threatened rising, 184
Guajira peninsula, 122–3
Guano Islands Act (1856), 251
Guantánamo Bay, 216, 221, 227, 249
Guerrier, Philippe, 190
Guevara, Che, 245, 248, 269
Gulf of Mexico, 16, 26–7, 85, 158
gunboats, steam-powered, 173
Gustavus III, King of Sweden, 140

Haile Selassie, Emperor, 230
Haiti, 189–92
    American intervention, 224,
        226–8
    Duvalier dictatorship, 254
    independence, 149, 161–2, 170,
        189–90
    recent crises, 274
    vodou, 150–1, 190
    see also Saint-Domingue rebellion
Hardwicke, Lord Chancellor, 126
Harrison, Benjamin, 214
Hatuey, 42
Havana cigars, 192
Hawai'ian archipelago, 44
Hawkins, Benjamin, 163
Hawkins, John, 52, 55
Hay, Michael, 103
Hay–Bunau-Varilla Treaty (1903), 222
Hay–Pauncefote treaties (1900–1), 218
Hearst, William Randolph, 214–15
Hein, Piet, 70
Heller, Joseph, 265
Hemingway, Ernest and Leicester, 251
Hennepin, Louis, 86

Hennessy, David, 199
Henriques, Moses Cohen, 9
Henry VIII, King, 51
Henty, G. A., 192
Herbert, John, 134
Hernández, Tony, 267
Hernández de Córdoba, Francisco, 42
Heureaux, Ulises, 208
HMS *Richmond*, 20
HMS *Spitfire*, 158
HMS *Surprise*, 153
hogs, feral, 68
homicide trials, 229
Hope, Bob, 234
Hopewell culture, 32
Hosier, Rear-Admiral Francis, 113
Howard, Edward, 180
Huastecs, 32
Hughes, Richard, *A High Wind in Jamaica*, 1–2
Huguenots, 6, 59
hurricanes, 1, 25–6, 64, 80, 175, 185, 195, 273, 290
Hutchison, Joseph, 165
Hyppolite, Florvil, 191

Ice Ages, 16, 27
Île-à-Vache, 204
Illinois, river, 85
Incas, 32
indentured labour, 194, 198, 231
indigo, 76, 100, 104, 179
Industrial Revolution, 155
influenza, 86
Inkle and Yarico, 95
Inter-American Peace Force, 254
intermarriage, 49–50, 131
International Monetary Fund (IMF), 262, 279
Iranian revolution, 255
Isabella, Queen of Castile, 40
Island of Fu Manchu, The, 234–5
Isle of Aves, 81
Isthmus of Tehuantepec, 30
Itza' people, 86

Jackson, Andrew, 163–4, 166, 168
Jackson, William, 90
Jamaica Train, 98

Jamaica, Maroon rising, 151–2
James II, King, 83
Javanese Wars of Succession, 118
jazz, 226
Jefferson, Thomas, 158–9, 161, 187
Jenner, Edward, 186
Jesuits, 71, 180
Jews, 72, 237
Jimémez, Marcos Pérez, 242
Johnson, Samuel, 56

Karankawa, 85
Kellogg, William Pitt, 209–10
Kennedy, John F., 247–9
Khrushchev, Nikita, 249–50
Kidd, William, 111
Kinglsey, Charles, *Westward Ho!*, 11, 56–7
Kinney, Henry, 202
Knights of Malta, 72
Knights of the White Camelia, 209
Kock, Bernard, 204
Kuna Indians, 273

La Salle, René-Robert Cavelier, Sieur de, 85–6
Lafitte, Jean, 160, 164, 168, 228
Lake Gatun, 26, 223
Lake Maracaibo, 33, 231, 261
Lake Péten Itzá, 86
Lambert, Major-General John, 166
Lansky, Meyer, 243
League of Coloured Peoples, 230
Leclerc, Charles, 148–9
Leeward Islands, 7, 18–19, 74, 80, 83, 102, 157, 186, 287
Légitime, François, 191
Légitimus, Hégésippe, 229
Leith, Lieutenant-General Sir James, 157–8
Lewis, Matthew 'Monk', 177
'Lighthouse to Columbus', 218
Ligon, Richard, 95
Lilly, Christian, 103
Lincoln, Abraham, 204–5
'lines of amity', 64
Llanos chiefdoms, 33
l'Olonnais, François, 90
López, Narciso, 201

Lords Commissioners for Trade and Plantations, 74
Louis XIV, King of France, 85
Louis XV, King of France, 105
Louis XVI, King of France, 147
Louis XVIII, King of France, 158
Louisiana
  coronavirus pandemic, 286
  desegregation, 266
  French settlement, 81, 85–6, 92, 104–6, 125
  Louisiana Purchase, 159–60, 170
  post-Civil War, 209–10
  slavery, 101, 139, 160–1, 164, 182, 194–5
  Spanish acquisition of, 127, 130, 135
  sugar cultivation, 179–80
  voodoo, 150–1
L'Ouverture, Toussaint, 22, 148
Lucas, Robert, 287

MacGregor, Sir Gregor, 171
Machado, Gerardo, 232–3
Machuca, Bernardo Vargas, 60
Madagascar, British invasion of, 237
Maduro, Nicolás, 261, 268
mahogany, 96, 114
Majapahit empire, 38
Mandela, Nelson, 252
Manet, Édouard, 203
Mao Zedong, 250
maps, 82, 104
Maracaibo, foundation of, 86
Margarita Island, 223
Marie-Galante, 157, 282
Mariel, battle of, 173
Marín, Luis, 237
Marlborough, John, Duke of, 108
Marley, Bob, 288
Maroons, 34–5, 60, 100–1, 103, 151–2, 175–6
Martelly, Michel, 274
Martí, José, 212, 216–17, 270
Martinique rising, 182, 184
Mary, Queen, 51
Matos, Huber, 245
Maximilian of Austria, Archduke, 203, 205–7
Maya, 6, 28, 30–2, 34, 37, 42, 45, 86–7

Melville, Alan, 233
Mendieta, Carlos, 233
Mercier, Louis Sébastien, 123
Mexican–American War, 145, 174, 215
Mexican Civil War, 23, 205, 210, 224, 289
Mexican independence, 162, 170
Middleton, Sir Charles, 136–7
Miller, Thomas, 128
Mississippi, river, 15–6, 30, 32, 85, 127, 165–7, 182, 199, 214
Mississippi Company, 105
Mississippian culture, 32–3
Mobilian tribe, 45
Modyford, Sir Thomas, 89
molasses, 73, 97
monogamy, 80
Monroe, James, 172
Monroe Doctrine, 168, 170
Mont Pelée eruption, 221
Montezuma, 42–3
Morant Bay uprising (1865), 57, 197–8
Morgan, Sir Henry, 9, 89–90, 103, 117
Morton, Jelly Roll, 226
Moscoso, Luis de, 45
Mosquito Coast, 21, 44, 70, 92, 117, 123, 125, 138, 142, 201–4
Mouchoir Banks, 16
Mount Pelée, 25
Moyne Commission and Report (1939), 230, 259
Mullins, Lieutenant-Colonel Thomas, 165
Murillo, Rosario, 8–9
Mustique, 5
Mutiny Act (1807), 152
Muzul Maya, 6
Myngs, Christopher, 89

Naipaul, V. S., 12
Napoleon Bonaparte, 124, 131, 148, 157, 159, 161, 169, 191, 196
Napoleon III, Emperor, 206–7
Narváez, Pánfilo de, 41–2
Navassa Island, 208
Navidad Banks, 16
navigation, 19–20

Navigation Acts, 134
Negro Fort, 168–9
Negro World, 221
'negroes' (the word), 78–9
Nelson, Admiral Horatio, 133–4, 141
Neville, Vice-Admiral John, 82
New Laws (1542), 49
New Mexico, 105
New Orleans, 25, 66, 105–6, 130, 149, 172, 178, 186, 199, 201, 209, 214, 265, 286
    and American slave revolt, 182
    and Civil War, 205
    and jazz, 226
    mid-century, 199
    and shipping, 238, 260
    strategic importance, 157–61, 163–7
    and tourism, 200, 272
New Orleans, battle of, 25, 124, 157, 163–7, 169, 283
New Virginia Colony, 206
Newcastle, Duke of, 124
newspapers, 103–4
Nicaragua
    American intervention, 255, 257
    anti-government protests, 289–90
    canal scheme, 278
Nine Years War, 82
Nisbet, Frances, 134
Nojpetén, 86
Nolte, Vincent, 167
Nonconformists, 7
Nootka Sound Crisis (1790), 138, 154, 159
Noriega, Manuel, 257
North American plate, 15
North Andros Island, 17
Notting Hill Riots, 262–3

Ochoa, General Arnaldo, 252, 257
O'Donnell, General Leopoldo, 204–5, 207
Olmecs, 28, 30, 37
Organisation of Eastern Caribbean States, 260
Orinqueponi chiefdoms, 33
orishas, 8
Ortega, Daniel, 9
Ostend Manifesto (1854), 200

Oxenham, John, 53–4
Ozama, river, 47

Pact of Zanjón (1878), 212
Pakenham, Major-General Sir Edward, 165–6
Palmerston, Henry, Viscount, 192
Pan-Africanism, 230
Panama, American intervention in, 257, 268
Panama Canal, 24, 26, 169, 222–4, 227, 231, 235–6, 254, 277–8
Parke, Daniel, 102
Parsley massacre (1937), 227
Peace of Amiens, 156
Peace of Nijmegen, 81
Peace of Paris, 104, 126–7, 135
Peace of Utrecht, 108, 110, 114
Penang, 154
Pentecostalism, rise of, 230
Philip, Duke of Orleans, 105
Philip II, King of Spain, 51
Philip V, King of Spain, 108
Philippines, 213, 216
Pierce, Franklin, 200, 202
Pierrot, Jean-Louis, 190
pimento, 76
pirates and privateers, 5–6, 9–11, 52–6
    black, 151, 171
    campaign against, 171–3
    eighteenth-century, 97, 107–8, 110–12, 115–16, 132, 136, 153, 159–60, 163, 168, 268
    end of privateering, 203
    female, 111
    seventeenth-century, 65, 67, 70, 80, 82–4, 87–91
Pirates of the Caribbean, 109–10
Plantation Act (1740), 102
Planter's Punch, 243
Platt, Charles, 172
Platt Amendment, 216, 233
Plessy v. Ferguson judgement, 209
Polo, Marco, 39
polygamy, 8, 80
polytheism, 8
Pontchartrain, Jérôme, Count of, 85
Porter, David, 172
Preston, Amyas, 56

Préval, René, 274
Priestley, Arthur, 287
privateers, see pirates and privateers
Providence Island, 65–7, 90, 168, 268
Ptolemy, 40
Puerto Rico, American annexation of, 216, 221–2, 237, 241, 273
Punta Ventana, collapse of, 25

Quitman, John, 202

Rackham, John 'Calico Jack', 111
Raizals, 66
Rastafarianism, 230, 288
rats, introduction of, 23, 68
Read, Mary, 111
Reagan, Ronald, 254–5
Reed, Major Walter, 223
Reform Act (1832), 183
reggae, 288
religion, 6–9
   see also Christian proselytism
repartimento, 49
Rhys, Jean, Wide Sargasso Sea, 4–5
Riché, Jean-Baptiste, 190
Richmond, Charles, 3rd Duke of, 136
Rigaud, André, 148
Rillieux, Norbert, 180
Rivers, Lieutenant-Colonel James, 22, 107
Rivière-Hérard, Charles, 190
Roatán, 122, 151, 272–3
Robert, Admiral Georges, 237
Rockingham, Charles, 2nd Marquess of, 24
Rodney, Admiral George, 21, 135
Rogers, Woodes, 111
Rohmer, Sax, 234
Roosevelt, Theodore, 214
Roy, Louis, 227
Royal African Company, 74
rum, 73, 96–7, 99
Rum Collins, 267
Rupert of the Rhine, Prince, 66
Russell, Major-General John, 227
Russell, Lord John, 204

Saba, 17, 69, 80, 157
Sabatini, Rafael, 54–5

Saget, Nissage, 191
St Barthélemy, 71–2, 140, 155, 184
St Croix, 72, 95, 114, 140, 156, 184–5
Saint-Domingue rebellion, 22, 101, 122, 130, 136, 138–40, 143, 146–51, 171, 189, 192
St Eustatius, 69, 80, 82, 93, 133, 157
St John, 100, 114
St Lucia rebellion, 151, 155
St Martin, 17, 25, 69, 71–2, 81, 152, 155, 157, 185, 197
Saint-Mery, Moreau de, 150
St Thomas, 65, 81–2, 84, 88, 93
St Vincent
   deportation of 'Black Caribs', 272–3
   rebellion, 151, 155
Sak Tz'i' kingdom, 30
Salnave, Sylvain, 191
Salomon, Louis, 191
Sam, Tirésias, 192
San Blas archipelago, 26, 273
San Domingo, battle of, 152–3, 156
Santa Clara, battle of, 245
Savannah, founding of, 94
Scott, Colonel John, 37
scurvy, 21
Second World War, 230, 234–9, 242
Selwyn, George, 11
Sergeants' Revolt, 233
Sert, José Luis, 261
Seven Years War, 104–5, 118, 123–4, 136
sex, interracial, 2–3
   see also intermarriage
Shakespeare, William, 3
Shelburne, Earl of, 137
shipbuilding, 238
Sicily, rebellion against Spanish rule, 84
Sierra Leone, 152, 194
Silver Banks, 16
Simolin, Ivan, 137
slave rebellions, 22, 50, 99–100, 114, 122, 130, 151, 155, 181–3, 187, 193, 200, 209
   Saint-Domingue rebellion, 22, 101, 122, 130, 136, 138–40, 143, 146–51, 171, 189, 192

slavery
  abolition of, 175–85
  and African American culture,
    79–80
  beginnings of, 49–52
  and black identity, 143
  British involvement in, 96–100
  continuation for in Spanish colonies,
    192, 211–12
  Dutch abolition of, 212
  and economy, 72–80
  female slave-owners, 174–5
  improved survival rates, 177
  and informal economy, 131
  justification for, 76
  lasting legacy of, 285–6
  legislation, 75–6, 78–9
  punishments, 79
  severity of treatment, 98–100
slaves, escaped, see Maroons
slaves, former, 193–5
smallpox, 43, 46, 86, 141, 157
Smith, Adam, 138
smuggling, 7, 9–10, 82, 142, 160, 168,
    172, 233, 252, 268
Sobers, Gary, 288
Socarrás, Carlos Prío, 243
Société des Amis des Noirs, 139
Somoza, Anastasio, 255
Sores, Jacques de, 54
Soto, Hernando de, 41, 45
Souloque, Faustin (Faustin I,
    Emperor of Haiti), 190–1, 203
South Carolina, 74, 81, 94, 96, 142
South Sea Company, 105
Spanish-American War, 21, 137, 215,
    218, 224
Spanish treasure fleet, Dutch capture
    of, 70–1
Spotswood, Lieutenant-Colonel
    Alexander, 22
Stamp Act (1765), 129
Stapleton, Sir William, 7, 99
strikes, 225, 228–30, 233
Suez Canal, 222–3
sugar, 23–4, 68, 72–7, 96–100, 104, 130,
    138–9, 142, 160, 176–7, 179–80, 184
  Cuba and, 192–3, 201, 211–12, 231–3,
    237

  decline in prices, 229
  sugar-beet production, 195–6
Sugar Duties Act (1846), 195
Swan Islands, 208

Taínos, 28–9, 36–7, 41–2, 48, 50–1
Tairona chiefdoms, 33
Tampico, 22, 170, 174
Taranto mutiny (1918), 225
Tehuantepec isthmus, 174
Tennyson, Alfred, Lord, 57
Teredo shipworms, 24
Texan independence, 162–3, 171
Thatch, Edward ('Blackbeard'), 112
Thirteen Colonies, 76, 129, 154
Thistlewood, Thomas, 99
Thompson, Robert, 39
Thornton, John, 82
Thurlow, Edward, Lord, 141
tobacco, 64–5, 68, 72, 74, 77, 81, 106,
    130, 179, 192, 212
Tobago conspiracy (1802), 175
Toltecs, 32, 37
Torrijos–Carter treaties, 223
Tortola, 93
Tortuga, 71, 81, 89–90, 278
tourism, 141, 200, 232, 263, 281
Trade Winds, 40
Treaty of Aix-la-Chapelle, 115
Treaty of Aranjuez, 131
Treaty of Cateau-Cambrésis, 88
Treaty of Comayagua, 207
Treaty of Madrid, 67
Treaty of Ryswick, 85, 131
Treaty of Tordesillas, 40
Treaty of Versailles (1783), 135
Treaty of Westphalia, 71
Trelawny, Colonel Edward, 100, 103
Trujillo, Rafael, 227, 237, 253–4
Truman, Harry S., 241
Trump, Donald, 271
Tugwell, Rexford, 237
Turks Island, 104, 129, 132, 134, 264
Turner, Lana, 251
typhus, 186

U-2 spy planes, 249
United States Constitution, 209
Urrutia, Manuel, 245

Ursúa, Martín de, 86
USS *Asheville*, 227
USS *Galveston*, 227
USS *Maine*, 214, 247, 268–9
USS *Memphis*, 227
USS *Ohio*, 174
USS *Oxford*, 248

van Walbeeck, Johannes, 70
Vanderbilt, Cornelius, 202–3
Vargas, Getúlio, 233
Vaughan, Lieutenant-General Sir
     John, 155
Velázquez de Cuéllar, Diego, 41
venereal diseases, 5, 112
Venezuela
     crisis (1895), 218
     government and economy, 261,
        268, 270, 281, 289
     oil production, 231, 235–6, 261
Veracruz Culture, 28
Vernon, Admiral Edward, 116, 141
Vietnam War, 254
Villette-Mursay, Philippe de, 92
Virgin Mary, 45
vodou (voodoo), 8, 150–1, 190, 282
volcanoes, 16–17, 29, 221

Wager, Rear-Admiral Charles, 108
Walcott, Derek, *Omeros*, 12
Walker, William, 202–3
Walpole, Horatio, 115
Walpole, Sir Robert, 56, 115
War of 1812, 163–7, 172
War of American Independence, 21,
     132, 138, 147, 158, 164

War of Jenkins's Ear, 21, 114, 117
War of the Austrian Succession, 117
War of the Quadruple Alliance, 113
War of the Spanish Succession, 107,
     112, 218
War of the Third Coalition, 159
Warner, Sir Thomas, 65
Washington, George and Lawrence,
     141
Waterloo, battle of, 157–8
Weeden Island culture, 32–3
Wentworth, Thomas, 24–5
Wesleyan Missionary Society, 183
West India Regiment, 152, 225
West Indies Federation, 259
West Indies Squadron, 172
Weyler, Valeriano, 213
whale-watching, 19
White League, 209
Wilkinson, Brigadier-General James,
     161, 164
William III, King, 83–4
Wollstonecraft, Mary, 174
World's Industrial and Cotton
     Centennial Exposition (1884), 214
Worth, General William, 173
Wrenn, Commodore Ralph, 83
Wright, Commodore Lawrence, 82–3

yellow fever, 22–3, 66, 158, 160, 177,
     186, 223
Yorktown, British defeat at, 133
Young, Sir William, 99

Zinglins, 190